CW01249833

Managing with Micros

MANAGING WITH MICROS
Management Uses of Microcomputers

Third Edition

COLIN LEWIS

Basil Blackwell
and
The Economist Publications

Copyright © C. D. Lewis 1983, 1984, 1986

First published 1983
Reprinted 1983
Second edition 1984
Reprinted 1985
Third edition 1986 (1987 in USA)

Jointly published 1986
Basil Blackwell Limited
108 Cowley Road, Oxford OX4 1JF, England
and The Economist Publications Ltd
40 Duke Street, London W1A 1DW

Basil Blackwell Inc.
432 Park Avenue South, Suite 1503
New York, NY10016, USA

All rights reserved. No part of this publication may be reproduced, stored in a retrieval system, or transmitted, in any form or by any means, electronic, mechanical, photocopying, recording or otherwise, without the prior permission of the publisher.

Except in the United States of America, this book is sold subject to the condition that it shall not, by way of trade or otherwise, be lent, re-sold, hired out, or otherwise circulated without the publisher's prior consent in any form of binding or cover other than that in which it is published and without a similar condition including this condition being imposed on the subsequent purchaser.

British Library Cataloguing in Publication Data
Lewis, C.D.
  Managing with micros : management uses of microcomputers.—3rd ed.
  1. Management—Data processing
  2. Business—Data processing
  3. Microcomputers
  I. Title
  658'.05416   HD30.2
  ISBN 0–631–15276–8
  ISBN 0–631–15277–6 Pbk

Library of Congress Cataloging-in-Publication Data
Lewis, C.D. (Colin David)
  Managing with micros.
  Includes index.
  1. Business—Data processing. 2. Management—Data processing. 3. Microcomputers—Programming. I. Title.
  HF5548.2.L425 1986   658'.05416   86-17469
  ISBN 0-631-15276-8
  ISBN 0-631-15277-6 (pbk.)

Typeset by Columns of Reading
Printed in Great Britain by Page Bros, Norwich

Contents

Foreword to the Third Edition		viii
Acknowledgements		x

A Microcomputers – General

1 ***Microcomputer systems – hardware and software*** — 3
   Hardware — 3
   Central Processing Unit (CPU) — 4
   Peripheral hardware — 10
   Microcomputer systems — 16
   Printers — 26
   Software — 32
   Conclusion — 42

2 ***The microcomputer industry and the choice of microcomputer system*** — 44
   Structure of the microcomputer industry — 45
   After sale support — 49
   Choice of microcomputer system — 52
   Conclusion — 58

3 ***The microcomputer as a communications device*** — 59
   Micro to micro communications –
     Local Area Networks — 59
   Micro to mainframe communications — 62
   General dial-up systems in the UK — 64
   Conclusion — 67

B General Purpose Applications Packages

4 ***Wordprocessing packages*** — 71
   General concept of word processing — 71

		Editing and presentation facilities	73
		Control and organization facilities	77
		Print quality and options	82
		Conclusion	84
	5	***Spreadsheet packages including graphics***	86
		The basic idea behind the spreadsheet concept	86
		Use of formulae and their replication	88
		Built-in functions	90
		Examples of spreadsheets	92
		Graphics	98
		Colour	100
		Macroprogramming	100
		Iteration control and forward referencing	101
		Simple database facilities	101
		Conclusion	101
	6	***Flexible database packages***	103
		Database terminology	104
		Classification of database packages	105
		Designing the record structure and/or layout	107
		Password access	111
		Sorting and indexing	111
		Searching for specified records	113
		Report writing	115
		Other facilities	121
		Conclusion	126
	7	***Integrated business packages***	128
		The concept of integration – advantages and disadvantages	128
		Integration from a user's point of view	131
		Disk based and RAM based integrated business packages	133
		Conclusion	136

C The Three Most Popular Packages

	8	***Payroll***	139
		Payroll packages	139
		Setting up a payroll system	142
		Week-to-week and month-to-month operations	149
		End-of-year procedures	159

9	**Sales, Purchase and Nominal Ledger**	163
	Ledger systems	163
	Main features	169
	Nominal ledger	171
	Sales ledger	180
	Purchase ledger	188
	Conclusion	189
10	**Stock control**	192
	Stock control packages	192
	Setting up a stock control system	194
	Day-to-day transactions	199
	End-of-month processing	200
	Reports available	202
	Trends and developments	207
	Conclusion	211
	Glossary of terms	212
	Index	218

Foreword to the Third Edition

In my foreword to the first edition of *Managing with Micros* I said that the principal focus of the book was not so much microcomputers themselves but, more particularly, the uses to which microcomputers could be put in management situations. Several years later, in spite of the many technological and market developments that have taken place, the applications for which managers are using microcomputers remain much the same as they were; but of course there are now far more applications in addition to these. Having said that the types of microcomputer applications in a management context are still largely the same, however, one has to realize that today's microcomputers are faster, larger in internal and external storage terms and generally more reliable than their predecessors – all of which has led to more efficient if not necessarily different solutions to management problems.

When the first edition of *Managing with Micros* was published in 1983 the microcomputer market was dominated by 8-bit machines with a maximum internal memory of 64 kbytes, twin 5.25 inch floppy disk drives and the CP/M operating system. By the time the second edition had appeared in 1984 one had seen the arrival of the 16-bit machines with their potential capacity for far larger internal memory but with hard disks still an expensive luxury. Today, in 1986, we see the consolidation of the 16-bit machine with up to 640 kbytes of internal memory and more particularly the move towards a 'standard' brought about by the increasing dominance of IBM PCs and their many 'compatibles', 'clones' and 'look-alikes' – all of which use the operating systems PC/MS-DOS. Hard disks are now far more commonplace with about a third of all business micros supporting such storage devices which offer from 10 to 50 Mbytes of external memory.

The two most significant changes to the microcomputer marketplace that have occurred since the second edition of *Managing with Micros*, however, have been the introduction of the so-called 'integrated business packages', which combine wordprocessing, spreadsheet, graphics and simple database facilities, and the increasing use of the microcomputer as a communications device to other computer systems in addition to its original role as an independent processor. Recognizing the significance of both these developments, this third edition devotes separate chapters to each of these topics.

Solihull   Colin Lewis

Acknowledgements

I am indebted to my many friends and colleagues both within academic life and within industry for their advice and comments often unwittingly given, which have influenced the content of this book. In such a fast-moving marketplace as the microcomputer field one is constantly picking up new developments and ideas from a myriad of sources too numerous to mention individually.

Section A

Microcomputers – General

1. Microcomputer systems – hardware and software
2. The microcomputer industry and the choice of microcomputer system
3. The microcomputer as a communications device

1

Microcomputer systems – hardware and software

All microcomputer systems consist of both the physical bits and pieces which make up the computer itself and, arguably of more importance, the programs which instruct the computer what to do. Since these two elements are, on the one hand, quite different but, on the other hand, totally dependent on each other, the physical bits and pieces are referred to as *hardware* and the controlling programs as *software*. The software can be further divided into applications software and systems software. *Applications software* consists of programs written for the particular application (stock recording, payroll, and so on) which have to be read into the computer from an external storage source (a disk). *Systems software* consists of programs which translate the applications software (by using interpreters and compilers), organize access to and from disk (by using a disk operating system – DOS) and also control the internal organization of the microcomputer's whole operating system. In a microcomputer, the systems software can either be permanently stored in the computer or read in from external disk storage.

To put microcomputers into the context of computers in general, at mid-1980s prices business microcomputer systems sold for between £1,000 and £15,000, mini-computers for more than £30,000 and mainframe computers for more than £100,000.

Hardware

While no single definition of a *microcomputer* has universal appeal, a widely accepted one is that a microcomputer is a computer based on a *single* microprocessor chip which performs arithmetic and logic functions and controls the operation of the

4   Microcomputers – general

central processing unit of the microcomputer. The *central processing unit* – CPU – is effectively the *brain* of the microcomputer. It controls all processing and also communicates with the various *peripheral devices* required to make up the hardware of a microcomputer system, principally:

a keyboard through which data or programs can be entered into the system;
an external storage device (usually a dual floppy disk drive or hard disk for most management applications) which can both enter previously stored data or programs into the computer's internal memory and receive and store data or programs currently held in the computer's internal memory;
a visual display unit (VDU) which temporarily displays information produced by the computer;
a printer which produces a permanent printed record of information produced by the computer.

Central processing unit (CPU)

Figure 1.1 shows the basic layout of a simple microcomputer system and demonstrates that the CPU consists essentially of four major components (in effect chips) connected by three buses (conceptually a group of wires carrying electrical signals) and synchronized by a clock. The function of these components is now discussed.

CPU chip or microprocessor unit – MPU

The MPU is the most important element in the microcomputer. It not only performs all the arithmetical operations required but also controls the flow of information between the other components of the CPU and, via the I/O (input/output) interface, controls the flow of information to and from the microcomputer system's peripheral devices (see p. 10 below). A typical MPU contains the equivalent of 20,000 transistors in a single chip.

While there are many microcomputer systems on the market, there are relatively few MPUs on which those computers are based, namely:
6502, 6504, 6800, 8080, Z80, 8085, Z80A, 6809 (8-bit)
MC68000, Z8000, NS16032, 8086, 8088, 80286 (16-bit)

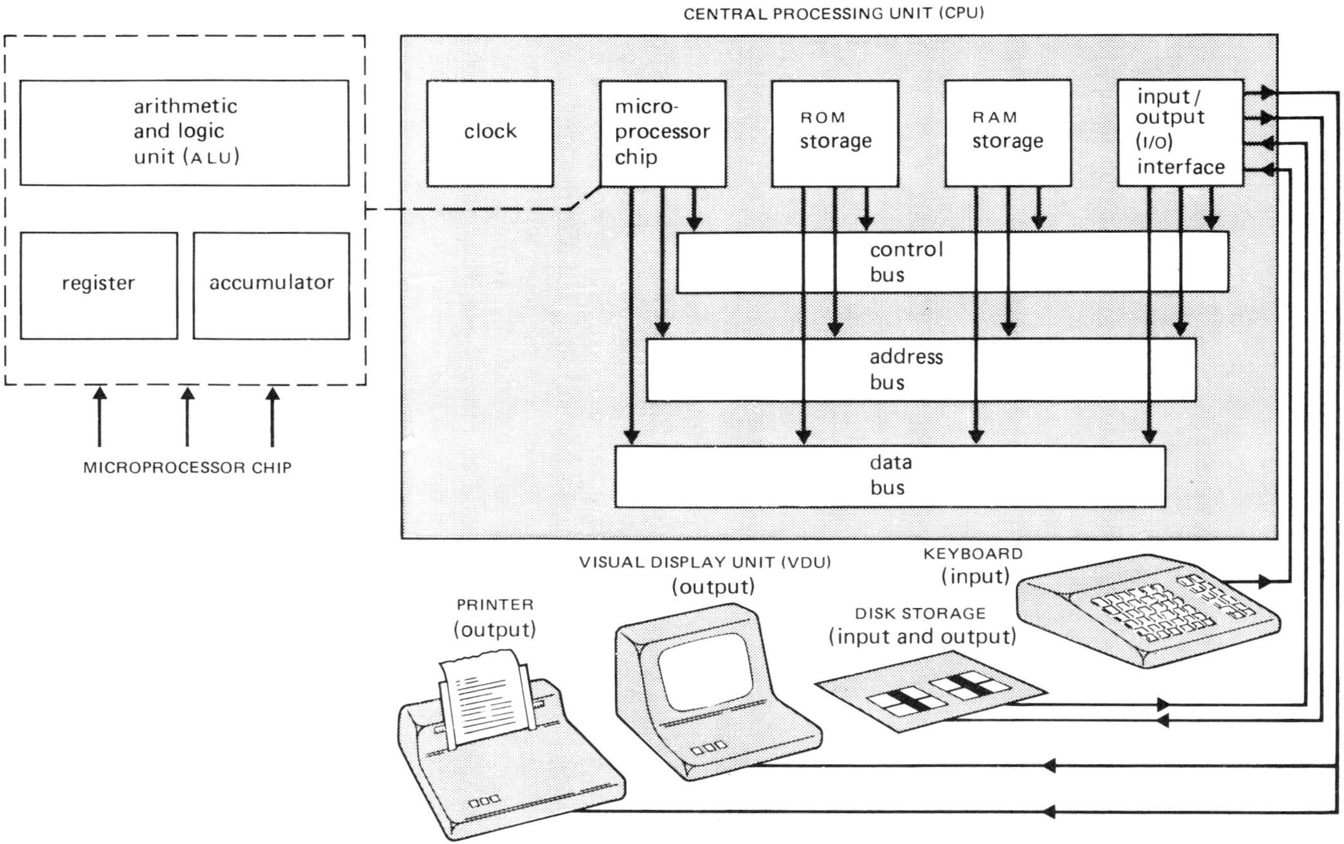

Figure 1.1 Basic components of a microcomputer system.

6 Microcomputers – general

The MPU recognizes only *binary numbers* (that is, numbers coded as a series of ones – 1s, and zeros – 0s) which are called *bits*. Originally all MPUs were *8-bit processors* since the basic unit of storage (that is, ten numbers 0–9, 26 alphabetic characters A–Z, arithmetic operators, punctuation marks, etc.) was made up of a code 8 bits long and referred to as a *byte*. Today, however, the majority of business microcomputers have *16-bit processors*. Their main advantage is that they permit a larger internal memory, as will now be explained.

The number of individual locations within a microcomputer's internal memory is controlled by the number of *address lines*. Since there are generally twice as many address lines as bits in a byte, this means that an 8-bit processor with 16 address lines can only control a range of addresses of individual storage locations from 0000000000000000 to 1111111111111111 in binary form or from 0 to 65,535 (i.e. 2^{16-1}) in decimal form. Thus at any instant in time the maximum amount of information that can be held in internal memory in an 8-bit machine is 64 kbytes, where 1 kbyte = 1024 bytes.

With a 16-bit machine, however, because there are more address lines, the number of individual storage locations within the internal memory is no longer effectively restricted by this constraint and is limited only by price. In practice, as will be seen later in this chapter, most 16-bit microcomputers start with a minimum of 256 kbytes of internal memory and currently have an effective maximum of 640 kbytes.

The size of a microcomputer's internal memory is most important and to a very large extent governs the applications for which a particular machine can be used and the speed at which it operates. This is because the internal memory has to accommodate not only the data relating to the particular application in hand, but also the applications programs and the systems software. For management applications 64 kbytes of memory (the amount traditionally available from 8-bit machines) was relatively little to meet these three requirements. In practice the machines could only be made to work satisfactorily by retaining the less frequently used elements of the applications program on disk (to be read in off disk as and when required, which slowed the system down considerably) and also by limiting the amount of data. (NOTE: The programs representing the operating system must always be stored in internal memory.)

Since 16-bit microcomputers generally start with a minimum of 256 kbytes of internal memory, for most applications it is now technically possible to have most of the applications program in memory, together with the operating system's programs and data, and hence theoretically have a much faster system.

Some of the integrated business packages such as Symphony and Framework (see chapter 7) are very demanding of memory, requiring up to 512 kbytes. PC/MC-DOS, currently the predominant operating system for business machines, can only use 640 kbytes but alternative uses are now being found for internal memory such as print buffer storage (in which files for printing are temporarily stored in internal memories, thus freeing the machine for other operations) and also 'RAM disk' (where memory is used effectively as a second disk drive – thus saving cost and improving performance). Within a microcomputer the type of internal memory into which data can be written, and from which data can also be read, is known as *random access memory* – RAM – although direct access memory would perhaps be a more meaningful name.

Each *location* within such memory has an *address* and the routing of data to and/or from a particular location is controlled by the MPU via the *address bus*, although the data itself travels along the *data bus* – a bus being a series of copper lines on a printed circuit board along which signals can travel between the various elements of the CPU. Whether data is to be read from or written to the memory is controlled by signals travelling along the *control bus* and, while reading a memory location does not alter the contents held there, writing obviously does.

Random access memory is *volatile*. It can only operate when the computer is switched on; and all information will be lost of the computer is switched off either deliberately or through an accidental failure of the mains supply.

Since applications programs and the associated data are different at each installation, such information can only be held temporarily in RAM during processing. However, programs associated with systems software for a particular microcomputer can be stored permanently. Hence, they can either be read into RAM from disk each time the computer is switched on, (more or less standard for business machines), or can be permanently stored in another type of memory known as *read only memory* – ROM, a system used more commonly with hobbyist or home computers.

Read only memory (ROM)

ROMs are memory chips which have information (usually programs) fixed into them permanently at manufacture and such information cannot be altered. This type of memory is known technically as *non-volatile* and is a slightly cheaper form of storage than RAM but, because programs are permanently recorded within the chip during the manufacturing process, it is only economic to produce ROM chips in reasonably large quantities.

Another type of read only memory chip is known as PROM (programmable ROM). These chips are produced with no program inside but can accept programs which are 'burnt' in using a special piece of equipment, sometimes linked to a microcomputer. Once a PROM is programmed, that program becomes permanent and cannot be altered or erased. Yet another type of chip, known as EPROM (erasable PROM), can have programs 'burnt' into it which can subsequently be 'erased' by exposing the chip to a very strong ultra-violet light for twenty minutes or so. EPROMs, therefore, can be used over and over again to store different programs, and generally have a memory capacity of 2 kbytes or 4 kbytes.

Programs which are held in read only memory, because they represent software which can be considered permanent, are often referred to as *firmware*.

Internal memory in general

Whether a microcomputer's internal memory is made up solely of RAM or of a combination of RAM and ROM, microcomputers using an 8-bit processor can, as we have seen, only normally address 64 kbytes of memory, whatever the type. Since, for management applications, one requires as much internal memory as possible, designers of business microcomputers (as opposed to hobbyists' machines) have had to decide whether to design a machine with a fixed operating system in ROM, usually leaving either 32 or 48 kbytes of RAM, or to use just RAM and to offer at least the opportunity of a variety of operating systems which could be loaded in from disk.

Historically the cheaper, more popular microcomputers which originated in the 4, 8 and 16 kbyte cassette-based, hobbyist market (such as Commodore/Pet, early Apple and Tandy machines) opted to incorporate their operating systems in ROM. However, once floppy disks became the main form of external storage – particularly for business applications – 'disk based' operating systems became the norm. With 8-bit microcomputers CP/M became the most popular operating system and currently with 16-bit machines MS-DOS, or its IBM equivalent PC-DOS, dominate the market. However, both MS-DOS and PC-DOS are essentially 'single-user' operating systems and a move towards multi-user systems in the future will require multi-user operating systems.

With all disk based operating systems, the main system files must be stored on the first disk which the computer finds when the machine is switched on, so that these files can be read into internal memory. Additional DOS files are also available for performing non-system tasks such as formatting, copying disks etc.

Input/output interface

The input/output interface contains the circuitry required to control and select the various peripheral devices connected to the microcomputer's CPU, namely: the keyboard, disk drive, visual display unit and printer. The basic function of the I/O interface is to ensure that the signals from the various peripheral devices can be made compatible with the CPU. The CPU operates in what is known as a *parallel* mode, while peripherals can operate in either a *parallel* or *serial* mode. So the I/O interface is made up both of chips that can handle serial to parallel conversions, such as UARTs (universal asynchronous receiver/transmitters) or ACIAs (asynchronous communication interface adaptors), and chips that can handle parallel to parallel conversions, such as PIAs (peripheral interface adaptors) or PIOs (parallel input/output devices). Serial data travels a bit at a time on two lines, whereas parallel data travels a byte (i.e. 8 bits) at a time on 8 lines.

Clock

The speed at which the CPU can operate is limited by the speed of the internal memory, which currently can be written to in about 200 nano seconds (i.e. 200×10^{-9} seconds). The operating frequency of the CPU is controlled by the *clock*, a chip which provides a regular high frequency pulse in much the same way as a chip in a digital watch. However, whereas in a watch the very high frequency (of the order of 4 Megahertz, or 4×10^6 cycles per second) has to be repeatedly divided to obtain a useful time pulse of one a second, in a computer processing does actually take place

10 Microcomputers – general

at a speed very near to that of the original clock pulse.

On average, each CPU instruction takes ten cycles or clock pulses. So, with a clock operating at a typical 4 MHz, a typical CPU can execute something like half a million instructions per second. This is much slower than a modern mainframe computer but, because a microcomputer usually only serves one user, it can appear as fast to that user as a mainframe computer does to one of its many users (often over a hundred).

Buses

The various elements of the CPU are connected by three buses, namely:

the data bus
the address bus, and
the control bus.

With the early 8-bit machines the S100 bus consisted of 100 lines, 16 for data – equivalent to two 8-bit characters – 16 in the address bus, 35 for the control bus and the remaining 33 for power supplies and other purposes.

With 16-bit machines a variety of bus systems are offered.

Physical construction of the CPU

The simplest CPUs consist of a single printed circuit board containing the microprocessor, memory, clock and interface chips with the interconnecting buses etched into the board's copper surface. More complicated CPUs have the individual elements of the CPU mounted on to separate circuit boards which plug into a base circuit board known as a motherboard.

Peripheral hardware

The visual display unit – VDU

The VDU contains a cathode ray tube and the associated circuitry necessary to display information in the form of *alphanumeric* (that is, A–Z and 0–9 etc.) or graphic characters on a screen. While many hobbyist machines have only 40 characters per line, it is generally accepted that business applications demand 80 characters per line (that is, 80 columns). When operating typically at 9600 baud (that is, 960 characters per second) a screen of 80 columns and 25 lines (a total of 2000 characters entered sequentially) can be filled completely in just over two seconds.

Single- or mono-colour screens generally produce a better definition than colour screens and are generally preferred for word processing. Colour screens, however, offer more interpretative facilities and are essential for business graphics.

The keyboard

The microcomputer's keyboard is usually based on the same layout of keys as a typewriter (QWERTY). In addition to the normal keys, all microcomputer keyboards include certain control keys such as RETURN (which is pressed at the end of each instruction), DELETE (DEL), ESCAPE (ESC), etc. Some keyboards are also furnished with special function keys whose operation can be controlled by the operating program and this facility is particularly useful in word processing applications. Increasingly, microcomputers intended for business use are fitted with a separate 'numeric pad' consisting of keys representing a decimal point and the numbers 0 to 9. This additional facility is particularly useful if large quantities of numeric data are to be entered via the keyboard. Where a numeric pad is included in a microcomputer keyboard, the number '5' key often has a raised nipple to assist touch typists. Similarly, on better keyboards the keys representing 'f' and 'j' may be sculpted slightly differently to assist touch and blind typists to locate the first fingers of both hands.

All alphanumeric and other characters entered at the keyboard have to be translated into a code of zeros and ones for sending to the CPU. The standard code for this is known as ASCII (American Standard Code for Information Interchange) which represents each letter, punctuation mark or other symbol as an 8-bit word (that is, one byte). The full ASCII code consists of 128 characters of which 96 are printing characters and the remaining 32 control characters. Being an American system, the one character the ASCII code does not accommodate is the pound sterling sign (£), so in place of the £ sign one often has to use a $ sign (not to be taken literally at the current rate of exchange) or a # (hash) sign.

Microcomputers – general

The mouse

A mouse is a small device used in conjunction with the keyboard and with software which requires a pointer to be manoeuvred to select items displayed on the screen. Physically small, a mouse usually fits easily into the palm of the operator's hand and consists of one or two switches and a moving ball arrangement which is rolled on a flat surface to achieve rapid movement of the pointer.

Disk storage

Although a few management applications packages can be operated using a cassette storage medium, it is generally accepted that, for the vast majority of business situations in which microcomputers are used, some form of disk storage is essential. While cassettes can be used to store a great deal of information, it is stored serially and can be read only at the relatively pedestrian pace of 250 baud, that is, 25 characters per second (cps). Typical read/write speeds for disks, however, range from 100 kbaud for 5¼ floppy disks to 8000 kbaud for a 'Winchester' hard disk. To read and load a 16 kbyte program from cassette at 250 baud would take 11 minutes, whereas the same program at 100 kbaud from floppy disk would just take 1.6 seconds. At the present stage of development most users find that floppy disks represent the cheapest form of storage in relation to performance.

5¼ inch floppy disk. The most popular disk currently used with microcomputer systems is the 5¼ inch floppy disk (sometimes referred to as a mini-floppy). At present the majority of microcomputer installations use 5¼ inch disks which, depending on whether the disks are single, double or quadruple density (quadruple means double density and double sided), can store from 100 kbytes up to about 800 kbytes each. A 5¼ inch floppy disk looks much like a smooth 45 rpm single record encased in a cardboard case. A slot exposes the surface of the disk, thus allowing the head of the disk drive's system to read information from and write information to the 30 to 70 individual tracks on the disk's surface. With 5¼ inch disks a *write protect* slot is also provided which must be covered with a protective adhesive strip to ensure that a programmed disk cannot subsequently be written on but can only be read. The Adler Alphatronic microcomputer flouts this convention by insisting that a *write enable* slot is covered to allow the disk to be written to. In the mid-1980s 5¼ inch floppy disks cost from £1 to £4 depending on the type and quantity purchased.

8 inch floppy disk. Similar in appearance to the 5¼ inch floppy disk, the 8 inch floppy disk, being considerably larger, can store more information at the same relative density. A double sided, double density 8 inch disk can typically store 1 Megabyte (i.e. 1000 kbytes). 8 inch disks are not yet quite as common as 5¼ inch disks for microcomputer applications, but do tend to be standard for dedicated word processors (see p. 85) where large amounts of text have to be stored. The convention with 8 inch disks is that they are normally write protected and the write enable slot therefore has to be covered before they can be written to. Currently 8 inch floppy disks cost from £2 to £5 depending on the type and quantity purchased.

3½ inch floppy disk. Now available from several manufacturers, the so called *micro-floppy* is not only physically smaller than the 5¼ inch disk but is housed in a rigid plastic container rather than a flexible cardboard envelope. In addition a metal slide is incorporated in this container which protects the read/write slot. Claimed to be more reliable and storing 360 kbytes in a single sided configuration, micro-floppies are available at much the same price as the better quality 5¼ inch disks. (Note: 3 inch micro-floppies are also used in some machines but are not as common as 3½ inch.)

Floppy disks in general. As far as the life of the disks themselves is concerned, a figure of 3.5 million passes per track can be interpreted in more practical terms as 160 hours of continual access to the same track. Another figure often quoted by disk manufacturers is that disks should be able to survive 20,000 uses (that is, in-and-out) of a disk drive. Currently some suppliers are offering two and five year guarantee periods for 5¼ and 8 inch floppy disks respectively. The higher the density at which the information is recorded on to disk, the higher the quality of disk required. While a single density disk will record at double density, corruption of information is much more likely to occur.

Unlike cassettes, before any information can be recorded on a disk, the disk must be prepared or *formatted*. This is done by loading the new, blank disk into the disk drive and running a special program. This program can take anything from one to eight minutes to complete the formatting of the disk, depending on the disk operating system – DOS – of the microcomputer being used. For disks to be used with the CP/M, MS-DOS and other oprating systems, the programs making up that system must be recorded on the disk in advance.

For virtually all microcomputer systems used in management applications, apart from those at the top of the range which use Winchester hard disks, the floppy disk provides the principal medium of permanent external storage for data and applications software. Since such disks can fail, it is essential to produce backup copies of disks at relatively frequent intervals. This can be done by loading the disk to be copied into one disk drive (by convention usually drive A) and the new, blank disk into the other disk drive (drive B) and then running a program provided with the operating system (e.g. DISKCOPY with PC-DOS) which copies tracks from the disk in the A-drive to that in the B-drive to produce an exact copy. Depending on the DOS (disk operating system), this process can take between two and ten minutes. In some systems it is possible to produce a backup disk with a *version number* which can indicate which of two apparently identical disks was copied from which. Such control of versions of copies can and should be implemented by correctly labelling disks at the time of backup. In all management applications using microcomputers, backup disks are essential to ensure that, if a disk fails entirely, the data lost on that disk can be recreated without too much bother. What 'without too much bother' means in practice depends on the application and the frequency at which new data is entered into the system, but as a rule of thumb most computer users can expect at least one disk failure per year.

For security, backup disks should always be kept in a different location from the original copy. Further guidelines for the care of floppy disks are:

> always keep the disk in its protective envelope when not actually in use;
>
> do not bend disks to prove that they are indeed floppy, and always insert disks into disk drives carefullly;
>
> never touch the disk surface through the read/write slot;
>
> do not store disks in extreme temperatures (i.e. lower than 10°C or higher than 52°C);

do not allow disks to be exposed to any magnetic source — particularly electric motors;

use either felt-tip pens or very light pressure when labelling the disk case itself. Write on the protective envelope *before* replacing the disk.

Readers should be warned that the storage capacities quoted for floppy disks are total or *gross* figures. Because the disk operating system must store additional information, such as the disk directory, the *net* available capacity will often be about 90 per cent of the gross figure.

The floppy disk controller and its associated mechanism are amongst the most sophisticated elements of a microcomputer system. The controller may well possess its own MPU and have an operating program equivalent in complexity to the one in the microcomputer's CPU.

Winchester hard disks. The so-called Winchester hard disk is similar in construction to the type of hard disks used on mini- and mainframe computers, the main difference being that a Winchester disk is permanently fixed in the microcomputer and cannot be removed.

Hard disk systems cost considerably more than floppy disk systems but, because the disk is contained in a sealed unit, much higher densities of information storage can be used. The Winchester hard disk can store typicaly between 5 and 30 Megabytes of information (that is, 5000 to 30,000 kbytes).

While floppy disks tend only to be rotated at between 200 and 360 rpm, and then only when a read or write procedure is in progress, hard disks run continuously and at much higher speeds, typically 3600 rpm. This considerably reduces the time of access and data transference speeds of up to 800 kbytes/sec are claimed, compared with 100 kbytes per second for mini-floppies.

Although hard disks are more reliable than floppy disks, it is still necessary to produce some form of backup copy of the information stored. Because of the comparatively large amounts of information that can be stored, the production of individual backup floppy disks becomes impractical, simply because of the numbers involved. Hence, such hard disks are usually backed up with magnetic tape using a high-speed read/write mechanism or occasionally by a magazine of floppy disks which are loaded automatically, although this latter system is generally associated with minicomputers. Because of the high price of Winchester disks, they are at the moment fitted only to the more expensive microcomputer systems but are becoming increasingly popular as prices fall.

The relative costs, storage capacities and speed of information transference for the various types of disk are summarized in table 1.1.

Table 1.1 Basic operating information of disk storage devices

Type of disk	Storage capacity	Speed of access	Cost
5¼ inch floppy (mini-disk)	100 kbytes to 500 kbytes (per disk)	100 kbaud to 500 kbaud (10,000 cps to 50,000 cps)	£250 (Dual Drive)
8 inch floppy disk	500 kbytes to 1.2 Megabytes (per disk)	500 kbaud to 620 kbaud (50,000 cps to 62,000 cps)	£500+ (Dual Drive)
5¼–8 inch Winchester hard disk	5 Megabytes to 40 Megabytes	8000 kbaud (800,000 cps)	£1,250+ (with facilities for producing a backup tape)

Microcomputer systems

With one or two exceptions (the OK800 microcomputer being one), printers are not generally physically integrated with the other peripheral components making up a microcomputer system. While some microcomputer manufacturers do produce their own printers, many more either come to an arrangement to stick their label on some other manufacturer's product, or simply allow the user to choose whichever printer seems appropriate.

Thus excluding the printer, a business microcomputer system typicaly consists of:

   central processor unit;

   visual display unit;

keyboard;

dual disk drive unit (i.e. two floppies or one floppy and a hard disk)

and these four major components can be packaged in various degrees of physical integration as illustrated in figures 1.2 to 1.9.

The Apple II machine shown in figure 1.2 demonstrates the lowest degree of physical integration. Only the CPU and keyboard are integrated, the two disk drives and VDU monitor all being separate units. The Apple II represents the early stages of microcomputer design. In many ways the development of microcomputers has mirrored that of domestic hi-fi systems which were originally made up of separate components such as the tuner, amplifier, etc. and then all these elements were integrated into music centres. Although by modern standards a rather antiquated machine, the Apple II still accounts for a significant proportion of

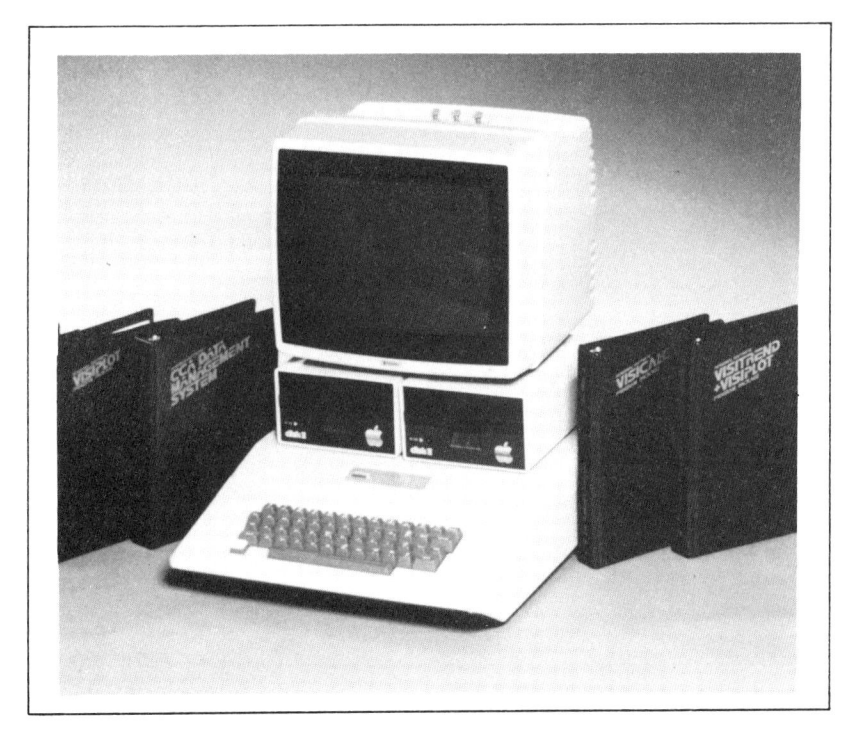

Figure 1.2 Apple II computer, two disk drives and Hitachi video monitor.

18 Microcomputers – general

Apple's sales and has been enhanced to ensure compatibility with the IBM PC. The various elements of the microcomputer are a little more integrated in the North Star Advantage shown in figure 1.3. This, like the Apple II, is an 8-bit machine which is therefore starting to show its age.

Figure 1.4 shows the Sirius 1 microcomputer, the first 16-bit machine to be widely available on the UK market. This illustration shows the physical separation of the VDU and keyboard from the main unit of the microcomputer, a design feature now generally adopted. A particularly interesting concept within the Sirius, unfortunately not adopted in subsequent manufacturers' designs, is the variable speed disk drives which allow information on the outer tracks to be recorded at the same density as that on the inner tracks, making it possible to store as much as 600 kbytes on a single sided floppy disk.

Figure 1.5 shows the Apricot microcomputer, claimed by ACT to be the 'first of the fourth generation of personal microcomputers', incorporating such features as 3½ inch micro-floppy disk drives, a microscreen – a unique two line Liquid Crystal Display (LCD) and six associated touch sensitive keys – and an internal modem. The latter enables the Apricot to act as an intelligent terminal or work

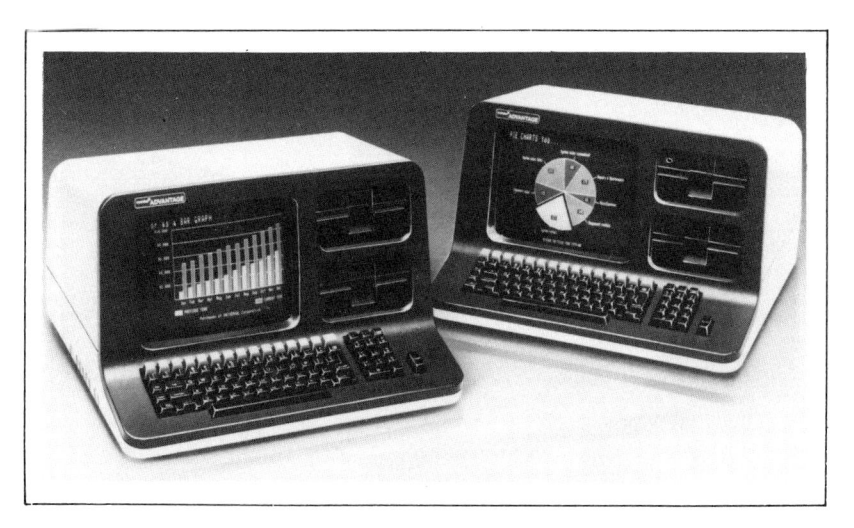

Figure 1.3 North Star Advantage microcomputer with dual 5¼ inch floppy disk drives (360 kbytes each). Business Graphics package featured. Courtesy: Comart Ltd.

Figure 1.4 Sirius 1 16-bit microcomputer starting with 128 bytes of RAM. Courtesy: ACT(UK) Limited.

station into either a Local Area Network (for more on LANs see p. 59) or any communication network using public telephone systems (see p. 64). While not portable as a single unit, the Apricot can easily be carried as two separate units and does provide a 9 inch screen which is intermediate in size between the standard 12 inch screen and the minute, eye-straining 5 inch screen of the first popular portable microcomputer, the now obsolete Osborne 1.

The Apricot was discontinued in mid-1986 due to market

20 Microcomputers – general

Figure 1.5 The Apricot personal computer with 3½ inch micro-floppy disks.
Courtesy: ACT(UK) Limited.

pressures. ACT announced at that time to continue with the Apricot Xen which is both a high powered, hard disk personal computer and also a cheap multi-user machine using the Xenix operating system to handle up to four remote terminals. ACT, the manufacturers of the Apricot range are one of the few British companies currently attempting to compete in the international microcomputer marketplace.

The machine that has had the largest impact on the UK business microcomputer market, however, is the IBM PC (Personal Computer), shown in figure 1.6. This machine represented IBM's first move into microcomputers (as opposed to minis and mainframe machines) in the UK. When originally introduced, initial reviews for this

Microcomputer systems 21

Figure 1.6 The IBM PC (Personal Computer)
Courtesy: IBM United Kingdom Ltd.

machine from the 'experts' were not very enthusiastic; and indeed, in retrospect it cannot be said that the IBM PC represented a breakthrough in microcomputer technology. However, in spite of the early criticisms, the IBM PC very rapidly gained for itself a major portion of the UK microcomputer market and it soon became evident to competitors that the reason for its success was not its technical specification but simply the fact that at last this machine represented a standard to which others would have to conform. It also became abundantly clear that this concept of a standard machine which would allow for interchangability of data was what the market had ben waiting for.

Following the initial launch in 1983 of the standard PC (pictured in figure 1.6), IBM have introduced three further PC machines to meet the specific needs of other perceived market sectors. The first of these additional models was the PC portable with a built-in 9 inch screen. Although at 28 lbs weight this is strictly speaking a 'transportable', the PC portable was launched to meet that market sector which required relatively frequent transportation of the source microcomputer – the market so successfully exploited originally by the 8-bit CP/M machine – the Osborne 1. The second addition to the IBM PC family was the PC XT which incorporated a hard disk and thus enlarged external disk storage from a mere 2 × 360 kbytes for the twin floppy PC and PC Portable to a relatively massive 10 Mbytes. This machine, apart from the addition of a hard disk, is a very similar hardware package to the standard PC and the PC Portable. All three machines use an Intel 8088, a 16-bit microprocessor chip, operating at a speed of 4.77 MHz and all operate with IBM's proprietary version of Microsoft's MS-DOS, namely PC-DOS.

The third addition to the IBM PC family was the PC AT (Advanced Technology), essentially a different machine from its three predecessors offering faster operating speeds, much improved keyboard and more storage. Viewed as a 'second generation' PC, the PC AT uses the powerful Intel 80286 processor and offers limited multi-user facilities. The role that this machine will fill in the microcomputing spectrum is at the time of writing not absolutely clear, but speculation has it that the typical AT user will be a 'power user', that is someone using large spreadsheet and 'number crunching' software and requiring the increased memory and speed of this machine which operates three times faster than standard IBM PCs. It is expected that the market for this machine will not be the casual microcomputer user, but rather data-processing managers, possibly replacing antiquated minis, requiring a gateway to the company mainframe machine or using the PC AT as a file-server for a local area network (see p. 59).

Since IBM – the largest computer company in the world – entered the microcomputer market, the name of the game for competitors in that market has become one of producing IBM 'compatibles', 'clones' or 'look-alikes' which, without contravening IBM's copyright, provide a machine which to the user does all that an IBM PC does but does it

faster,

cheaper,

with free (or bundled) software,

with more storage for the same price,

with better keyboards, video displays, etc.

Microcomputer systems 23

Technically it is not difficult to produce an IBM PC 'compatible' and also to present it to the potential customer either at an attractive price or as an attractive package; a potential target that some market pundits have referred to as '10 per cent better and 10 per cent cheaper'. The real problem for each competitor, however, is to make PC 'compatibles' in large enough numbers and with sufficient backup to convince the business and industrial market sectors that they represent a solid and reliable company able to survive in the marketplace well into the future.

One of the most successful companies in the IBM compatible sector has been the COMPAC Computer company which originally produced a portable machine generally reckoned to be superior to the IBM equivalent and sold so successfully as to establish COMPAC as one of the few originally small microcomputer manufacturers that have been able to survive in the business microcomputer marketplace. This company now offers a whole range of machines, one of which, the COMPAC Plus, is shown in figure 1.7. This machine competes directly with the IBM XT and incorporates a 10 Mbyte hard disk.

The Apple Computer company is the most successful microcomputer manufacturer of those which have pursued a development policy independent to that of IBM and the many companies producing IBM compatibles. This company's very successful Macintosh microcomputer has its own user friendly operating system within which, by using a 'mouse' (see p. 12) to point at 'icons' (small picture symbols) on the screen, the user can perform many selection tasks without having to resort to using the keyboard. However, in spite of the Macintosh's success as an identifiably different machine to the IBM PC series and its many clones, it has been recognized that a large sector of the microcomputer market is closed to this machine if it is not IBM compatible. This restriction has now been overcome by the introduction by the Mitsui Company of MacCharlie – a hardware and software product which enables the Apple Macintosh to use software written specifically for the IBM PC whilst maintaining the integrity of the Macintosh. This is achieved, as can be seen in figure 1.8, by providing an expansion unit that physically connects to the right side of the Macintosh and provides 640 kbytes of RAM and dual 5¼ inch floppy disk drives (whilst preserving the normal Apple 3½ inch drive) and also by providing a keyboard extension (into which the normal Apple keyboard slides) which contains 10 function keys and an 18 key numeric keypad. It is claimed by Mitsui that:

Figure 1.7 The COMPAC Plus – a portable 16-bit micro with a 10 Mbyte hard disk.
Courtesy: COMPAC Computer Ltd.

MacCharlie has been designed to satisfy the needs of three major groups of people. Macintosh owners who would like to use some specific MS-DOS software; potential Macintosh buyers who are concerned about having to sacrifice MS-DOS compatability for Macintosh's ease of use and committed MS-DOS users who can improve their productivity by making use of the Macintosh's graphic capabilities, desktop accessories and its ability to integrate data between different unrelated application packages.

The Wang company, with a strong reputation in offic automation, has a range of machines which are IBM compatible. The Wang PC (Professional Computer) incorporates an advanced, ergonomically designed monitor which can be mounted either on a pedestal base as here (figure 1.9) or on an optional monitor arm and desk clamp. Wang is a multinational company based in the USA offering a range of machines starting with an internal memory of 128 kbytes

Figure 1.8 The Apple Macintosh with the MacCharlie Coprocessing System offering IBM compatibility.
Courtesy: Apple Computer (UK) Ltd and Mitsui Co Ltd.

expandable up to 640 kbytes and supports both MS-DOS and CP/M-80 operating systems. Like the IBM PC, the Wang PC can also operate as a 'stand-alone' machine, as a work station within a local network or as an intelligent terminal communicating with a large host computer.

Printers

Microcomputer printers can most easily be classified by the mechanism used to produce printed hard copy. On this basis there are essentially five categories of printer, namely:

impact dot-matrix;
daisy-wheel (or thimble);

26 *Microcomputers – general*

Figure 1.9 The Wang PC (Personal Computer) on pedestal base. Courtesy: Wang (UK) Ltd.

thermal;

ink-jet;

laser.

Of these five categories, dot-matrix printers represent the vast majority of printers used for business applications where 'correspondence quality' printing is considered to be adequate. Daisywheel printers are used in most business applications where 'letter quality' is required, and the poorer correspondence quality of the average dot-matrix printer is not considered suitable. (See figures 4.3 and 4.4 for comparison.)

Impact dot-matrix printers

This type of printer has a print-head formed by a *matrix* of pins individually raised to form the character to be printed. The printing of the character is effected by physically *impacting* the print-head against a carbon ribbon as in traditional typewriter technology. Because a dot-matrix printer is usually designed to print 'on the fly' with the print-head moving at a uniform horizontal velocity and also bi-directionally (both forwards and backwards), it can achieve speeds of up to 200 characters per second (cps).

The print quality of dot-matrix printers can be improved by the use of multiple passes, but this obviously reduces operating speeds. A more effective means of improving print quality is to increase the size of the print matrix by increasing the number of pins incorporated. Such an arrangement can produce an acceptable *near letter quality* print.

Dot-matrix print-heads do wear, and under a very heavy workload may need replacing once a year at a cost of 5–10 per cent of the cost of the whole printer, but in less arduous working situations they can last for the effective life of the printer itself.

Daisy-wheel (or thimble) printers

A daisy-wheel printer uses a set of characters embossed on the tips of individual spokes of 'petals' of a wheel. The wheel is rotated so that the correct character is positioned in front of a hammer which strikes the tip of the petal when the wheel is momentarily stationary, and thus, via a carbon ribbon, produces an image of that selected print character. Daisy-wheel printers usually operate at about 50 cps and so are rather slow compared with dot-matrix printers but the quality of print is very good. Hence, this type of printer is normally used in word processing applications.

Because individual daisy-wheels are removable, many different typefaces can be offered. One manufacturer offers 72, varying from traditional British Pica 10 to the more exotic Dual Gothic 12/Multilingual A and including, on the way, Canadian Bilingual which is naturally only recommended for special machines!

One of the biggest disadvantages of these type of printers is that they cannot print graphical symbols and, hence, graphs.

Laser printers

Whilst very expensive, these printers – which use photocopier technology – can print up to 12 complete A4 pages a minute. Laser printers offer a very good print quality, fast speed and quiet operation.

Thermal printers

Thermal printers use a dot-matrix principle, where the pins are heated to produce an impression on heat sensitive paper. Because of the cost of this special paper is quite high, thermal printers are not used extensively in business applications.

Ink-jet printers

Ink-jet printers are a relatively new development and fairly expensive by microcomputer standards. Their main asset would appear to be quietness of operation and speed of printing (210 cps). Their one drawback is that since 'jets' of ink are used to form the printed character there is no physical impact, so that multiple printed copies cannot be produced using multi-part stationery.

Printers in general

For some business applications, printers capable of printing up to 120 characters per line are required. Line widths of printers tend to be either 80 or 132 characters per line, so for business use the latter is usually specified, unless condensed print on a smaller printer is acceptable.

Business applications also increasingly require the printing of graphs and this has tended to bias business users towards dot-matrix machines which can now also produce a very acceptable near letter quality print.

Figure 1.10 illustrates the Epson FX80 dot-matrix, economy printer and its more expensive cousin the LQ1500. Both offer a variety of fonts, graphics and a 'near letter quality' mode which is nearly as good as that produced by daisy-wheel printers. This type of printer can also cope with foreign print characters and mathematical symbols.

Figure 1.11 illustrates a very robust dot-matrix printer of the type used for business applications. The Tandy TRS-80 heavy-duty, bi-directional dot-matrix printer operates at 120 cps which, in more practical terms, means that it can print 48 lines per minute. With 132 characters per line at a print density of either 10 or 15 characters per inch, this type of machine would be suitable for most applications packages.

Figure 1.12 shows the Tandy TRS-80 Daisy-wheel II printer

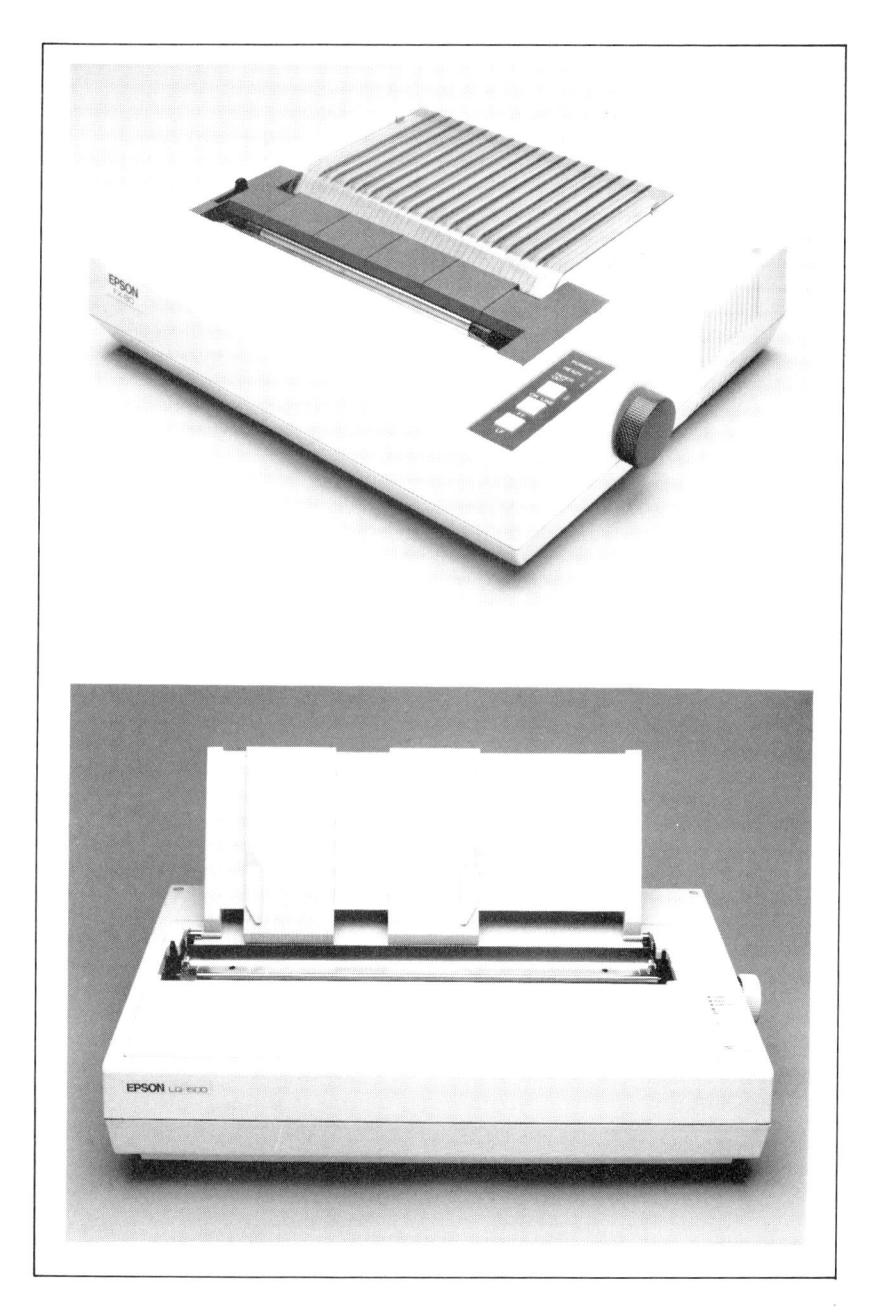

Figure 1.10 The Epson FX-80 impact dot-matrix economy printer (above) and Epson LQ500 24 pin impact dot-matrix printer with near letter quality mode (below).
Courtesy: Epson (UK) Ltd.

30 Microcomputers – general

Figure 1.11 Tandy TRS-80 heavy duty bi-directional dot-matrix printer (120 cps).
Courtesy: Tandy Corporation (Branch UK).

which was developed specifically for word processing applications and has a print speed of 43 cps. An individual daisy-wheel is shown (inset); it can be changed easily to produce different typefaces such as Courier Prestige Elite and Madeleine Proportional Space Print.

Figure 1.13 illustrates the NEC spin writer, a high quality thimble printer with a print speed of 55 cps. While the thimble uses a similar printing technology to the daisy-wheel, the makers claim that the shape and construction of the thimble allows 128 different characters to be produced compared with the daisy-wheel's 96.

Finally, Figure 1.14 shows, in diagrammatic form, the technology used in ink-jet printing. These printers are relatively expensive compared with the equivalent dot-matrix printer but, at 210 cps and 132 characters per line, this notably quiet printer would be suitable for most applications packages.

As a conclusion to this section on printer/typewriters used with

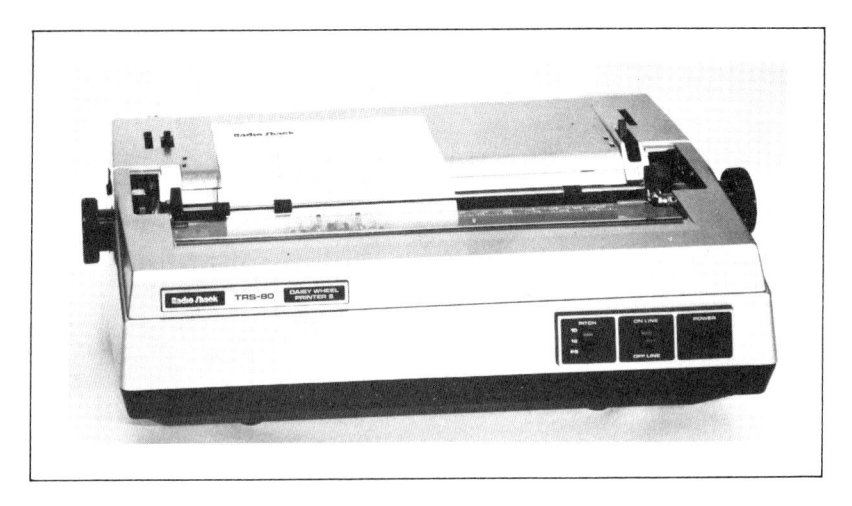

Figure 1.12 (above) Tandy TRS-80 Daisy-wheel II printer with a print speed of 43 cps and 136 characters per line; (left) print daisy-wheel. Courtesy: Tandy Corporation (Branch UK).

microcomputer systems, table 1.2 summarizes the main characteristics of the five principal types.

Software

Software is the overall name given to programs which either provide computer instructions for a particular application (hence *applications software*) or translate a higher level computer language

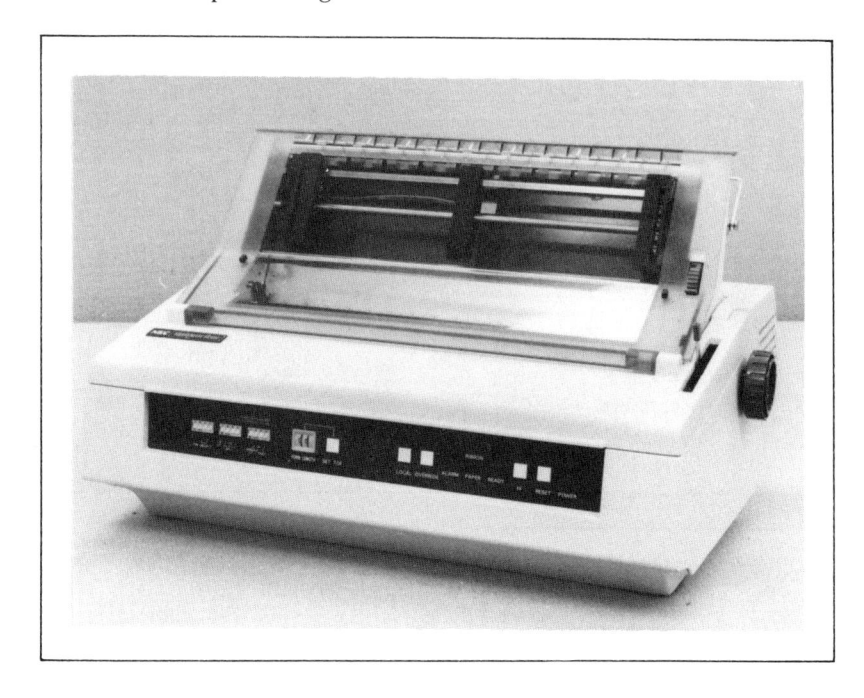

Figure 1.13 (above) NEC spin writer, high quality thimble printer (55 cps); (left) print thimble.
Courtesy: Thame Systems Ltd.

into a lower level language, organize the flow of information between peripheral devices and the computer's CPU and in general control the computer's overall operating system (hence *systems* or *operating software*).

A program is a series of instructions written in a computer language which at the higher level can be understood by the human

Microcomputer systems 33

Figure 1.14 (left) The 'noiseless' AJ 650 ink-jet printer (210 cps); (below) ink-jet mechanism.
Courtesy: Anderson Jacobson Inc.

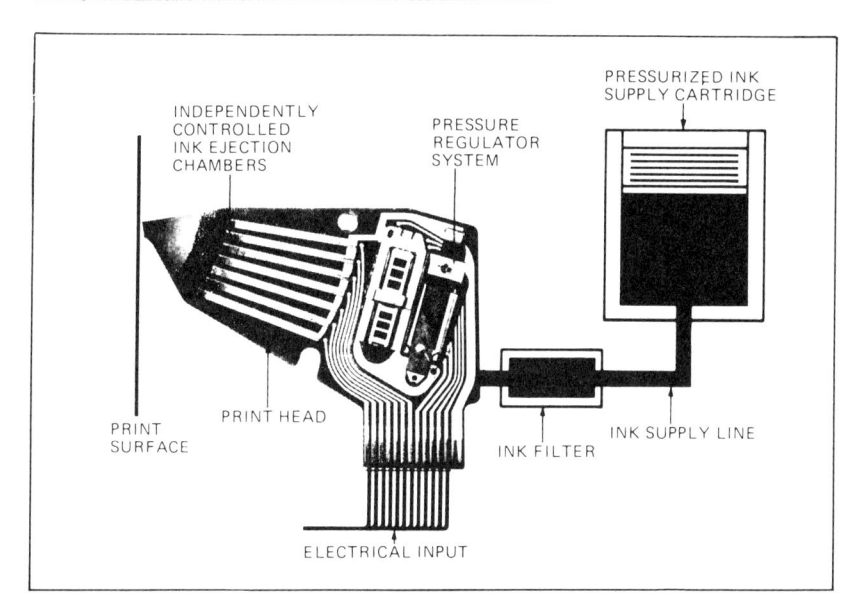

[Diagram labels: PRESSURIZED INK SUPPLY CARTRIDGE; INDEPENDENTLY CONTROLLED INK EJECTION CHAMBERS; PRESSURE REGULATOR SYSTEM; PRINT SURFACE; PRINT HEAD; INK FILTER; INK SUPPLY LINE; ELECTRICAL INPUT]

programmer and at the lower level can be understood by the microcomputer's CPU.

Figure 1.15 shows in diagrammatic form the sources and levels of programming language in a microcomputer and indicates how a higher level language, such as BASIC, is eventually converted into a series of codes of 0s and 1s that can be understood by the CPU.

Table 1.2 Classification of printers by print mechanism

Print mechanism	Speed (characters per second)	Print quality	Line width (characters)	Price range (1985)	Comments	Manufacturers
Impact dot-matrix	30 cps to	'correspondence' quality (near letter quality with larger matrix print heads)	80	£300 to £500	able to print graphics	Epson Centronics Anadex IBM
	300 cps		132	£500 to £1,500	limited print-head life	Microline Texas Tandy Commodore
Daisy-wheel or Thimble	55 cps (typical) 80 cps (maximum)	'letter' quality	80–132	£1,700 to £2,000	can be used as a typewriter no graphics	Olympia, Tandy Qume, Commodore Diablo, NEC, Olivetti Ricoh, IBM
Laser	12 pages per minute	'letter' quality	80–132	£2,500+	fast, quiet, superb graphics	Apple, Canon Hewlett Packard Ricoh
Ink-jet	210 cps	'letter' quality	80–132	£2,000+	quiet cannot produce direct copies	Anderson Jacobson Epson
Thermal	40 cps	acceptable	80	£400+	no direct copies and expensive paper	Apple Epson IBM

Systems software

The functions of systems software are mainly technical and therefore of little interest to the potential business user. However, in choosing a microcomputer system two features of systems software are particularly important and these will be examined here before we enter into a wider discussion of applications software.

Flexibility versus inflexibility. As we have seen (p. 9) the programs representing systems software can either be permanently stored in the computer in a read only memory chip (ROM) or be read in from disk into the computer's main random access memory chip (RAM) using a small program stored in ROM called a resident monitor.

Historically, when cassettes were the only form of external storage medium for microcomputers, it was only practical to record the programs representing the operating system permanently in ROM (read only memory) chips which to all intents and purposes meant that the machine's operating system was fixed, unless one physically inserted different chips.

However, with the development of floppy disks which permitted the operating system to be read into internal memory in a matter of seconds rather than minutes, there was a general move towards disk based operating systems. With 8-bit machines the predominant disk based operating system was CP/M (Control Program for Microprocessors) and with 16-bit machines a variety of operating systems are available, such as CP/M-86, PC-DOS, MS-DOS and Unix. Many of the more sophisticated business microcomputers can accommodate more than one operating system which greatly increases the number of applications packages that are potentially available to those machines.

Disk operating system (DOS). One of the most important elements systems software for business microcomputers is the disk operating system (DOS). This is a series of programs which organize how information is stored on disks and which, therefore, control the speed at which information can be written to or read from disk.

In business applications where information is *not* continually being transferred from disk to internal memory, for example, in word processing (chapter 4) or numerical analysis using electronic

```
                                                                    ┌──────────────┐
                                                                    │  TRANSLATORS │
                                                                    └──────┬───────┘
                                                                           │
```

HIGHER LEVEL PROGRAMMING LANGUAGE	
BASIC (C-BASIC) FORTRAN COBOL PASCAL	BASIC (M-BASIC)
a programming language using English command words whose syntax permits programs to be written with little reference to the machine to be used. Designed for ease of programming rather than computational efficiency. One high-level instruction may represent many machine readable code instructions	

COMPILER	INTERPRETER
converts whole program into a machine readable code and removes superfluous logic to speed up program operation	converts program into machine readable code statement by statement, rather than all at once as in a compiler

LOWER LEVEL PROGRAMMING LANGUAGE
ASSEMBLY LANGUAGE
a language where instructions are represented by mnemonics, usually machine specific

ASSEMBLER
translates an assembly language instruction into a machine readable code instruction usually on a one-for-one basis

MACHINE READABLE CODE (OF BINARY OF MACHINE CODE)
codes of 0s and 1s which the cpu can understand directly

(APPLICATIONS SOFTWARE)

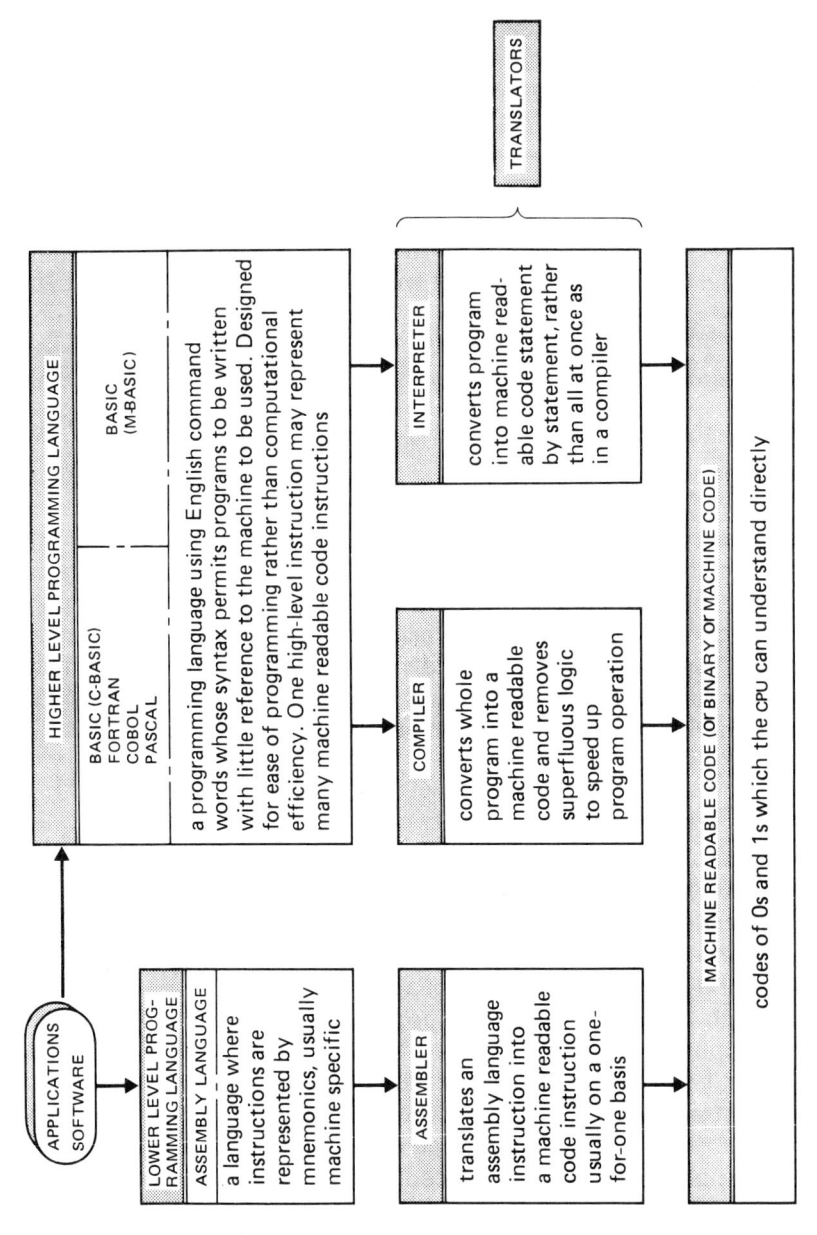

Figure 1.15 Sources and levels of programming languages in a microcomputer.

spreadsheet programs such as Lotus 1-2-3 (chapter 5), the speed of the disk operating systems is not too important. However, in situations where many individual records (such as stock, personnel, accounts records, etc. *are* continually being pulled in from disk to be processed by sections of applications programs selected via a menu (a listing on the computer screen of the programs available) which will also have to be pulled in from disk, the speed of the disk operating system can become crucial. Unfortunately, sales demonstrations do not usually highlight the difference in speeds between different disk operating systems, simply because such demonstrations usually only involve a handful of records. A discussion with another business user of a microcomputer system operating with a large number of records on a similar application to that intended by the prospective purchaser is the only way of really finding out how quickly one can, for instance, process and update 250 personnel records in a payroll system. The time required to produce a backup disk could also be a reasonable indicator of the operating systems speed.

Applications software

Applications software can either be acquired in the form of a proprietary package ('canned program' in American usage) or can be written specifically for the potential user as a *'bespoke' package* tailored to his or her particular requirements. Because professional programmers cost £20,000+ *per annum* with overheads and the development time is rarely less than six months, bespoke packages tend to be expensive, especially when related to the cost of hardware. Proprietary packages, on the other hand, because their development costs can be recovered over many copies, tend to be priced between £100 and £1,000, and for the business applications considered in this book the following range of values applied in the mid-1980s:

electronic spreadsheet (numerical analysis and graphics)	£90–£350
payroll, stock recording	£250+
database management and information retrieval	£200–£500
integrated ledger/accounts	£350–£600
word processing, integrated business package	£450+

38 *Microcomputers – general*

A proprietary applications package usually comes as a set of pre-programmed floppy disks together with an instruction manual and, sometimes, a security device such as a ROM chip or 'dongle' (see p. 41). The quality and comprehensibility of instruction manuals is most important for management applications and does vary considerably. Some can baffle anyone whose mind does not work like a professional programmer's; others are excellent.

Programming language

The programs in most applications packages are written in a *higher level language* such as BASIC, FORTRAN or COBOL but some are written at a *lower level* or *assembly language* (see figure 1.15) which in general terms will tend to be quicker and more efficient than the equivalent higher level language program.

Although BASIC – the most popular higher language used for microcomputers – is much abused by programming buffs, it soldiers on, particularly for business applications, in spite of the rival claims of its nearest competitors FORTRAN, COBOL, ALGOL and PASCAL. Because most BASIC programs are *interpreted* one program line at a time, when microcomputers were first introduced commercially BASIC was the only higher level language that could be used. With the subsequent development of *compilers*, which translate all the instructions in a program into a complete 'compiled' form before the program is run, FORTRAN, COBOL, ALGOL and even compiled BASIC could also be run on microcomputers. Yet, having been first in the field, interpretative BASIC still has a strong hold on the applications software market.

Applications packages

Figure 1.16 summarizes results from the magazine *Personal Computer World*'s bi-monthly 'packages' feature which surveys business packages that are available on the open market and have been used for at least six months in a minimum of five sites.

From this survey it is immediately apparent that a large proportion of the available applications packages on the UK software market fall into five broad catagories, namely:

integrated accounts and ledger (various)   31%

stock recording and control   12%

database, lotteries, mailing list   10%

payroll   9%

word processing   8%

Two omissions from this survey are the spreadsheet and integrated business packages, most of which have been developed in the USA.

It can be seen that the vast majority of business applications fall into seven major categories; this book provides information on and examples of all of these. Chapter 4 deals with wordprocessing; chapter 5 spreadsheets with graphics; chapter 6 database management and information retrieval; and chapter 7 with integrated packages, which combine these four functions in a single package. The more specifically business orientated packages such as Payroll, Accounts Ledger and Stock Control are described in chapters 8, 9 and 10 respectively.

Software protection

All software houses that produce applications packages face the problem of software piracy – the copying of programs. Having invested considerable sums of money developing a program, which, incidentally, cannot be patented, it is obviously in the software house's interest to ensure that only registered users who have purchased a package through the normal channels should be able to use it.

Several methods of software protection have been developed to counter software piracy and these are now briefly discussed.

ROM protection.   One method of protecting a program is to arrange that a small but necessary part of the program is stored in a ROM chip, so that the main program will only operate on a microcomputer with that chip plugged into the appropriate socket inside the machine. Because chips can be copied this method of protection is not foolproof, but it will deter the less enthusiastic potential pirate. VISICALC was an example of a well known program that used this form of protection.

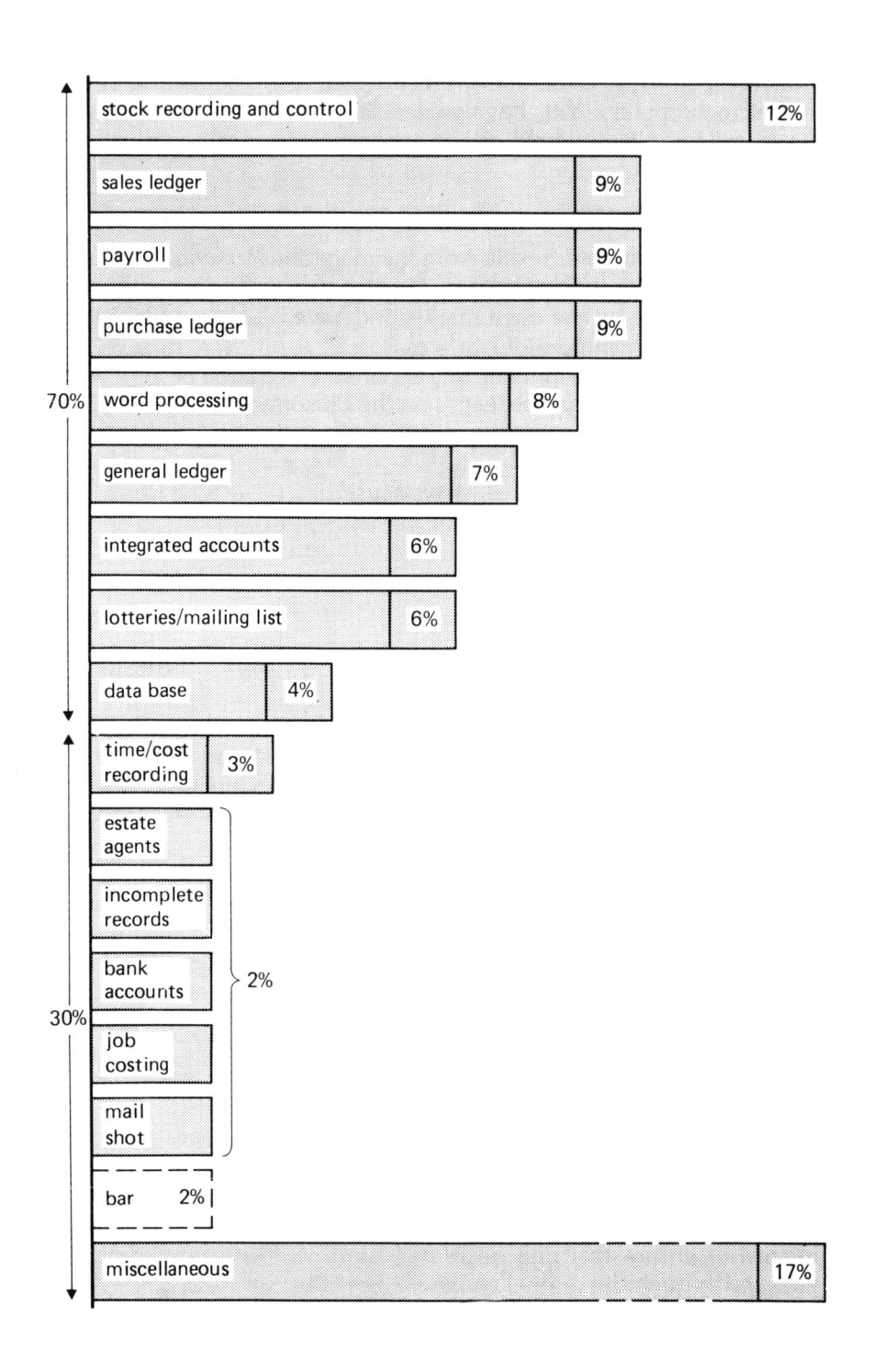

Application	%
stock recording and control	12%
sales ledger	9%
payroll	9%
purchase ledger	9%
word processing	8%
general ledger	7%
integrated accounts	6%
lotteries/mailing list	6%
data base	4%

70% (stock recording and control through data base)

Application	%
time/cost recording	3%
estate agents	2%
incomplete records	2%
bank accounts	2%
job costing	2%
mail shot	2%
bar	2%
miscellaneous	17%

30% (time/cost recording through miscellaneous)

'Dongle' or stunt box protection. With this method of protection a small device consisting of an encapsulated piece of circuitry is plugged into one of the sockets on the outside of the microcomputer and the program in question will run only when the device is in position. Because these devices, called variously dongles or stunt boxes, have no rigid design they are not easily copied and this form of protection is therefore more foolproof than the security ROM chip. For the properly authorized user, dongle protection is also more convenient because dongles can easily be moved from one microcomputer to another (of the same type) if the user has several machines on the same site, whereas chips can easily be broken in an attempt to move them. The word processing package *Wordcraft* inaugurated dongle protection.

Uncopiable disks. Although technically speaking no disk is uncopiable, programmers are currently developing methods which make it increasingly difficult for potential pirates to produce usable copies. At the end of the day, if it is more costly in time to break a system of protection than to buy the software, there is no point, in commercial terms, in making the attempt even though the technical challenge may remain. In practice, rather than make the master disk uncopiable, software developers generally allow the user to produce a working copy which will only 'boot up' (i.e. start) when the original master disk is in the other disk drive.

Registered user. If a software house provides a valuable backup service to its users, such as answering queries or providing updated copies of the program, there is little or no incentive to produce pirated copies. All payroll packages are sold on a registered user basis and, because of this, pirating of payroll packages is virtually unknown.

Conclusion

All microcomputer systems require both hardware and software. In spite of the great emphasis placed on hardware – particularly in

Figure 1.16 Top 83 per cent of microcomputer applications packages available in the UK for a minimum of six months in a minimum of five sites.
Source: Personal Computer World 1981/82.

trade journals – it is the choice of software which is more likely to be the deciding factor in the purchase of a business microcomputer system.

In 1980 it was claimed that 11,000 microcomputers of all types were in use in the UK; in 1982, *Dataguide*, a trade directory indicated that there were well in excess of over 100,000 *business* machines in use. More recently, ROMTEC, a market research company, is predicting quarterly sales of business microcomputers of over 21,000! Whilst a few of these machines are still being programmed in languages such as BASIC by individual users for very specialized applications, the vast majority are operating with standard applications packages in such areas as:

word processing;

spreadsheet (usually with graphics);

database management;

payroll;

ledger systems;

stock control.

Because such packages are sold in hundreds (and sometimes even in many thousands) they are much cheaper than 'bespoke' – specially written – software. The most significant advantages of purchasing a proprietary applications package, from the business user's point of view, are that the package will:

a   have had most, if not all, the operating difficulties ironed out as a result of earlier exposure in a real business environment and its resultant user feedback; and
b   unless the particular application for which it is proposed to use the package is virtually unique, should also make good business sense and be acceptable to other business organizations such as auditors, suppliers and customers.

The entry of the large, multinational computer companies – particularly IBM – into the business microcomputer market has led to a welcome degree of standardization, such that it is now possible to exchange information between machines much more easily than was possible previously. This development, together with technical improvements in communications, has led to the increasing use of the microcomputer as a communications device as well as an independent processor, its principal role hitherto. Over the next few years one will see an rapid expansion in the use of microcomputers exchanging business information with other machines either locally, nationally or internationally.

2

The microcomputer industry and the choice of microcomputer system

The UK business micro- (as opposed to the mini- or mainframe) computer industry has grown from virtually nothing in the late 1970s into what is now a multi-million pound market. A recent report by Pedder Associates revealed that in the UK, at the end of 1984, 874,000 business microcomputers were installed with an overall value of £2.2 billion. During 1984 this installed base was increased by over 60 per cent in units and 57 per cent in value as users bought 341,000 business micros valued at £831 million. In addition, in spite of the increased proportion of sales of hard-disk machines and also multi-user systems, the average cost of a system fell from £2,661 in 1983 to £2,437 in 1984. Technologically the market has expanded from the bottom upwards, from hobbyist machines, which typically had 4 kbytes of internal memory, through 8 kbytes and 16 kbytes up to the accepted minimum for a business machine of 256 kbytes. From the applications point of view, however, the market has developed from the top downwards by adapting applications, such as stock control and ledger systems, which were previously feasible only on mini- or mainframe computers. The operating differences that remain are caused mainly by the relatively limited external storage devices currently used with microcomputers.

Thus the microcomputer market covers an extraordinary range of expectations. On the one hand is the ex-mainframe specialist who is accustomed to capital investment of £100,000 or more, virtually unlimited storage facilities and hardware and software support thrown in *as of right*. On the other hand, is the upgraded hobbyist revelling in 256 kbytes of internal memory, at a minimum two floppy disk drives as opposed to outdated cassettes and increasingly, in comparative terms, virtually unlimited external storage in the form of hard disks. This mixture of upgraded hobbyist and downgraded mainframe specialist may explain to the bewildered newcomer to the market why one group claims that virtually no business problem exists that cannot be solved using a microcomputer, while the other group recounts horror stories or disastrous attempts to use microcomputers in business.

Of course, the true picture lies somewhere between the optimistic and pessimistic extremes. This is illustrated by a survey entitled *Small Computers in Small Companies* made by Lancaster University's Marketing Department (1982) which indicated that out of 100 selected computer users, 92 companies considered computerization was a success even though 84 had no previous experience. While this survey included computers costing up to £30,000 which can hardly be regarded as microcomputers, 17 of the companies had machines costing less than £4,000 which certainly could, at 1982 prices.

Structure of the microcomputer industry

Figure 2.1 provides a diagrammatic representation of the structure of the microcomputer industry and, although a gross over-simplification, it does identify the major categories of service company in the industry likely to be encountered by the prospective business user.

Systems houses

Although systems houses obviously vary, both in size and in service offered, a good systems house can probably offer all the services required to implement a business application on a microcomputer system. These would extend from the initial analysis of the situation before computerization, through to continued hardware and software support afterwards. Such a complete package of services is often referred to as a 'turn-key' package – presumably on the optimistic hypothesis that the user simply turns the key to switch the system on and the system is guaranteed to work – eventually!

Services offered by a good systems house would be:

consultancy advice on the suitability of the proposed application for computerization and recommendations on any changes required in current procedures before implementing a computer solution;

OVERSEAS MANUFACTURERS
manufacture hardware and peripherals

UK SUBSIDIARIES
suppliers of hardware and peripherals

UK IMPORTERS
suppliers of hardware and peripherals

UK MANUFACTURERS
manufacturers of hardware, peripherals and some software

EXPORT

OVERSEAS SOFTWARE HOUSES
produce proprietary applications packages

UK AGENTS or CONCESSIONAIRES
suppliers of software

UK SOFTWARE HOUSES
producers of proprietary applications packages giving software support to dealers or direct to customers

EXPORT

SYSTEMS HOUSES
offer
1 consultancy service
2 hardware supply and service
3 software supply and support (bespoke and proprietary)
4 training

MAJOR DEALERS
offer
1 hardware supply and service
2 software supply and support (occasionally)

RETAIL OUTLETS and MINOR DEALERS
offer
1 hardware supply and possibly some services
2 software supply but little direct support

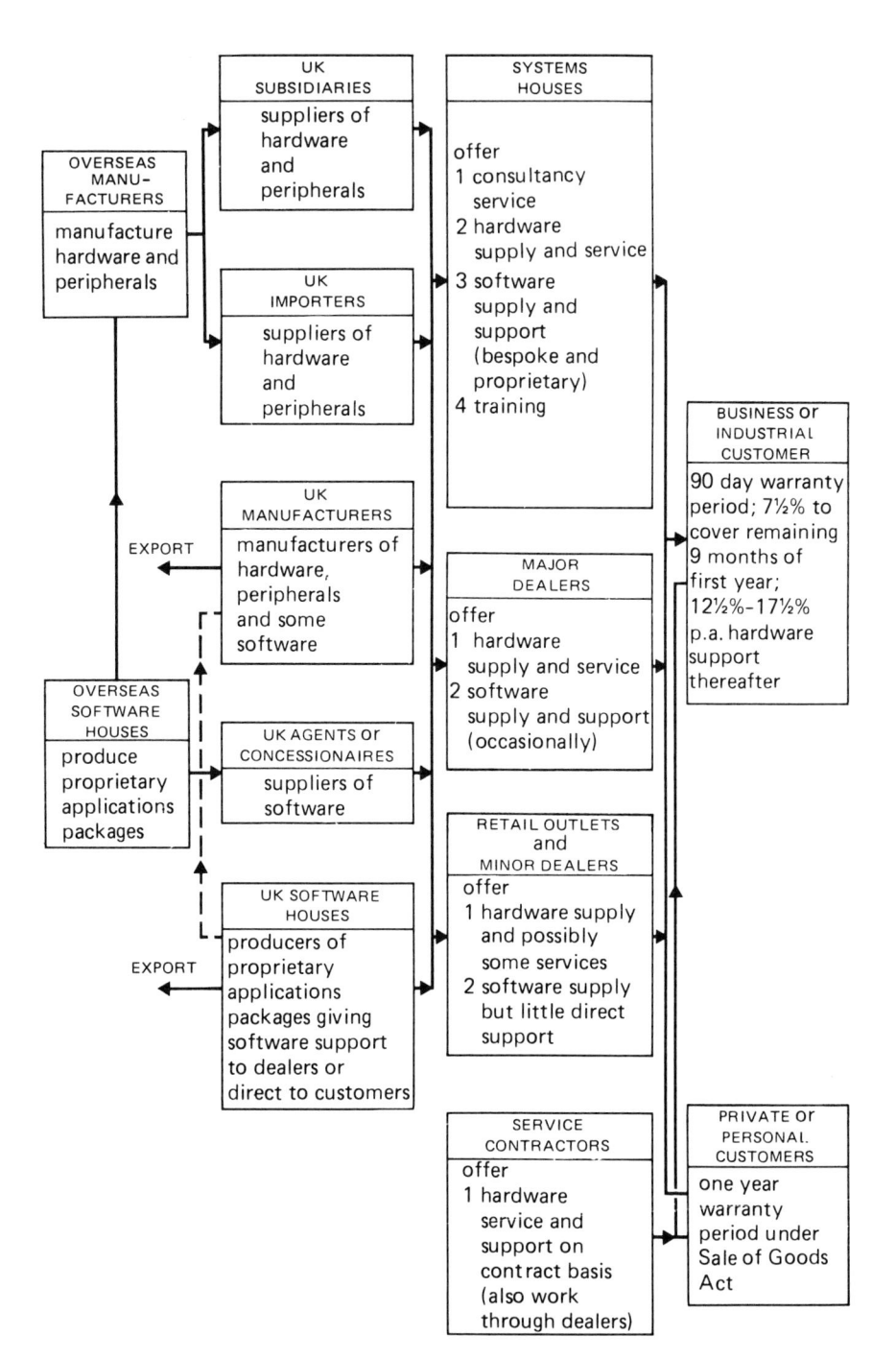

SERVICE CONTRACTORS
offer
1 hardware service and support on contract basis (also work through dealers)

BUSINESS or INDUSTRIAL CUSTOMER
90 day warranty period; 7½% to cover remaining 9 months of first year; 12½%-17½% p.a. hardware support thereafter

PRIVATE or PERSONAL CUSTOMERS
one year warranty period under Sale of Goods Act

Figure 2.1 Simplified structure of the UK microcomputer industry.

recommendations of suitable software/hardware packages. The software may be a proprietary system of which the systems house has operating experience, or bespoke, specially designed software written by the systems house's own programmers (see p. 37). The hardware recommendation will generally be from a range of machines with which the systems house is familiar and may even be labelled with its own name and/or logo;

assistance in 'going live' with the microcomputer system and accepting responsibility for ironing out the inevitable practical problems encountered;

provision and responsibility for continued hardware and software support and also pre-printed stationery if that is required;

training of a general nature.

The sevices of a systems house are not cheap and generally speaking it would not be worth using one unless the cost of the software/hardware system being purchased exceeded £10,000 since the cost of the supporting services offered, although less than the software/hardware costs, will be of the same order of magnitude.

Major dealers

A *major dealer* in microcomputers is, by contrast, mainly concerned with selling hardware rather than consultancy services. To help sales of hardware, however, he or she has to provide software advice and this advice will usually centre around a series of proprietary applications packages with which the dealer has a reasonable working knowledge. A major dealer should be able at least to demonstrate applications packages although, because the profit margin on packages is very low, the demonstration will generally be at the dealer's site rather than at that of the prospective user.

A major dealer will generally have a service department and so will be able to offer continued hardware support. Only the very largest dealers offer software support on a contractual basis. In addition most major dealers should be able to offer more than one hardware system in a particular price range.

To summarize, the services offered by a major dealer would be:

a limited choice of hardware systems in a particular price range;

recommendations as to suitable applications packages with limited immediate support and, occasionally, longer term support on a contractual basis;

hardware support (i.e. servicing of equipment) on a contractual basis.

Most major dealers have managed to achieve their standing in the industry by offering specialist software which ensures that purchasers are tied to buying the appropriate hardware from the same source.

This state of affairs, on reflection, is a natural reaction to the market situation in which price undercutting by newcomers with low overheads is a permanent feature, as exemplified by the fact that many small dealers in the microcomputer market trade for less than two years.

Retail outlets and minor dealers

While systems houses and major dealers cater almost exclusively for business clients, *retail outlets* and *minor dealers* serve both the home computer/hobbyist market and the lower end of the business market which tends to be made up of small businesses encountering microcomputers for the first time. Although often disparagingly referred to as 'box shifters', retail outlets and minor dealers, because of the volume of trade they generate in terms of individual microcomputer systems, can offer very competitive prices.

The services normally offered by retail outlets and minor dealers in the microcomputer market are:

usually only one make of microcomputer in a particular price range;

supplies of proprietary software packages but no formal software support;

no hardware support, although as agents they can arrange hardware support through a service contractor (see below).

Service contractors

A microcomputer contract servicing company provides hardware servicing on a contractual basis, usually for a limited range of machines. Its services are often limited to a particular geographical region and the degree of support offered and the promptness with which it is provided vary considerably. Some of the larger manufacturers of peripheral equipment, such as printers, offer a national network of servicing.

Software houses

A *software house* essentially consists of a company which employs programmers producing either bespoke software to customers' specifications or standardized, proprietary applications packages. Generally, a company will tend to specialize in one or the other. Most bespoke work is for existing computer users who wish either to enlarge their current system or to develop new systems. The most useful proprietary packages have been developed mainly in the stock recording, sales/purchase/nominal ledger and payroll applications areas (see chapters 8–10) or in a specialization for which the software house has developed a particular reputation such as hotel booking and account systems, estate agents systems, etc.

Although payroll packages are always contractually supported by the originating software house or its agents at about £200 *per annum*, the degree of support offered for other types of package varies widely.

A software house can vary in size from a single person developing a single package on a single machine to a relatively large organization with packages running on several different machines at over a thousand installations. The larger software houses offer a range of packages on a range of machines and some offer free training courses.

Table 2.1 summarizes, in broad terms, the microcomputer market, showing the types of equipment and support services different kinds of user are likely to be able to obtain. These services are discussed in more detail below.

After sale support

Hardware

Most microcomputer hardware is sold to business users on a basis of a 90 day warranty period. Although 90 days may appear a

Table 2.1 Overview of microcomputer users in the UK

	Users of microcomputers			
	Home hobbyist and personal market	Main industrial and business market	'Heavy' end of the market	
Hardware (price range 1985/86)	£300 to £1,200	£1,200 to £6,000	£6,000+	
External storage medium	cassette	floppy disk and increasingly hard disk	floppy and hard disk	
Applications	games, domestic systems, hobbies	stock control, sales ledger, payroll, purchase ledger, word processing	general ledger, lotteries/mailing list, database, time/cost recording	
Software (price range 1985/86)	self written, from magazines/ books etc, pre-programmed cassettes (£10 to £100)	mainly standardized software purchased through dealers/retailers (£200 to £1,000)	standardized software and specialized or bespoke software written by software/ systems house (£1,000+)	
Hardware support	no	usually	yes	
Software support	no	payroll – yes others – perhaps	yes	

relatively short time compared with other equipment warranty periods, most incipient faults in a microcomputer system tend to make themselves evident straight away and faults that occur after the warranty period are usually as a result of 'wear and tear' and, hence, not properly the direct responsibility of the supplier.

To obtain hardware service, either from the original supplier's service department or an independent service contractor, will usually cost in the order of $7\frac{1}{2}$ per cent of the hardware purchase price for the remaining nine months of the first year, and from $10\frac{1}{2}$ per cent to $17\frac{1}{2}$ per cent thereafter, depending on the speed of call-out offered.

In microcomputer systems, the electro-mechanical devices are the most likely to fail. Listed according to their relative reliability, these are the central processing unit (CPU) (the most reliable), visual display unit (VDU), printer, keyboard, and floppy disk drive (the least reliable).

Although routine maintenance of microcomputer hardware by servicing engineers does not yet appear to be a feature of the market, some basic preventative measures can be taken by the user. These are:

> do not switch the microcomputer on and off if use is intermittent but leave it on all day – power consumption is very small;
>
> try and keep the surrounding temperature at a reasonable level – neither too hot nor too cold – and ensure that if fan cooling is provided no obstructions prevent the cooling system from functioning efficiently;
>
> if dust is a problem, ensure that dust-covers are fitted when the machine is not in use
>
> be particularly gentle with disks (see p. 14) and disk drives. If it is relatively easy to gain access to the read/write heads, clean them regularly following the service engineer's instructions.

Software

Where software support is not included in the overall package (as it is, for example, in a 'turn-key' arrangement offered by a systems house), only very limited software support is offered by either software houses or major dealers. Such support is on a contractual basis after an initial warranty period of one year.

52 *Microcomputers – general*

The one exception to the general rule is a payroll package which is always supported. For about £200 *per annum*, users are provided with the following support services:

a telephone 'hot-line' during normal working hours for sorting out operating difficulties, queries, etc.;

an update service to cover such things as tax changes issued by the Inland Revenue and national insurance changes issued by the Department of Health and Social Security;

guaranteed sales of pre-printed stationery for pay advice slips, bank giros, etc.

Choice of microcomputer system

Since a microcomputer system comprises both hardware and software, the initial problem in choosing an adequate system is whether it is the hardware of software that should determine the choice. It is now generally agreed that *software* is the more important. Some of the essential considerations in choosing software packages are discussed briefly here.

Software

Although much has been written on the topic of choosing software (see, for example, J. E. Lane's *Choosing Programs for Microcomputers*, 1980, published by the National Computer Centre), surveys such as the one referred to earlier conducted by the Marketing Department of Lancaster University appear to show that the majority of potential users ignore such advice and simply go out and buy microcomputer systems (both software and hardware) with no formal feasibility study and often without even seeing the machine in action.

I shall not, therefore, enumerate here all the theoretical points one might consider in choosing software. The bulk of this book is in any case concerned with explaining what the more popular packages actually do, which will be of far greater benefit to the potential users. I will restrict myself here to a brief consideration of *stand-alone* versus *integrated* packages.

Well before a potential user reaches the stage of comparing various applications packages, he or she should determine in non-computing terms exactly what it is the company wants to computerize. The particular application may stand alone or may, now or later, need to be integrated with further applications. For example, a small company could well decide to computerize its payroll function and, if this is all it is ever likely to want to computerize, there is absolutely no reason why it should not purchase a proven payroll package and the appropriate hardware from its local retailer and get on with the job – as many small companies have successfully done. However, if at a later stage they discover it would be useful to have the payroll function reporting to a nominal ledger, and they had chosen a payroll package that was not part of an integrated system, it would be impossible to obtain that reporting facility at that stage without changing to a completely new payroll package. A similar argument would apply to stand-alone versus integrated sales and purchase ledgers.

Hardware

If one accepts that the choice of software is of prime importance in deciding on a particular microcomputer system, the choice of hardware is mainly a matter of determining the size of the system in terms of external storage, which then largely determines *price* rather than which particular *make* of computer.

Broadly speaking microcomputer systems can be classified as:

small – 300 kbytes to 1 Megabyte of external storage;

medium – 1 Megabyte to 5 Megabytes;

large – 5 Megabytes to 15 Megabytes;

multi-user – 15 Megabytes to 96 Megabytes.

At the top end the distinction between microcomputers and minicomputers does admittedly become rather blurred. Table 2.2 gives some basic information on the differences between these four categories of microcomputer system.

The size of a microcomputer system is perhaps most critical in accounting applications such as operating purchase and sales ledgers (possibly reporting to a nominal ledger) and also stock recording. In these situations each supplier, customer and stock item will require an individual record within a file and this feature can be used as a basis for estimating the overall size of the files and, hence, the storage required.

Table 2.2 Classification of microcomputers by size (excluding printer)

Category	Internal memory RAM	External storage	Principal user languages	Price range
Small (personal, desktop, low cost entry etc.)	64 kbytes to 256 kbytes	dual 5¼ inch floppy disks 300 kbytes to 1 Megabyte (i.e. 1000 kbytes)	BASIC ASSEMBLER	£2,000 to £2,500
Medium	256 kbytes to 512 kbytes	dual 5¼ inch floppy disks up to dual 8 inch floppy disks 1 Megabyte to 5 Megabytes	BASIC FORTRAN COBOL PASCAL	£2,500 to £5,000
Large	up to 640 kbytes	5¼ inch or 8 inch floppy disk and 5¼ inch Winchester hard disk up to 15 Megabytes	PILOT APL LISP	£5,000 to £10,000
Multi-user, multi-task		up to 8 inch Winchester hard disk 15 Megabytes to 96 Megabytes	ASSEMBLER	£10,000 to £15,000

User company size				Proportion	Machines
Payroll (employees)	Ledger Customers	Suppliers	Maximum stock items	of the business user market (installations)	
250	500	150	1500	50%	Zenith Research Machines Commodore Amstrad PCW 825 Apple Macintosh Tandy Comart Olympia Xerox Epson Taxi DEC Rainbow Sanyo ACT-Apricot Merlin Tonto
400	1000	500	10000	25%	Olivetti M24 Commodore Apple Macintosh Tandy IBM PC and compatibles Compac Wang PC Ericsson DEC Professional
400+	1000+	500+	10000+	15%	Apricot Xen ITT Extra IBM XT and compatibles Kalamazoo Eagle Altos
400+	1000+	500+	10000+	10%	Sperry Cromenco Future Altos Onyx IBM AT and compatibles

56 Microcomputers – general

J. Mike Eaton has proposed a very simple method of file size estimation in his excellent pamphlet *How to Choose your Small Business Computer* (1981, available with an accompanying voice cassette, from the National Computer Centre, Manchester) and allows 150 bytes per customer/supplier, 90 bytes per service offered to customers and an additional 50 bytes per service which is an item held in stock. The method, having established what is effectively a minimum file space, then takes into account the operating requirements of the applications software and allows room for expansion by multiplying this minimum by a factor of three to arrive at the overall storage requirement.

Thus for a company with 3,000 customers and 1,000 suppliers, offering customers 2,000 items/services of which 600 are stocked, the arithmetic would be:

   3000 customers @ 150 bytes/record   450,000
   1000 suppliers @ 150 bytes/record   150,000
   2000 items/services @ 90 bytes/record 180,000
   600 stock items @ 50 bytes/record   30,000
   Minimum storage   810,000 bytes

   Total storage requirement = 3 × 810 kbytes
                             = 2500 kbytes

Since 2,500 kbytes (or 2.5 Megabytes) represents five or more 5¼ inch floppy disks, the potential user in this example will require a microcomputer system in the medium-to-large microcomputer range at a cost (in 1982) of at least £5,000, plus £2,000 for a heavy duty dot-matrix printer.

A slightly more sophisticated approach to the same problem can be seen in figure 2.2 which shows for approximately the same input data the printout of the Bytesoft Business System Configurator which is Bytesoft's programmed version of much the same idea. It is interesting that both methods arrive at a similar overall price.

A further example would be a company with only 500 customers, 150 suppliers and 800 items/services all of which are stocked where the total storage requirement comes out by the same calculation at 600 kbytes. This could certainly be accommodated by a small microcomputer system. Figure 2.3 indicates that the Bytesoft estimate for a similar size of system would (in 1986) be

The microcomputer industry 57

```
                    BYTESOFT BUSINESS SYSTEM CONFIGURATOR

Bytesoft Business System, comprising:                              6755.00
    64K system, 2 790K disk-drives                                 ex. VAT
    green-phosphor screen, 24 lines of 80, numeric pad
    120cps dot-matrix printer, 132ch platen, tractor-feed
    all necessary cables.
    one box of paper (2000 sheets), 2 spare printer ribbons,
    2 boxes of diskettes (total 20).
    Bytesoft Business System (Sales, Purchase & Nominal) holding:
        50 nominal accounts,
        500 customer accounts,
        500 supplier accounts
        non-stock invoicing sub-system
        stock sub-system, with full stock-control, sales orders,
        purchase orders, all fully integrated into the ledger system
        capacities: 200 purchase orders, 200 sales orders,
                    10 stock categories, and 2000 stock lines.
    4 half-days' on-site installation support
    Mounted in specially-designed system desk,
    and 1 full year's hardware and software maintenance.
This quote is subject to confirmation and applies for a maximum of 30 days.
```

Figure 2.2 Estimating hardware size and price for a medium to large system using the Bytesoft Business System Configurator.

```
                    BYTESOFT BUSINESS SYSTEM CONFIGURATOR

Bytesoft Business System, comprising:                              4750.00
    64K system, 2 390K disk-drives                                 ex. VAT
    green-phosphor screen, 24 lines of 80, numeric pad
    110cps dot-matrix printer, 80ch platen, sprocket feed
    all necessary cables.
    one box of paper (2000 sheets), 2 spare printer ribbons,
    2 boxes of diskettes (total 20).
    Bytesoft Business System (Sales, Purchase & Nominal) holding:
        40 nominal accounts,
        500 customer accounts,
        150 supplier accounts
        non-stock invoicing sub-system
        stock sub-system, with full stock-control, sales orders,
        purchase orders, all fully integrated into the ledger system
        capacities: 60 purchase orders, 60 sales orders,
                    1 stock categories, and 800 stock lines.
    4 half-days' on-site installation support
    Mounted in specially-designed system desk.
This quote is subject to confirmation and applies for a maximum of 30 days.
```

Figure 2.3 Estimating hardware size and price for a small microcomputer system using the Bytesoft Business System Configurator.

£4,750, which certainly confirms that the system does fall within the category of small microcomputers (printer included).

Upward compatibility

If a range of microcomputers is available, it is often useful to know whether a package under consideration for one of the smaller machines in the range can subsequently be used on a larger machine, if required. Such a facility is referred to as upwards compatibility and depends on a common *file structure* which is independent of the size of machine.

Conclusion

In spite of the claims of advertisements, microcomputer hardware is becoming more standard in performance, if not in appearance. Prices are largely controlled by the amount of external (disk) storage which is required to retain – in the business environment – the necessary customer, supplier and stock records. For most practical purposes, as we have seen, systems can be categorized as small, medium, large or multi-user. Although, currently, software is much cheaper than hardware, the choice of software should come before the choice of hardware.

3

The microcomputer as a communications device

The majority of the business and management applications of microcomputers has so far been based on the microcomputer's power as an information processor. With the rapid improvements in methods of communication taking place, however, the microcomputer is now acquiring an increasingly important role as a communications device as well as an independent processor.

The theory of computer communications is technically complex requiring the synchronization of many elements, at hardware level, the operating system level and the applications software level. It is theoretically possible to link most computer based devices to most others, and this chapter touches briefly on the necessary technical requirements of communication. The chapter concentrates, however, on the two principal roles currently being acquired by microcomputers as a communications device within the business and commercial environment, namely:

  micro to micro communications,

  micro to mainframe communications.

Micro to micro communications – Local Area Networks

A Local Area Network or LAN allows from two to 200 microcomputers to be connected to each other for data communication purposes within a limited locality. Such LANs operate by physically connecting microcomputers to each other by a cable so that each computer within the network can then share:

  information/data, or

a relatively expensive central resource such as a fast printer or large hard-disk facility.

Ideally a LAN manages the traffic between the various microcomputers and peripherals connected to the system whilst at the same time allowing each microcomputer to act as an independent processor. The distance over which microcomputers can be linked to each other on a local network without any signal boosting is usually about 1,000 ft but this can be extended up to about 5,000 ft if boosters are incorporated in the system.

In practice there are three basic LAN layouts:

bus – a single length of cable to which each micro (which can now be regarded as a station within the network) is connected. When a station wishes to send a message to another on the bus, it waits for the bus to be clear of other messages and then sends its message to the appropriate destination;

ring – a loop of cable to which all micros are attached. Messages travel around the loop in one direction only. Each station reads every message and recognizes those addressed to itself;

star – as the name suggests, this network configuration connects all machines or stations through a single central point, usually a microcomputer which acts as the file server or shared disk storage.

All LANs consist not only of the cable providing the physical link between machines but also:

in all but the simplest LANs, an individual plug-in card or board enabling each microcomputer to be connected to the LAN;

a central host microcomputer controlling the network and usually providing the central hard-disk facilities required by the network to save the data files to be exchanged between stations connected to the system;

software mounted on both the central host and individual microcomputers.

A typical layout of a small LAN, in which a single IBM XT or AT is used as a central host and file server for a small network of several IBM PCs or compatibles sharing a printer, is shown in figure 3.1.

At the time of writing there are a multitude of local area network systems available on the market and even IBM is supporting two different systems, namely PC network and Tapestry. An added complication in choosing an appropriate system is that there are reportedly up to two dozen different network technologies in use.

The quality of a local area network depends on the services offered in terms of the management of the system. In very simple LAN systems microcomputers can be connected to the system through their standard RS232 port (thus obviating the cost of special plug-in boards) and allocated space on a single hard-disk (file server). In more complicated LAN systems, stations can gain access to the same files on a central file server and when conflicts arise – such as two users attempting to alter the same record in a database file – the management of the system has to be able to cope and allocate priorities.

In business and management situations, the motivation for investing in a local area network facility will depend on whether the benefits of shared facilities offset the costs of providing the facilities allowing that sharing to take place.

The costs involved in setting up a local area network will obviously depend on the size of the network and the facilities offered, but as a generalization it can cost between £800 and £1,200 per microcomputer connected. Additional costs will also be involved in providing a central host microcomputer – if one is not already available – and software for the central host. In practice, the

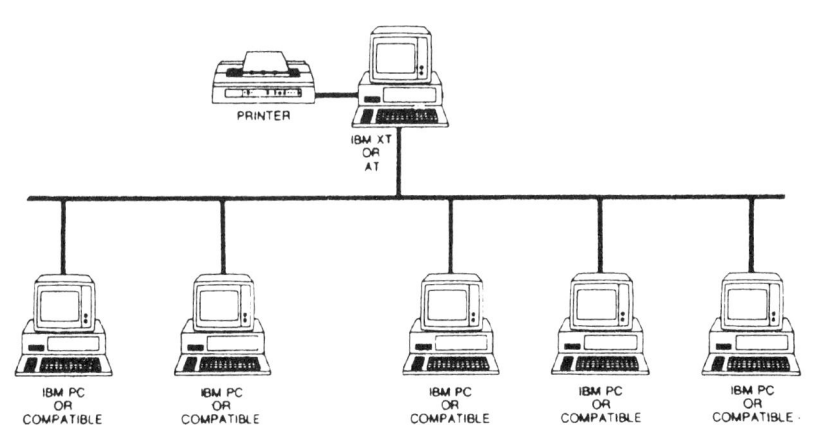

Figure 3.1 A simple LAN with an IBM XT or AT acting as a central host and file server for several IBM PCs or compatibles.

62 Microcomputers – general

minimum size of such a central host will be an IBM XT or equivalent.

Some of the principal benefits of incurring such costs, which have caused users to invest in LANs in business and management situations, are:

> to allow several secretaries operating IBM PCs (or compatibles) as word processing stations, to share a relatively expensive printer, such as a fast laser printer costing in the order of £5,000;

> to allow several users to share the facililties of common database files;

> to allow several users to be connected to a local Electronic Mailing system.

Micro to mainframe communications

Ignoring the fact that a microcomputer can be made to operate as a 'dumb' terminal and be connected to an 'in-house' mainframe computer, the majority of micro to mainframe applications occurs where a microcomputer is used to access a remote mainframe machine (often, in practice, a large mini) via a telephone system.

For a microcomputer to be connected to a telephone system, the digital signals of the computer have initially to be converted to sound signals which can be transmitted along normal telephone lines. The most common device used to achieve this signal conversion is known as a modem (for modulator/demodulator) and such a device must obviously be available at both ends of the communication link, i.e., at the microcomputer and the mainframe. The modulator section of a modem converts digital signals from the computer into acoustic signals acceptable for transmission on the telephone network and the demodulator section converts acoustic signals received from the telephone system into digital signals acceptable to the computer. Modems operate at different speeds (known as baud rates) both in transmitting and receiving information and it is obviously necessary to ensure that the speeds set on the modem (usually by switches) and within the associated software match those of the system being accessed. The three most popular baud rates (i.e., evaluated as the number of characters transmitted per second multiplied by ten) are 300/300, 1200/75 and 1200/1200 – the two numbers in each case referring to the receive and transmit baud rates respectively.

Modems are relatively cheap devices ranging from £100 to about £400 at the top of the range. At the top level the best modems will autodial one of several previously stored numbers, recognize an engaged signal and keep retrying, and when eventually connected transmit an automatic log-in sequence. Some will even recognize the baud rate of an incoming call and respond accordingly.

Modems connect to the RS232 port of the microcomputer, which must be fitted with an asynchronous communications plug-in board, and through a jackplug to the telephone system's standard wall socket. Currently, a set of rules for controlling modems known as the Hayes protocol has become the *de facto* industry standard for these devices. Lotus 1-2-3, for instance, uses Hayes protocols within its communications facilities as do many other application packages. In purchasing a modem, therefore, it is now sensible to ensure that the equipment is Hayes compatible.

Modems are the most reliable method of connecting a microcomputer to the telephone system, but where such a 'hardwired' (i.e., direct) connection cannot be made it is possible to use the normal telephone handset as the connecting device in conjunction with an acoustic coupler which is provided with two rubber 'cups' designed to fit the microphone and earpiece or speaker of the handset. Acoustic couplers can be used wherever there is a normal telephone but they do cost more than modems and they are not quite as reliable, particularly over long distances. This slight lack of reliability is caused by the possible interference that can occur in the process of converting the digital signals from the computer to the acoustic signals required for transmission via the microphone, and converting the received acoustic signals into digital signals via the earpiece or speaker. Whether a modem or an acoustic coupler is used for connecting a microcomputer to a telephone system, an appropriate software package will also be required.

The cost of using a telephone system (such as British Telecom) to connect a microcomputer to a remote mainframe computer depends as in the case of ordinary speech based calls on the duration of the connection, the distance involved and the time of day at which the connection is made. However, most of the mainframe computer systems offering a service via British Telecom can be accessed by a local call.

Where the required mainframe computer is not located in the UK, however, an international service called Packet Switch Stream (PSS) is available to avoid astronomic telephone bills for Europeans contacting the US. This service, which obviously charges, is a specialized form of telephone system specifically for computers. To use the system, a local telephone call connects the user to the nearest national PSS 'node' – an access point where the normal telephone system is connected to the PSS. Once in communication with the node and having entered an acceptable personal code, the user enters the address number of the system required, and PSS then makes the necessary national connection, or IPSS in the case of an international connection. Because the PSS system is much faster and is more reliable than a direct phone call it does offer a very competitive service. It is also truly international and allows connection to mainframe services anywhere in the world, particularly to the US where IPSS offers one of the few practical means of accessing the powerful dial-up computer services available there.

General dial-up systems in the UK

Mainframe computer services available to users via a dial-up connection in the UK offer two main services:

electronic mail, and/or telex

database information provision, or

a combination of both the above.

For the business user the major advantage of using an electronic mail service provided by a third party (as opposed to operating a system on the company's in-house machine) is that the user only pays rental, not the capital cost, and also avoids the long-term overhead costs of maintaining hardware, software and databases where provided. Additionally, if the user's organization operates at a number of geographically well-spread sites, it is easier and cheaper to dial into a large central system.

Some of the advantages of electronic mail for business purposes are:

speed of communication;

sender and receiver do not have to be available at the same time – as with normal telephone calls. This is particularly advantageous when communicating across many time zones;

costs of electronic mail systems can be very competitive

Microcomputers and communications

compared with other forms of communication when using a micro as messages can be prepared 'off-line' using the micro's own word processing facilities and then transmitted very rapidly (in a matter of seconds).

There are four major dial-up systems offering electronic mail facilities in the UK:

Telecom Gold. This service is aimed squarely at the business user, its main facility being electronic mail. The system can be accessed via 300/300 baud 1200/75 baud and 1200/1200 baud as well as PSS. Gold is therefore readily accessible and, after rather a slow start, it is now relatively popular amongst the business community – so much so that at peak times the system's response time can be quite slow.

Users of Gold are divided into groups – usually based on companies subscribing to the system – with a 'manager' who has special facilities and is responsible for looking after the group's mailboxes. Each user of the system has a six-figure identification number, the first three figures being common to the group, together with a password access.

Outgoing telex facililties are also available on this system as is access to some of the major US database systems – thus it provides an alternative form of access to PSS/IPSS.

Prestel. This is essentially an information provision service and offers both graphics and colour on local access to 96 per cent of the UK telephone population. The system is based on 'pages' (i.e., a screenful of information) and the user is provided with page numbers (there are currently 330,000) as a means of identifying the information required.

Information on Prestel is supplied by 'Information Providers' (IPs) – usually companies or groups providing information about their specialized goods or services. A provider is allocated (and charged for) a certain number of pages and can make changes as and when required and can impose a charge for access to the information displayed on specified pages. If an access charge is imposed, the rate is displayed on the screen. The information provided by Prestel is very diverse and is very large in terms of pages and this can make it slightly difficult for the novice user to navigate the system efficiently. Some of the more important subjects available on the Prestel index are:

Air Travel, Air Lines, Airports, Assurance
Bank Services, Building Societies, Business Information
Car Hire, Career Advice, Colleges of Higher Education
Computing Services, Conference Facilities, Customs
Development Corporations, Education, Entertainment
Ferries, Financial Times Index, Government Information
Health & Safety, Holidays, Immigration, Information Services
Insurance, Law, Legal Advice, Mail Order, News
Package Tours, Pensions, Port Information, Rail Travel
Restaurants, Road Haulage, Road Maps, Teleshopping
Viewdata Services, Weather Forecasts, Zoos

In addition to public access areas – such as those indicated above – Prestel also provides pages which can only be accessed by authorized users. Prestel does offer electronic mail facilities but its predominant use is as an information provider.

Originally regarded as an expensive 'white elephant' Prestel recently announced that it had begun to make a profit on its day-to-day operations. This has been brought about mainly by the increasing use of Prestel in homes rather than offices. This increase in the home use of Prestel – now about 45 per cent of total subscriptions – results from the dropping of computer-connection charges outside business hours. Recently a 24-hour supermarket ordering system for food and groceries has been launched through Prestel which is available to subscribers in five London boroughs.

Easylink. Primarily a system geared to sending and receiving telex messages amongst the 1,600,000 telex users world-wide with the support of a back-up electronic mail service. The system's particular feature is that it can offer microcomputer users access to a well-established business communication system traditionally based on relatively expensive telex equipment.

Easylink is generally regarded as relatively cheap – particularly for the low volume user – and offers an efficient service in the restricted area of processing telex-style messages. It currently claims over 50,000 subscribers in the US and is pushing strongly for a greater foothold in the UK. Easylink offers users a cheap connection to the US telex system and it is even possible to send messages to recipients not connected to either Easy link or the telex system using a Mail-Gram service which guarantees next day delivery to the specified address. Easylink also offers a translation service to and from English and French, German, Spanish, Italian, Dutch, Portuguese, Danish, Swedish and Norwegian.

One-to-One. A relative newcomer to electronic mail, One-to-One claims to offer a wide range of facilities within a very user friendly environment. The facilities currently on offer from this organization are:

  electronic mail-box with password security,

  access to the world-wide telex system,

  radio paging for urgent telexes or messages,

  mailing list service to send messages to a pre-prepared list of customers or clients,

  priority postal letter service to link with clients who are not subscribers to One-to-One,

  courier letter service for personal delivery of documents.

Conclusion

The microcomputer is being used increasingly as a communications device as the technical difficulties of providing communication links between such devices are being overcome at reasonable costs. Micros can be linked to other micros in the locality using a LAN (Local Area Network) which allows for the sharing of facilities such as:

  expensive peripherals (fast printers or large disk storage facilities); or

  information (either in the form of an in-house database or electronic mail).

Microcomputers can also be connected to mini- or mainframe computers either directly over a telephone network or through a packet switching system. This method of connection offers a wide variety of information facilities to the business or commercial user both nationally and internationally.

Section B

General Purpose Applications Packages

4 Word processing packages
5 Spreadsheet packages including graphics
6 Flexible database packages
7 Integrated business packages

4

Word processing packages

General concept of word processing

Word processing is the most popular of microcomputer applications. For the professional typist a word processing package offers both improved quality of output and increased productivity. For the 'two-fingered' amateur a word processing package offers a facility for achieving a printed document of professional quality within which the accuracy of spelling can also be checked. For both amateur and professional, with text stored as files on disk, existing documents can be completely reconstructed and new documents formed from sections of several existing documents. This ability to manipulate textual information can cut down enormously on the amount of time required to produce printed documents, particularly those which have features in common with previously created documents: a common situation in a business environment.

For the business user of a word processing package on a personal computer a feature known as 'mailmerging' allows him or her to print what appear to be personalized individual letters to all, or alternatively a selected group of, customers or clients. A similar facility can of course also be used to send general sales literature by printing all or selected customer addresses onto adhesive labels mounted on continuous stationery.

On microcomputers with 5¼ inch disks, the equivalent of about 500 A4 sized pages at approximately 2,000 characters per page can easily be held on a single disk. Where a substantial amount of printing is involved, it is possible to transfer to a printer buffer in a matter of seconds text which may take up to ten minutes to be printed. Such printer buffers can either be incorporated in the printer or purchased as a separate hardware item. This facility frees the microcomputer for further work while printing is in progress.

72 General purpose applications packages

Word processing packages tend to cost between £250 and £450 depending on the range of facilities offered. In particular 'mail-merging' and 'spellchecking' are usually offered (if they are available for the package in question) as additional packages. Most word processing packages can accept files from spreadsheet packages for incorporation into reports, etc., but such files must have been saved originally from the spreadsheet package as text files suitable for such transfer.

Since the advent of 16-bit microcomputers with their additional storage facilities, a larger portion of which can now be reserved for supporting the screen, many word processing packages can now display text on the screen in the exact form that that text will appear when printed. This so-called 'WYSIWYG' (pronounced Wizzywig) presentation — where WYSIWYG stands for What You See Is What You Get — is able to display italics, superscript, subscript, etc., either as they would appeaar when printed or appearing in different colours. Older style packages from the 8-bit microcomputer era and those which have not been updated to make full use of the additional storage facilities offered by 16-bit machines generally make use of embedded control characters on the screen to indentify such print characteristics.

A feature which may be required of a word processing package, particularly for business applications, is that necessary for the preparation of long documents for which it is often sensible (or sometimes necessary if there is a file size limit) to store the completed text of the document in several different files. Where this is done, it is necessary, if page numbering for the complete document is to remain consecutive, to be able to specify within each constituent file at what number page numbering should start. If such documents also require 'headers' — text which is repeated at the top of every page — it is essential to ensure that the package under consideration incorporates this facility.

Another useful facility, which is not available in all word processing packages, is the ability to save small sections of frequently used text to be stored on disk and retrieved into a new document by the pressing of a single key combination. This is a particularly useful facility in the preparation of letters where address and style of ending (i.e., Yours faithfully, yours sincerely, etc., followed by the writer's title) can be held in this way. For readers who already have a word processing package which does not have this facility, it is possible to purchase a separate, general purpose package such as Prokey, Smartkey, Magic Keyboard and

Keyworks costing in the region of £75, which will operate in conjunction with most other packages – including word processing – and which can be used to store a series of characters under any specified key combination for subsequent recall.

Obviously, for single page letters, it is also necessary to exclude automatic page numbering, while another useful facility which is not available in all word processing packages, but which is of particular use to authors, is a word count.

As well as using a specific word processing package, all integrated business packages offer a word processing component which is linked with spreadsheet, graphics and database components. The facilities offered in the word processing component of such integrated packages are not generally as good as those in packages that only perform word processing, except where that word processing component can operate as a stand-alone word processor in its own right. (See page 129 for a discussion of disk based integrated business packages.)

Editing and presentation facilities

The following editing and presentation facilities are available on most word processing packages, the better of which display the document being typed on the microcomputer's screen as it will appear when printed together with additional information for control functions:

Corrections. The cursor's position controls where characters are placed and since the cursor can be positioned anywhere on the computer screen, corrections are effected simply by typing over the incorrect character (i.e., the cursor is said to be in an 'over-type' mode). Although the appearance of the cursor varies, in many systems it is represented by the underline character and in some configurations it flashes on and off.

Insertions and deletions. Single characters, whole words, sentences or paragraphs can be deleted using control commands. In many packages insertion is effected by putting the cursor in the 'insert' mode, after which inserted text moves existing text to the right to make room. In some packages, on insertion existing text following the position of insertion is temporarily moved to the bottom of the screen.

Search/find and/or replace. Where a particular word or series of characters (a name, part number, specification number, etc.) appears repeatedly in a document and requires changing, the operator can specify the word to be changed and the new word to replace it and the word will be automatically located and optionally replaced for all occurrences throughout the document. By specifying that partial words be replaced both plural and singular versions of nouns can be accommodated.

Moving. Where a section of text has to be moved from one part of a document to another, the operator can indicate the starting and finishing points of the text to be moved and the position to which it is to be moved. Such a section of text can be replicated in several different places within a document and also saved to disk as a new text file if required.

Paging. As soon as one page is full, a new page is automatically initiated, but a new page can be 'forced' at any time if this is required for clarity of presentation, context, etc.

Justification. Justification of the right-hand margin is normal on most word processing packages but can be removed if required. A letter looks more personal without right-hand justification, whereas a formal report appears much tidier with it (compare figures 4.2 and 4.4).

Centring, underlining and highlighting. Headings can be emphasized using any of these three facilities. Centring ensures that a heading will remain at the centre of the page irrespective of the page width. Headings can be highlighted by underlining or by overprinting so that the *emboldened* heading appears in more prominent characters. With some printers it is possible to achieve a *reverse* heading, that is, white on black.

Line spacing. Text is normally stored on a basis of single spacing but can subsequently be printed double or triple spaced.

Proportional spacing. On a printer with the ability to space characters proportionally, the product can look more like print than typing. Narrow characters such as 'i' take up less space than larger ones such as 'm' instead of all printed characters requiring equal (maximum) spacing.

Page width. Word processing packages allow the user to vary the page width. This facility may be necessary for different printers and/or different widths of stationery.

Page offset. To accommodate the printing of text material to be copied back-to-back for inclusion in bound documentation, some packages offer a page offset facility which operates on alternate pages.

Tabbing and indentation. Tabs can be set in much the same way as on a traditional typewriter. However, an advantage of the word processing package is that the positions of tab setting can be indicated on the screen. Decimal tabs can also be set to ensure that in a column of figures the decimal place remains in the same relative position and right-handed tabs ensure right-hand justification of text entries at the position of the tab setting.

Indentation is, in effect, an automatic tabbing facility which can be turned on and off and is used to indent subparagraphs, etc. It differs from tabbing, however, in that in subsequent editing the indentation controls the whole paragraph rather than individual lines within that paragraph.

Setting headers and trailers. Particularly for document work, a header (a heading at the top of the page) and/or a trailer (a heading at the bottom of the page) can be printed on every page simply by keying in the heading at the beginning. For documents produced in book form, left- hand and right-hand headers can be printed on alternate pages.

Page numbering. For long documents which have to be saved as several text files, it is necessary to be able to specify the page number at which numbering for each file starts so that overall numbering within the document appears sequentially. For single page letters it is necessary to suppress page number printing.

Buffered keys. Because key depressions put information into the computer's store, rather than, as in the case of conventional typewriters, directly on to paper via a mechanical or electromechanical linkage, there is no effective speed restriction as to how fast information can be keyed into a word processing package. While there might be a delay in the keyed character appearing on the computer screen, the buffer store ensures that all characters

Instruction Manual Test Document

This document is provided with the WORDCRAFT 80 word processor and is intended to show you how to use many of WORDCRAFT 80's features.

> Note that this section of the document is written in the middle of a page. This has been achieved by using the RULER facility so that the left and right hand margins have been reset to column 20 and column 50 respectively.

Page widths can be altered at any time either for the entire document by changing the total number of columns available or by using the RULER facility.

Note that the document is now limited to 35 columns wide, this was achieved by changing the right hand margin to column 35 and leaving the left hand margin at 5.

The table of numbers below was produced using the TAB settings of the RULER:

500	3000	4000	8000	250
8520	8954	7854	8564	7410
	8974	8965	8520	9630
789	8745	595	25	89521

Note here that a straightforward use of the TAB feature does not align the decimal point; this can be done using the DECIMAL TAB feature as shown on the next page.

78.50	2.25	56.32	89.56
2.50	89745.2564	5.0	1.2
4568.0	25.0	63	75.20
.5682	.002	32.1	

You will notice that all the decimal points have now been aligned - this was done automatically by WORDCRAFT 80.

Besides the normal TAB facilities it is also possible to use INDENTATION as in the example below:

> This paragraph has been set to start at column 10 and end at column 50 - this was achieved by resetting the left and right hand margins. We may now wish to have sub-paragraphs within this paragraph, each of which may require a heading.
>
> a) This has been done by using the INDENTATION feature, so that after the heading letter, the rest of the sub paragraph is indented from the left hand margin.
>
> b) Here we have a second sub-paragraph complete with its own sub-heading.
>
> c) These RULER facilities are extremely useful in the production of technical documents and manuals - such as the one you are reading about WORDCRAFT 80.

Figure 4.1 *Illustration of some of the facilities available on the word processing package WORDCRAFT.*

keyed in are retained. This allows typists to operate more quickly with the assurance that any mistakes caused by the higher typing rate can easily be corrected.

Example. Many of the facililties of a typical word processing package are demonstrated in figure 4.1 which was produced by the WORDCRAFT package. Note the high quality of print produced by a daisy-wheel printer.

Control and organization facilities

Once a document has been created and stored on disk by a word processing package, the following control or organizational facilities are usually available. It is these facilities which really differentiate a word processing package from an electronic typewriter.

Merging files. Since it is possible to extract sections of existing text files and save them to disk as small, renamed files, it is subsequently possible to create new documents by combining these smaller files. This ability to manipulate sections of text for the creation of new documents is a tremendous source of time-saving in many business and management situations since in practice it is found that many new documents are very similar in content to previously created documents.

Printing files. Once a completed document has been saved as a named file, which can normally consist of up to 20 pages of A4 text, it can be printed on a dotmatrix printer with 'correspondence' or 'near letter' quality print or on a daisy-wheel printer with 'letter' quality print.

Stationery. If continuous stationery is used, printing can also be continuous. For single sheets, the printer will pause as the end of each page for a fresh sheet of paper to be inserted. A slightly more expensive solution is to use a cut sheet feed, a hopper fed device which allows the printing of up to 500 single A4 sheets treated, in effect, as continuous stationery. The use of single sheets allows headed notepaper to be used. For repeated printing of a specific document, such as an invoice, the user can purchase continuous pre-printed continuous stationery.

Mailmerging

As has been indicated earlier, one of the most useful organizational facilities available in a word processing package for business applications is the ability to send what appear to be personalized letters to all, or selected, customers or clients. This mailmerging facility, which is either provided as an integral element of the basic word processing package or as an optional extra to the main package, provides the following facilities.

Fill points. Where a standard letter is stored as a document it is often necessary later to insert small sections of text such as the current date individually. This is achieved by creating, in advance, 'fill' points where such information can be specifically inserted. In the specimen letter shown in figure 4.2, such fill points are shown by the characters ← and in the completed letter (figure 4.4) the two fill points have been used to enter the current date and the date of a telephone conversation.

Address points. So that the same letter can be sent to a number of different people, address points can be specified and filled automatically from a file of addresses. In figure 4.2 the positions of address points are specified by the characters ←A, ←B, ←C and ←D. These address points indicate where the address is to be typed so that it can line up with the transparent section of a window envelope.

Greeting points. A separate character ←E allows for the insertion of the appropriate greeting, formal or informal. Such a greeting will be filled from a greeting (American: Salutation) field held as part of the addressee's record in the appropriate data base file.

Lists of addresses and greetings. To insert addresses and greetings automatically into standard letters it is first necessary to create a file of such addresses and the appropriate greetings as shown in figure 4.3. Once such a file has been created and stored, letters can be sent either to all addressees, or those specified by number or only those meeting certain criteria such as all customers in Birmingham or all customers with an annual turnover in excess of £50,000.

Word processing packages   79

```
←A
←B
←C
←D

Dear ←E

     Further to our telephone conversation of ←, I have pleasure in
enclosing some brochures describing the micro-computer equipment that
Brown & Plank Systems could provide.

     The details of the services we can provide can best be presented by
your visiting our establishment where we maintain a fully equipped
demonstration room with all the latest hardware and software.Should this
not be convenient, we can arrange for one of our senior representatives to
visit you but, as you will readily understand, with the small profit
margin involved it will be necessary for us to make a charge for such a
visit. The amount of the charge will depend on distance and time taken.

     We look forward to your response.

                              Yours sincerely,




                              P. G. Brownly,
                              Sales Director.
```

Figure 4.2 Specimen letter with fill, address and greeting points. The letter was printed by an Olympia electronic typewriter using a daisy-wheel.

Examples of the final version. Figure 4.4 is a completed version of the letter illustrated in figure 4.2. The letter has been dated 12th October, 1981; the date of the phone call specified as 2nd October; and then the address and greeting points have been filled, automatically in this case, from the third address in the file illustrated in figure 4.3. The completed letter, figure 4.4, has been left *unjustified* (ragged at the right-hand margin) which is claimed to give a more *personal* appearance than the fully justified presentation shown in figure 4.2.

80 *General purpose applications packages*

```
Mrs. Brown,
17, The Drive,
Barwell,
Leicester,
Mrs. Brown,


Mrs. D. Green,
26, Barrett Rise,
St. James Park,
Malvern,
Mrs. Green,


Dr. Colin D. Lewis
6, Oakley Wood Drive,
Solihull, West Midlands,
B91 2PH.
Dr. Lewis,


Mr. C. Smith,
106, Bridle Mead,
Kings Norton,
Birmingham,
Mr. Smith,
```

Figure 4.3 List of addresses and greetings held on file for automatic insertion into a letter. This is done after fill points have been inserted. The printer used is an Anadex dot-matrix printer. Compare the quality with that of the daisy-wheel used for figure 4.2.

Printing of labels. Where general publicity material, identical letters, etc., are to be enclosed in plain envelopes, addresses can be printed directly on to adhesive labels mounted on continuous

12th October 1981

Dr Colin D Lewis
6 Oakley Wood Drive,
Solihull, West Midlands,
B91 2PH.

Dear Dr Lewis,

Further to our telephone conversation of 2nd October, I have pleasure in enclosing some brochures describing the micro-computer equipment that Brown & Plank Systems could provide.

The details of the services we can provide can best be presented by your visiting our establishment where we maintain a fully equipped demonstration room with all the latest hardware and software. Should this not be convenient, we can arrange for one of our senior representatives to visit you but, as you will readily understand, with the small profit margin involved it will be necessary for us to make a charge for such a visit. The amount of the charge will depend on distance and time taken.

We look forward to your response.

Yours sincerely,

P.G. Brownly

P. G. Brownly,
Sales Director.

Figure 4.4 Completed letter with fill, address and greeting points utilized. Printed using a high quality Qume Sprint daisy-wheel printer.

stationery. Such labels, which can be arranged in rows of ones, twos or threes, can subsequently be transferred to the envelopes by hand.

Letters composed of standard paragraphs. Where letters can be composed of standard paragraphs, for example, after an interviewing session, where some applicants are being accepted and others rejected, a file of standard paragraphs can be created and stored and then appro-priate paragraphs can be specified and collected to compose an 'individual' letter.

82 *General purpose applications packages*

Spellchecking

Spellchecking (i.e., checking the spelling of words in a document (file) is usually offered as an additional facility (as is mailmerge) with many word processing packages.

A spellchecking package usually has an initial vocabulary of some eighty thousand commonly used words and occasionally a facility for adding additional words. In operation the package can correct the spellings of words it knows (i.e., those held in the vocabulary) and provide a list of those it has been unable to identify. Because such packages check every word in a document they tend to be rather slow and really are not necessary for everyday business use other than in report publishing applications.

A small warning to British users of spellchecking packages. Since many of the word processing packages available in Great Britain originate in the USA, the associated spellchecking packages would insist on correcting 'centre' and 'labour' to 'center' and 'labor' respectively.

Print quality and options

In the past when printing from a word processing package the choice has essentially been:

> correspondence or draft quality print at high speed from a dot-matrix printer, with options controlled by the word processing software of bold face, double strike, restricted and double width print options of the same basic type font (see upper half of figure 4.5); or

> letter quality print at slow speed from a daisy-wheel printer.

Now, however, with the development of more sophisticated dot-matrix printers (see p. 27 for more details) it is possible to obtain fast correspondence quality print and slow near letter quality print from the same printer, the choice of quality being controlled either directly on the printer or indirectly through the software. Most dot-matrix printers are now sold with this facility built in and they cost only marginally more than those printers which can only produce correspondence quality. Whilst the professional printer might be

```
             Correspondence quality print
                      (fast)

                   ABCDEFGHIJKLMNOPQRSTUVWXYZ
    Draft          abcdefghijklmnopqrstuvwxyz

                   ABCDEFGHIJKLMNOPQRSTUVWXYZ
    Boldface       abcdefghijklmnopqrstuvwxyz

                   ABCDEFGHIJKLMNOPQRSTUVWXYZ
    Double strike  abcdefghijklmnopqrstuvwxyz

                   ABCDEFGHIJKLMNOPQRSTUVWXYZ
    Restricted     abcdefghijklmnopqrstuvwxyz

                   ABCDEFJHIJK
    Double width   abcdefghijk


             Near letter quality print
                      (slow)

                   ABCDEFGHIJKLMNOPQRSTUVWXYZ
    Courier        abcdefghijklmnopqrstuvwxyz

                   ABCDEFGHIJKLMNOPQRSTUVWXYZ
    Cubic          abcdefghijklmnopqrstuvwxyz

                   ABCDEFGHIJKLMNOPQRSTUVWXYZ
    Elite          abcdefghijklmnopqrstuvwxyz

                   ABCDEFGHIJKLMNOPQRSTUVWXYZ
    Italic         abcdefghijklmnopqrstuvwxyz

                   ABCDEFGHIJKLMNOPQRSTUVWXYZ
    Orator         abcdefghijklmnopqrstuvwxyz

                   ABCDEFGHIJKLMNOPQRSTUVWXYZ
    Typewriter     abcdefghijklmnopqrstuvwxyz
```

Figure 4.5 *Different forms and fonts of dot-matrix print.*

84 *General purpose applications packages*

able to discriminate between true letter quality print, as produced by a daisy-wheel printer, and near letter quality as produced by a dot-matrix printer, as can be seen in figure 4.5, the standard of near letter quality as produced by the current generation of dot-matrix printers is very good and more than satisfactory for the majority of business applications.

Most dot-matrix printers that do offer near letter quality print usually offer a single font style, often Elite or Courier, but Metatext, a novel piece of software used in conjunction with a gravity switch, offers a choice of six different fonts in near letter quality (see bottom half of figure 4.5) in addition to normal correspondence quality. This device with its associated software works on the principle that a combined plug and socket attached to a gravity switch is interposed between the microcomputer's printer socket and the printer cable plug. The gravity switch takes the form of a small tablet which sits on the desk alongside the microcomputer and in one position produces correspondence quality print and when turned over to the alternate position produces near letter quality print.

For business applications in particular, one would anticipate that in future dot-matrix printers will tend to increase their already substantial proportion of the microcomputer printer market, given the improving quality of near letter quality print as produced by dot-matrix printers and the additional ability of such printers to produce graphics – taken in conjunction with their low cost relative to daisy-wheel printers (which cannot produce graphics). This, of course, will happen simultaneously with the growth of laser printers, which although very expensive at the moment will come down in cost and can produce an even better print quality of both text and graphics.

Conclusion

A word processing package for a microcomputer offers word processing facilities at about two-thirds of the price of a dedicated word processor. While the commands used by such a package are slightly more difficult to learn than on a dedicated system, the facilities offered are very similar and, of course, the microcomputer retains its flexibility to operate with packages other than word processing.

Such packages are therefore often the answer where the workload does not justify the purchase of a dedicated word processor or where the use of other packages is required.

Typical business and management applications of word processing on a microcomputer are to produce:

documents,
contracts,
mailing lists,
price lists,
accounts,
standard letters to many addresses,
technical reports.

Although word processing packages currently on the market offer to business microcomputer users broadly the same facilities, some are designed specifically for office use and others are oriented more towards the professional author. Those designed more for office use tend to have a wider range of mailing facilities, whereas those aimed more at the professional author tend to allow large amounts of text to be stored.

5

Spreadsheet packages including graphics

The spreadsheet concept was introduced originally in 1978 with the development of the package VISICALC which was followed in 1980 by SUPERCALC, both of which have sold several hundreds of thousands of copies world-wide. Subsequently many other packages have been developed along broadly similar lines to exploit the original spreadsheet concept, which, more than any other, has stimulated sales of microcomputers – particularly to first-time users. So popular has the spreadsheet concept become, there are now something of the order of 200 different packages available.

Currently one is seeing increasing use of 'super' spreadsheet packages such as Lotus 1-2-3, VisiOn, Visicalc IV and Supercalc 3 which take the original simple concept further and now include:

graph drawing capabilities,

colour,

macro programming,

iteration control and forward referencing,

simple database functions.

The basic idea behind the spreadsheet concept

The basic concept behind the spreadsheet is that the user is presented with a large 'electronic' sheet marked out as a grid of a minimum of 56 alphabetically labelled columns and 250 numbered rows. The novel concept of the spreadsheet is that numbers or variables within the sheet are both identified and named by their position relative to the columns and rows respectively. Thus the

Spreadsheet packages including graphics 87

numeric value entered at the intercept of column B and row 7 is automatically referred to as B7 from then on. If the variable B7 occurs either on its own or as a variable within an equation elsewhere within the spreadsheet, any change to the value of the entry in B7 will be reflected throughout all the other cells within the spreadsheet that depend on B7.

Thus in the simple sheet shown as figure 5.1a, the entry in cell C7 which is a formula A7*B7 appears as 25 simply because A7 is 5 and B7 is also 5.

```
      A          B          C         D         E
1 : Number    Multiplier   Product
2 :---------------------------------------------------
3 :   1           3           3
4 :   2           2           4
5 :   3           6          18
6 :   4           4          16
7 :   5           5          25
8 :
```

Figure 5.1a Spreadsheet showing dependence of one entry (C7) on two others (A7) and (B7).

```
      A          B          C         D         E
1 : Number    Multiplier   Product
2 :---------------------------------------------------
3 :   1           3           3
4 :   2           2           4
5 :   3           6          18
6 :   4           4          16
7 :   5          10          50
8 :
```

Figure 5.1b Spreadsheet showing effect of changing a number at entry B7 and the resultant effect on a dependent entry or cell C7.

If either the value of A7 or B7 is altered then the result in C7 will also alter. This effect is shown in figure 5.1b by altering the entry at B7 from 5 to 10.

Each location within a spreadsheet (i.e., the intercept of a row and a column) is usually referred to as a cell (or sometimes entry) and the contents of a cell can be:

text – normal alphanumeric text mainly used for identifying numerical data;

numbers – numerical values which when changed will affect all those cells dependent on the cell whose value has been changed.

This effect is often referred to as 'if what', that is, if this value is changed what effect does it have? Numbers can be formatted to appear as integers, as percentages, to a fixed number of decimal places (i.e., two decimal places for monetary values), etc.;

formulae – within which variables are referred to by their cell name such as A4, B7, etc. Formulae can contain all the usual four basic functions as well as logical operators, trigonometric and special functions. A formula's size will normally be limited to something like 120 characters.

Use of formulae and their replication

Formulae within a spreadsheet can be reasonably complicated with the normal four functions of + (addition), − (subtraction), * (multiply) and / (divide) to which are usually added raising to a power, natural logarithms and logarithms to base 10. The great attraction for the user of a spreadsheet package, however, is that a single formula once entered into a cell can be replicated into either a column or row and, moreover, that a column or row of formulae can be replicated into a block or rectangle. For instance, in figures 5.1a and 5.1b the formula entered as A3*B3 at C3 was subsequently replicated into the row of cells from C4 to C7 with a single instruction.

Another point worth noting is that in this case not only has a formula been replicated into several other cells, but the new formulae have also been automatically adjusted to match the grid. Thus in the cell C4 the formula derived originally as A3*B3 has automatically become A4*B4. This effect is illustrated in figure 5.2 where those formulae underpinning the spreadsheet are shown rather than the results from the formulae such as was shown in figures 5.1a and 5.1b.

	A	B	C	D	E
1	Number	Multiplier	Product		
2	---	---	---		
3	1	3	A3*B3		
4	2	2	A4*B4		
5	3	6	A5*B5		
6	4	4	A6*B6		
7	5	10	A7*B7		
8					

Figure 5.2 *Illustrating the replication of a formula in cell C3 into cells C4, C5, C6 and C7.*

In the example shown in figure 5.2 it was necessary for both the variables in the formulae to be adjusted relative to the grid, i.e., A3 became A4, etc. However, in some situations it may be necessary for some variables to be adjusted relative to the grid but for others to remain fixed. Within spreadsheet packages a facility is built in to allow the user to select for each variable within a formula whether it should be adjusted or not. This feature is demonstrated in figures 5.3a and 5.3b where 'factor' in B1 is common and must therefore remain as B1 after replication and not change to B2, B3, etc.

	A	B	C
1	Factor= 7		
2	----------	----	---
3	1	7	
4	2	14	
5	3	21	
6	4	28	
7	5	35	
8	6	42	
9	7	49	
10	8	56	
11	9	63	

Figure 5.3a Demonstration of a simple spreadsheet where Factor in B1 should not be adjusted in formula B3 to B11.

	A	B	C
1	Factor= 7		
2	----------	--------	---
3	1	B1*A3	
4	2	B1*A4	
5	3	B1*A5	
6	4	B1*A6	
7	5	B1*A7	
8	6	B1*A8	
9	7	B1*A9	
10	8	B1*A10	
11	9	B1*A11	

Figure 5.3b Formulae underlying figure 5.3a illustrating that Factor in B1 is not adjusted when formulae are replicated.

Built-in functions

As well as allowing equations to be constructed using the usual algebraic and trigonometric functions, most spreadsheets provide a range of built-in functions which can be incorporated into formulae and also replicated as shown above. Some of these built-in functions are listed below together with their more traditional form:

Summation:

$$\text{SUM}(X1:X20) = \sum_{J=1}^{20} X_J$$

Mean:

$$\text{AVERAGE}(X1:X20) = \bar{X} = \sum_{J=1}^{20} X_J/20$$

Net present value:

$$\text{NPV}(i, X1:X20) = \sum_{J=1}^{20} X_J/(1+i)^J$$

The Net Present Value function in a single formula allows the variables X1 to X20 to be simultaneously discounted at an interest rate i and summed over the range 1 to 20. The effect of this at an interest rate of 10 per cent is illustrated in figure 5.4a supported by figure 5.4b which shows the underpinning formulae and illustrates that the single formula NPV(C1/100, B5:B14) in cell C19 performs the same function as the formulae in cells C5:C14 and C16.

Maximum and minimum functions are also generally available and take the form of either:

MAX(A1:A20)

which selects the maximum value in the range A1 to A20 or:

MIN(Exp1,Exp2,Exp3 etc)

which selects the expression with the minimum value where the expressions can be individual values, formulae or ranges.

Spreadsheet packages including graphics 91

```
    !    A    !!    B    !!      C       !
 1 !INTEREST RATE PER ANNUM :   10
 2 !==========================================
 3 !         YEAR      INVESTMENT     PRESENT VALUE
 4 !==========================================
 5 !           1          1000              909
 6 !           2          1200              992
 7 !           3          1500             1127
 8 !           4          1000              683
 9 !           5          1300              807
10 !           6          1600              903
11 !           7          1700              872
12 !           8          1900              886
13 !           9          2000              848
14 !          10          2100              810
15 !==========================================
16 !TOTALS              15300             8838
17 !==========================================
18 !
19 !NPV(C1/100,B5:B14)...   8838
20 !
```

Figure 5.4a Demonstration of ability of the NPV function to replace separate discounting and subsequent summation.

```
    !    A    !!    B    !!      C       !
 1 !INTEREST RATE PER ANNUM :   10
 2 !==========================================
 3 !         YEAR      INVESTMENT     PRESENT VALUE
 4 !==========================================
 5 ! 1                   1000          B5/(1+C1/100)^(A5)
 6 ! 1+A5                1200          B6/(1+C1/100)^(A6)
 7 ! 1+A6                1500          B7/(1+C1/100)^(A7)
 8 ! 1+A7                1000          B8/(1+C1/100)^(A8)
 9 ! 1+A8                1300          B9/(1+C1/100)^(A9)
10 ! 1+A9                1600          B10/(1+C1/100)^(A10)
11 ! 1+A10               1700          B11/(1+C1/100)^(A11)
12 ! 1+A11               1900          B12/(1+C1/100)^(A12)
13 ! 1+A12               2000          B13/(1+C1/100)^(A13)
14 ! 1+A13               2100          B14/(1+C1/100)^(A14)
15 !==========================================
16 !TOTALS          SUM(B5:B14)    SUM(C5:C14)
17 !==========================================
18 !
19 !NPV(C1/100,B5:B14)...   NPV(C1/100,B5:B14)
20 !
```

Figure 5.4b Spreadsheet formulae underpinning figure 5.4a.

92 General purpose applications packages

An additional function specific to spreadsheets is the LOOKUP function defined as:

LOOKUP(n,X1:X20)

which can be interpreted in columnar mode as, find the value between X1 ascending to X20 which is nearest to n and produce the value opposite this value in the adjacent column Y, i.e., if X10 then Y10. This function is most useful in identifying the position of a numerical occurrence in tables, etc., as it occurs in price-break situations. It is illustrated in the third of the examples now described to demonstrate applications of spreadsheet packages in business and management situations.

Examples of spreadsheets

Example 1 Stock portfolio

Some of the basic spreadsheet facilities already described are incorporated in the stock portfolio example shown in figure 5.5 which represents a hypothetical holding of shares in beers, wines and spirits, and shows the valuation of the portfolio (using prices published by the *Financial Times*) on Thursday, 17 September, five days later on Tuesday, 22 September and three days later on Friday, 25 September 1981.

Within this example, any change of any value in either the Qty (Quantity) or Price columns automatically causes a change in the corresponding row of the Value column which derives from the formula Qty × Price/100. Any resulting change of an element in the Value column then automatically alters the total which is the summation of the ten Values.

Observers of the Stock Market scene may recall that there was a general drop in share prices in September 1981 since the four main clearing banks raised their interest rates from 12 per cent to 14 per cent. This caused a sudden drop in share prices overall and, hence, a drop in the value of this portfolio from £4,920.66 to £4,852.20 to £4,576.54.

Incorporated within this example are just a few of the basic facilities already described, in particular multiplication and summation.

Once the original portfolio has been stored on disk, reloading allows the user to update any price or quantity quickly, and immediately evaluate the new, current value of the portfolio.

Spreadsheet packages including graphics 93

```
STOCK PORTFOLIO (BEERS,WINES & SPIRITS)         17/09/81
------------------------------------------------------------
        NAME            QTY         PRICE           VALUE
------------------------------------------------------------
    1   AllBrew         1000         72              720
    2   Bass             700        216             1512
    3   Border            50        100               50
    4   Bulmer           175        267              467.25
    5   City Lon          79         79               62.41
    6   Guinness         200         58              116
    7   Highl'd          300         87              261
    8   IrishDis        1000         50              500
    9   Morland          560        190             1064
   10   Vaux             120        140              168

                                    -----------------------
                                    TOTAL   ........  4920.66
------------------------------------------------------------

STOCK PORTFOLIO (BEERS,WINES & SPIRITS)         22/09/81
------------------------------------------------------------
        NAME            QTY         PRICE           VALUE
------------------------------------------------------------
    1   AllBrew         1000         69.5            695
    2   Bass             700        212             1484
    3   Border            50         88               44
    4   Bulmer           175        265              463.75
    5   City Lon          79         75               59.25
    6   Guinness         200         58              116
    7   Highl'd          300         81              243
    8   IrishDis        1000         52              520
    9   Morland          560        190             1064
   10   Vaux             120        136              163.2

                                    -----------------------
                                    TOTAL   ........  4852.2
------------------------------------------------------------

STOCK PORTFOLIO (BEERS,WINES & SPIRITS)         25/09/81
------------------------------------------------------------
        NAME            QTY         PRICE           VALUE
------------------------------------------------------------
    1   AllBrew         1000         68.5            685
    2   Bass             700        200             1400
    3   Border            50         83               41.5
    4   Bulmer           175        245              428.75
    5   City Lon          79         71               56.09
    6   Guinness         200         54              108
    7   Highl'd          300         76              228
    8   IrishDis        1000         47              470
    9   Morland          560        180             1008
   10   Vaux             120        126              151.2

                                    -----------------------
                                    TOTAL   ........  4576.54
------------------------------------------------------------
```

Figure 5.5 Stock portfolio example of some basic spreadsheet facilities.

Example 2 Cash flow anaysis

Figure 5.6 illustrates a typical use of a spreadsheet from which the cash flow situation within a company can be analysed. In this hypothetical example, the management of a small company intend to ask the bank for a two-year loan and are analysing their cash flow situation to help decide what size of loan to ask for, and also to help convince the bank manager to make the loan. The table drawn up by the spreadsheet package indicates the expected income from sales over the next 12 months and also expenditure.

LOAN: 10000   INTEREST RATE (pa) 14   TOTAL REPAYMENT OVER TWO YEAR PERIOD   12996

PERIOD	1	2	3	4	5	6	7	8	9	10	11	12	TOTAL	PERCENT
SALES	10000	10000	10000	10000	10000	10000	10000	10000	10000	10000	10000	10000	120000	
MORTGAGE	600	600	600	600	600	600	600	600	600	600	600	600	7200	6.00
UTILITIES	140	140	80	80	40	40	85	85	50	50	100	140	1030	0.86
TELEPHONE	75	75	75	75	75	75	75	75	75	75	75	75	900	0.75
SALARIES	8000	8000	8000	8000	8000	8000	8000	8000	8000	8000	8000	8000	96000	80.00
CLOTHING	120	120	120	120	120	120	120	120	120	120	120	120	1440	1.20
RATES	80	80	80	80	80	80	80	80	80	80	80	80	960	0.80
INSURANCE	160						160						320	0.27
POSTAGE	150	150	150	150	150	150	150	150	150	150	150	150	1800	1.50
LOAN REP.	542	542	542	542	542	542	542	542	542	542	542	542	6498	5.42
CASH FLOW	134	294	354	354	394	394	189	349	384	384	334	294	3852	3.21

LOAN: 13000   INTEREST RATE (pa) 14   TOTAL REPAYMENT OVER TWO YEAR PERIOD   16894.8

PERIOD	1	2	3	4	5	6	7	8	9	10	11	12	TOTAL	PERCENT
SALES	10000	10000	10000	10000	10000	10000	10000	10000	10000	10000	10000	10000	120000	
MORTGAGE	600	600	600	600	600	600	600	600	600	600	600	600	7200	6.00
UTILITIES	140	140	80	80	40	40	85	85	50	50	100	140	1030	0.86
TELEPHONE	75	75	75	75	75	75	75	75	75	75	75	75	900	0.75
SALARIES	8000	8000	8000	8000	8000	8000	8000	8000	8000	8000	8000	8000	96000	80.00
CLOTHING	120	120	120	120	120	120	120	120	120	120	120	120	1440	1.20
RATES	80	80	80	80	80	80	80	80	80	80	80	80	960	0.80
INSURANCE	160						160						320	0.27
POSTAGE	150	150	150	150	150	150	150	150	150	150	150	150	1800	1.50
LOAN REP.	704	704	704	704	704	704	704	704	704	704	704	704	8447	7.04
CASH FLOW	-29	131	191	191	231	231	26	186	221	221	171	131	1903	1.59

LOAN: 11000   INTEREST RATE (pa) 18   TOTAL REPAYMENT OVER TWO YEAR PERIOD   15316.4

PERIOD	1	2	3	4	5	6	7	8	9	10	11	12	TOTAL	PERCENT
SALES	10000	10000	10000	10000	10000	10000	10000	10000	10000	10000	10000	10000	120000	
MORTGAGE	600	600	600	600	600	600	600	600	600	600	600	600	7200	6.00
UTILITIES	140	140	80	80	40	40	85	85	50	50	100	140	1030	0.86
TELEPHONE	75	75	75	75	75	75	75	75	75	75	75	75	900	0.75
SALARIES	8000	8000	8000	8000	8000	8000	8000	8000	8000	8000	8000	8000	96000	80.00
CLOTHING	120	120	120	120	120	120	120	120	120	120	120	120	1440	1.20
RATES	80	80	80	80	80	80	80	80	80	80	80	80	960	0.80
INSURANCE	160						160						320	0.27
POSTAGE	150	150	150	150	150	150	150	150	150	150	150	150	1800	1.50
LOAN REP.	638	638	638	638	638	638	638	638	638	638	638	638	7658	6.38
CASH FLOW	37	197	257	257	297	297	92	252	287	287	237	197	2692	2.24

Figure 5.6 Simple cash flow example.

In the example the amount of the loan to be requested can be varied, as can the accompanying interest rate. The total repayment over a two-year period is then automatically calculated, and the resulting figure, divided by 24, automatically becomes the monthly loan repayment – the last entry in the expenditure column. The resulting cash flow, the difference between sales income and total outgoings, is then calculated automatically for each month. Yearly totals are also calculated at the right-hand side of the tableau and the percentage these totals represent of total income is also calculated. If either the loan or the interest rate is altered, the resulting changes are computed immediately.

It is apparent that a £10,000 loan at a 14 per cent interest rate (compounded over two years) would cause no cash flow problems, but at the same interest rate a £13,000 loan would create an overdraft situation in period 1. An £11,000 loan at a pessimistic 18 per cent interest rate causes no monthly overdraft situations and, therefore, might be an appropriate figure on which to base the management's loan request.

Another feature of this particular worksheet is that if the company's mortgage were to be increased in period 6, a new entry in that position would be replicated over the remaining periods of the year, that is, from period 7 to period 12.

Since most of the figures are large cash values these are only shown as integers, except in the percentage column where values are shown to two decimal places. However, the global use of an integer format can cause apparent arithmetical anomalies due to rounding errors (as can be seen here) and should only be used where the requirement for simple presentation overrides that of accuracy.

Example 3 Breakeven analysis

In marketing a product, to ensure a profit it is always necessary to know when sales income starts to offset incurred fixed costs. This type of traditional breakeven analysis can be simply implemented within a spreadsheet as is shown in figure 5.7.

In this example the profit or loss for producing a quantity of 9,000 in cell C3, say, is calculated as Qty (Price – Variable Cost) – Fixed Cost which in spreadsheet form is

C3*(B4−B18)−B11

96 General purpose applications packages

```
 !           A            ! !      B        ! !    C      ! !    D     !
 1!Break Even Analysis for New Product         Qty. Prod.    Profit/Loss
 2!_____
 3!Product Name/Number:- Bi-metallic detector    9000        -4200.00
 4!Proposed Retail Price £              72.00    9100        -3780.00
 5!                                              9200        -3360.00
 6!Fixed Costs £              (Totals)           9300        -2940.00
 7!   Design, dvelopment     20000.00            9400        -2520.00
 8!   Cost of manuf. plant   10000.00            9500        -2100.00
 9!   Set-up costs            5000.00            9600        -1680.00
10!   Marketing, advertising  7000.00            9700        -1260.00
11!TOTAL Fixed Cost          42000.00            9800         -840.00
12!                                              9900         -420.00
13!Variable Costs £           (Per Unit)        10000            .00
14!   Material costs             45.30          10100          420.00
15!   Labor costs                13.20          10200          840.00
16!   Overhead costs              3.00          10300         1260.00
17!   Profit margin               6.30          10400         1680.00
18!TOTAL Variable Cost           67.80          10500         2100.00
19!                                              10600         2520.00
20!                                              10700         2940.00
21!                                              10701         2944.20
22!COST if not manufactured  27000.00           10702         2948.40
23!                                              10703         2952.60
24!    Start quantity:           9000           10704         2956.80
25!    Increment quantity:        100           10705         2961.00
26!                                              10706         2965.20
27!=========================================================================
28!
```

Figure 5.7 *A traditional breakeven analysis implemented as a spreadsheet.*

When this formula is replicated only the variable C3 will be automatically adjusted to C4, etc.

Within this example it is evident that with the costs as specified the breakeven quantity is 10,000 at a proposed retail price of £72.00; below that a loss would be made. If a potential customer were to require, say, 9,800 to be made, it would be necessary to increase the price (i.e., the contents of cell B4) to guarantee a profit. The response of the spreadsheet to such changes is so rapid that this type of price negotiation could be proceeding over the phone with the manufacturer manipulating figures within the spreadsheet in response to the potential customer's reactions.

Example 4 Forecasting analysis

Figure 5.8 shows a spreadsheet which incorporates the relatively complex calculations required to evaluate a forecast based on an exponentially weighted average formula together with ancillary analyses. The response of such a forecast depends wholly on the value of Alpha (the exponential smoothing constant) which in this example is set at a typical value of 0.2.

	A	B	C		J	K	L
1	---------------------------------			1	-------------------------		
2			DEMAND ANAL	2	Alpha fixed at 0.2		
3	---------------------------------			3	-------------------------		
4			1	4	8	9	10
5				5			
6	1.Current Demand Value		55	6	49	58	68
7	2.Current Forecast		50	7	56	55	56
8	3.Error		5	8	-7	3	12
9	4.Squared Error		25	9	49	9	144
10	5.Cumulative Sq Error	0	25	10	1403	1412	1556
11				11			
12	6.Alpha*Error		1.00	12	-1.40	.60	2.40
13	7.(1-Alpha)*Past Sm Error		.00	13	2.71	1.05	1.32
14	8.Current Smoothed Error	.00	1.00	14	1.31	1.65	3.72
15				15			
16	9.Alpha*/Error/		1.00	16	1.40	.60	2.40
17	10.(1-Alpha)*Past MAD		4.00	17	6.64	6.43	5.62
18	11.Current MAD	5.00	5.00	18	8.04	7.03	8.02
19				19			
20	12.Current Std Dev		6.25	20	10.05	8.79	10.03
21				21			
22	13.Tracking Signal		.20	22	.16	.23	.46
23	14.Cumulative Error		5	23	27	30	42
24				24			
25	15.Alpha		.2	25	.2	.2	.2
26	16.Alpha*Current Demand		11.00	26	9.80	11.60	13.60
27	17.(1-Alpha)*Past Forecast		40.00	27	44.80	44.00	44.80
28	18.Next Period's Forecast	50.00	51.00	28	54.60	55.60	58.40
29	---------------------------------			29	-------------------------		
30				30			

Figure 5.8 Forecasting analysis based on an exponentially weighted average and illustrating the use of windows.

Because this particular spreadsheet is much wider than can be accommodated on the computer screen, a window facility has been used which provides the user with two smaller versions of the spreadsheet – both of which can be moved separately. This ensure that a user can arrange to see widely spaced elements of the spreadsheet simultaneously on the screen. In this particular instance it would be useful to know which value of Alpha (located in C25) produces the smallest sum of squared forecasting errors over the period of the forecast. This value, which occurs in period 10, is

98 *General purpose applications packages*

located in cell L10, and whilst normally these two cells could not be viewed simultaneously, inspection of figure 5.8 shows that they can be so viewed if the window facility is used. Note that figure 5.8 has been printed with a border (i.e. rows numbered, columns lettered) whereas this has been excluded in several of the previous examples.

Whilst the examples discussed earlier in this chapter can be produced using the facilities available in virtually all spreadsheet packages, the more advanced facilities which will now be briefly discussed are only available in the latest 'state-of-the-art' packages.

Graphics

Spreadsheet packages with graph drawing facilities allow the user to define the ranges of data within the spreadsheet which are required to be displayed in the graph and offer the user various facilities to enhance the graphical presentation of those data which can initially be displayed on the computer's screen prior to printing. Up to six different graphical formats can be saved within a single spreadsheet file and the additional facilities offered allow the user to choose:

graph type (i.e., line, bar, stacked bar, pie, etc.),

headings (i.e., main, sub, axis, etc.),

variable identifiers (i.e., a key).

Some of the graphical output forms available from spreadsheet packages are now illustrated.

Figure 5.9 shows a pie-chart derived from the stock portfolio example originally shown as figure 5.5. This graph shows the relative sizes of the various stockholdings in the portfolio and also allows one to be highlighted by separating it from the main structure of the pie.

Figure 5.10 is a simple bar-chart derived from the cash flow example originally shown as figure 5.6 and shows the cash flows resulting from borrowing £10,000 at 14 per cent interest over two years. In this example bars are presented vertically. Alternative forms of presentation allow for horizontal bars and 'stacked' bars (in which bars representing more than one variable are stacked on top of one another).

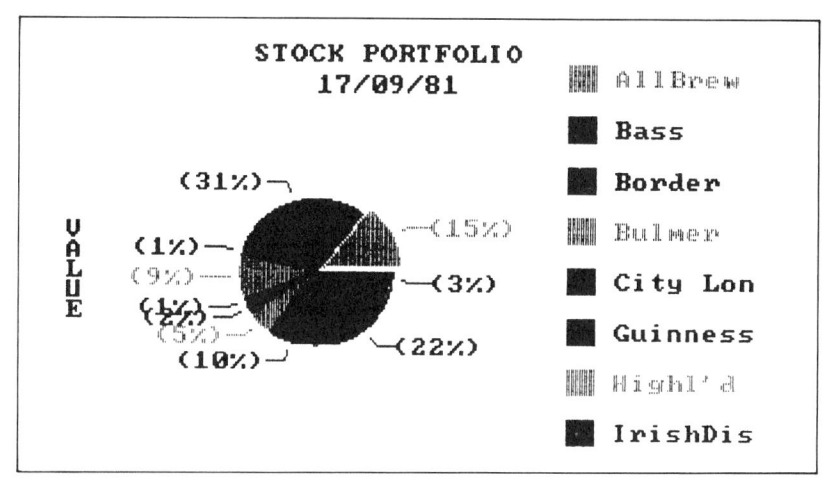

Figure 5.9 Pie-chart derived from stock portfolio example.

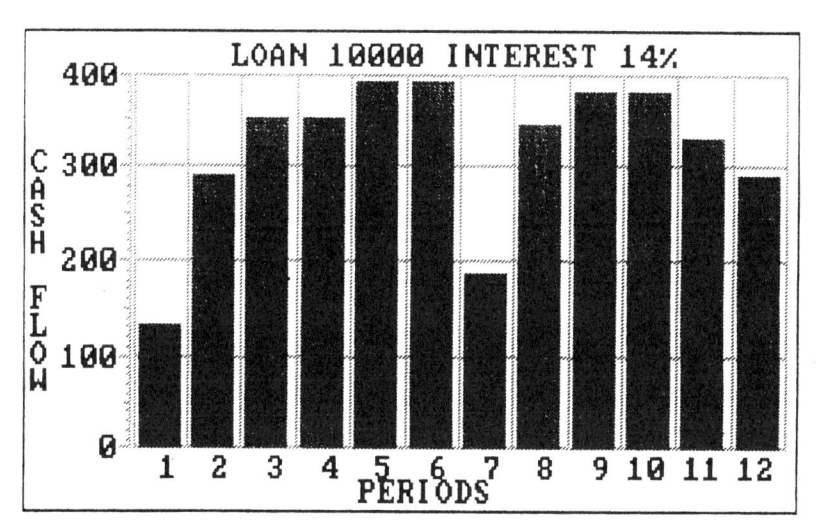

Figure 5.10 Bar-chart derived from cash flow example.

The final example of a graph derived from a spreadsheet is shown in figure 5.11 as a simple line graph derived from the forecasting analysis originally shown as figure 5.8. This example shows the forecast response of an exponentially weighted average based on an Alpha value of 0.2.

SIMPLE EXPONENTIAL SMOOTHING

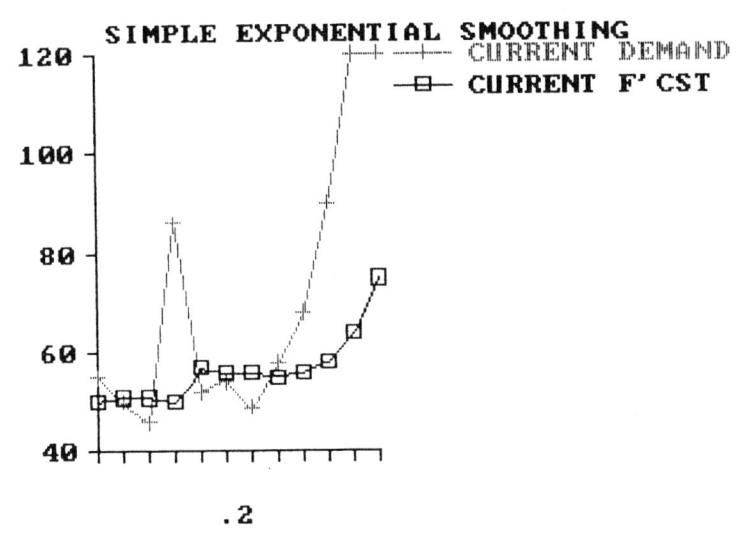

―+― CURRENT DEMAND
―□― CURRENT F' CST

.2

Figure 5.11 Line graph showing response of an exponentially weighted average forecast using an Alpha value of 0.2.

Colour

Most spreadsheets operating on 16-bit microcomputers make use of the additional storage available to display information within a spreadsheet in colour. Thus negative values, protected cells (i.e., cells which contain formulae, etc., which are then protected from mistaken attempts to add further information) can be made to appear in a colour different from normal text or numeric values in order to aid interpretation. Perhaps the most advantageous use of colour, however, is in the graphical displays where colour representation improves discrimination between closely plotted variables.

Macroprogramming

A macroprogramming facility within a spreadsheet allows the originator of a spreadsheet to store in a text file what, to the naive user, would be the actual key strokes that would be required to execute a prescribed set of instructions or manoeuvres. This facility allows for the development of relatively sophisticated spreadsheet work by untutored users and is particularly useful where the same analysis is used regularly.

Iteration control and forward referencing

In general, spreadsheets perform calculations either in row or column sequence. For example, in the demand analysis worksheet exhibited as figure 5.8, it is evident that calculations must be performed in column order if forecasts are to be calculated correctly. In some spreadsheets it is not possible to evaluate all calculations correctly in a single iteration of the spreadsheet, such as in situations described as 'forward referencing'. In such situations it would be necessary with the older packages to 'force' further calculations manually to obtain correct results. More recent spreadsheet packages with iteration control can automatically detect such situations and perform the necessary number of iterations to obtain valid results. A further iteration control facility is to define the size of a numeric value by specifying the size of the value stored in a specified cell at which to end iterative calculations – this facility allows the user to develop 'goal searching' analyses.

Simple database facilities

Some spreadsheets now incorporate simple database facilities based on the concept that a row within the spreadsheet is defined as a record and the cells within the row as fields. Simple search and sorting (or ordering) facilities are then offered. It would appear, however, that most users of microcomputers with database applications prefer to use a proper database package (see chapter 5) rather than the rather limited database facilities provided within a spreadsheet package.

Conclusion

Spreadsheet packages are one of the most popular microcomputer packages and it is claimed that the development of the spreadsheet concept has been largely responsible for the rapid growth of the microcomputer industry. Certainly many business and management problems can be expressed in a spreadsheet form and one foresees spreadsheets becoming an essential part of curricula for many courses in the future.

6

Flexible database packages

One of the most useful features of any computer is its ability to store large amounts of information and to retrieve specified sections of that information rapidly. Correspondingly one of management's greatest problems is, having accumulated vast amounts of information over the years, then to gain access rapidly to that information as and when required.

Not surprisingly, therefore, the majority of microcomputer application packages in the business and management area tend to be designed for database management and information retrieval applications of one sort or another, a database being defined as 'a file of data structured to allow a number of applications to access the data and update them without dictating or constraining the overall design of the content'. Such packages can either be tailored to cope with a specific but fairly common area of application or flexible, general purpose packages which allow the user to 'design' a data management and information retrieval system to suit his or her particular problem. These latter are variously termed FMS (File Management Systems) DBMS (Data Base Management Systems), etc.

While this chapter is concerned with the flexible type of package, it is still relevant to point out that many management applications of microcomputers are fixed design (bespoke) versions of database management and information retrieval packages:

purchase and sales ledger packages – designed to hold information on the financial transactions of a company with its suppliers/customers for goods and services received/supplied,

stock control packages – designed specifically to store information on stocked items and products, and to permit the normal transactions that take place such as allocations, withdrawals, receipts, etc., payroll packages – designed to hold information on employees and to maintain and record details of remuneration, PAYE tax contributions and other monetary deductions.

Such specialized, proprietary packages have a fixed record design or format and the method by which transactions are performed with those records is correspondingly restricted. Nevertheless, the software houses designing these packages naturally design them to be suitable for as many practical applications as possible.

When such proprietary packages prove unsuitable in a particular situation or when the area of application is so unusual that the software houses have not produced a relevant package, a flexible database management and information retrieval package may well come in useful. Certainly, there are more than enough such packages on the market.

Typical applications of flexible database management and information retrieval microcomputer-based systems are:

establishing personnel files in virtually any type of company or organization with more than 50 personnel,

recording students/fees/courses, etc., in universities and colleges,

matching clients to jobs in an employment agency, potential buyers to houses at an estate agent or potential spouses to each other in a 'dating' service,

keeping records of patients/treatment/drugs, etc., in hospitals or clinics and establishing appointment schedules,

monitoring mailing lists of customers/clients, directories of telephone extensions, etc.,

maintaining lists of equipment purchased indicating date of purchase, supplier, current location, etc.

Database terminology

To the layman intending to use a microcomputer for database management, it is of paramount importance that the relevant terminology first be understood.

There are essentially four levels of information in a database system.

Flexible database packages

Characters or bytes. These are essentially either alphabetic (A–Z) or numeric (0–9).

Fields. Several characters make up a data field and data fields can be of the following form:

alphanumeric – containing either alphabetic or numeric characters. Date fields which can take the form MM/DD/YY (American) or DD/MM/YY (European) are also treated as alphanumeric fields;

numeric containing only numeric characters together with the decimal point (.) or period (American). Alphabetic characters are specifically prohibited since it is possible that a numeric field will be used for arithmetic calculations. Monetary values are generally expressed as numeric to two decimal places;

key – an alphanumeric field which is sometimes used to label (i.e., identify) each record individually.

Records. Several fields make up a *record*. A typical record can have from ten to 50 fields, which will be a mixture of alphanumeric and numeric.

Files. Many records (typically 500 up to 1,000) make up a file. Files, therefore, consist of records with a common subject.

Since several data files, each containing up to 1,000 records, can be stored on a single floppy disk, a physical analogy of a database management storage system could be represented as in figure 6.1.

Classification of database packages

Flexible database packages can be broadly categorized into three levels or classes:

Level 1   Allows the user to create a record designed to his or her requirements and to enter information into that record structure, thus creating a simple database. Records can be selected by simple or conditional criteria and records can be sorted into alphanumeric or numeric order.

Level 2   As level 1 but with the addition of a report generator – this latter being a small program created from the responses

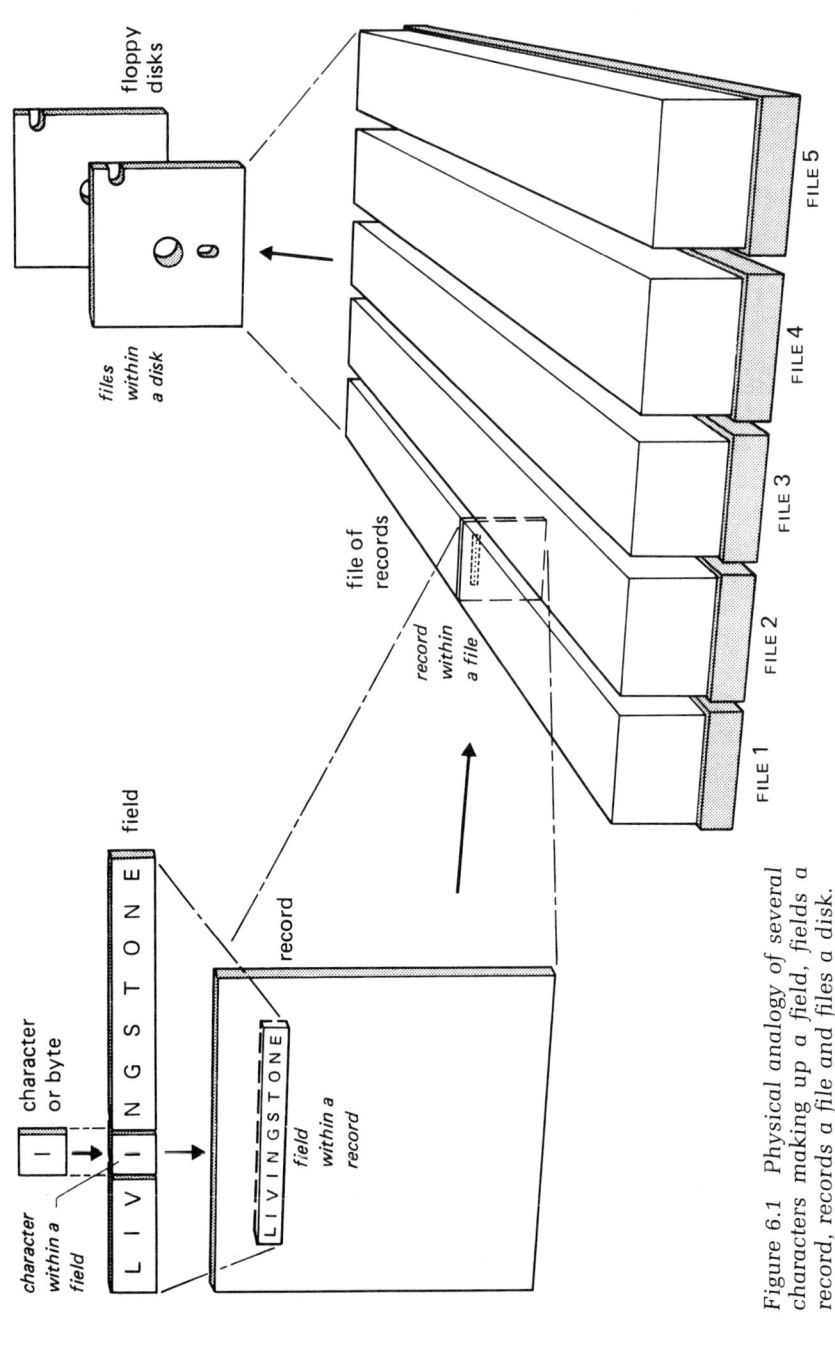

Figure 6.1 Physical analogy of several characters making up a field, fields a record, records a file and files a disk.

provided to a series of questions relating to the design of the report. This report form program can be saved on disk and re-used to produce the same style of report at any time in the future.

Level 3 As level 1, and usually including a report generator (level 2), but with the additional facility that commands can be saved as instructions within a high-level program (macroprogram) which can be used to design a bespoke database system. The advantage of using a specialized, high-level programming language for database work is that development times for new systems can be cut down considerably compared with using low-level programs such as BASIC.

Within the three levels of packages mentioned above, commands can be effected either by selection through a menu (hence, menu driven) or by keying in the command words themselves (command driven). Menu driven packages are generally more user friendly but tend to be rather cumbersome to operate for the experienced user who would generally prefer the directness of a command driven package.

Designing the record structure and/or layout

The first task in creating an information system based on a flexible database package is to design the record structure by specifying:

the number of fields per record,

the name and type of fields,

field lengths – if the package is of a fixed field length structure.

Subsequently it may be possible to design the layout of how each record appears on the screen. In many packages a fixed or standard layout is offered as a default with a personalized or bespoke layout being offered as an option. This latter is achieved by providing the user with an initially blank computer screen and then, following instructions or prompts which appear at the bottom of the screen, he or she can locate the position of the contents of individual data fields and also, where required, the position of the labels or headings associated with those data fields within the screen or record format.

108 *General purpose applications packages*

```
RECORD £ 00014
COMPANY    : EURO MICRO:
DIVISION   : EXPORT:
DEPT       : R & D :
NAME       : BROWN R F :
SALARY     :  14678:
```

Figure 6.2 Personnel record shown in the standard editing format style of dBASE2.

Figure 6.2 illustrates a standard layout as produced by dBASE2 which can be contrasted with the bespoke record formats shown in figures 6.3 and 6.4.

Size restrictions

Within any flexible database package, there will usually be some size restrictions such as the number of

bytes (characters) per field,

fields per record,

characters per record,

records per file,

although in practice the size limitation of a database file will be imposed generally by disk size rather than by the package.

Size of record. Having specified the size and number of fields that constitute a record (and if required completed the design of the record display) it is essential to know how many bytes (characters) have been reserved to represent a single record. For some packages a running total of the bytes used appears during the design stage.

Size of file. Because files of records are stored on disk, packages are structured around the size of a disk's block size of 256 bytes, and, although in general the bigger the size of record the fewer records can be held per file, this relationship is not strictly linear.

'Within record' calculations

The estate agent record shown as figure 6.3 contains 13 fields, all independent of each other, so that information has to be specifically keyed in for each. A slightly more complex record could contain *within record' calculations* whereby, for example, the entry in one field could be the product of two other fields. Figure 6.4 is an example of a stock record with four built-in calculations which are:

With VAT   = 1.15 × Sell Price

Cost Value = Cost Price × Stock

Sell Value = Sell Price × Stock

Mark Up   = 100 × (Sell Price/Cost Price −1)

With such a record structure entries into fields which are calculated as functions of other fields are made automatically by the computer when information in the other fields becomes available.

Obviously, in this example, any withdrawal of stock would be entered as a reduction on the Stock figure and would produce an

```
05/11/81   Example of a record from the Houselist file

Address              :Greenways  -  Old Warwick Road
District             :Lapworth
Asking Price         : 76000      Date accepted :09/08/81
Reception  : 3                    Bedrooms   : 4
Bathrooms  : 2                    Garage spaces: 3
Detached or semi   :Det
Garden(small/medium/large):Large
Annual rates  :865
Reference No.  :S1005    Comments :Rural outlook
```

Figure 6.3 *Example of a simple record design as used by an estate agent (record length 183 bytes).*

110 *General purpose applications packages*

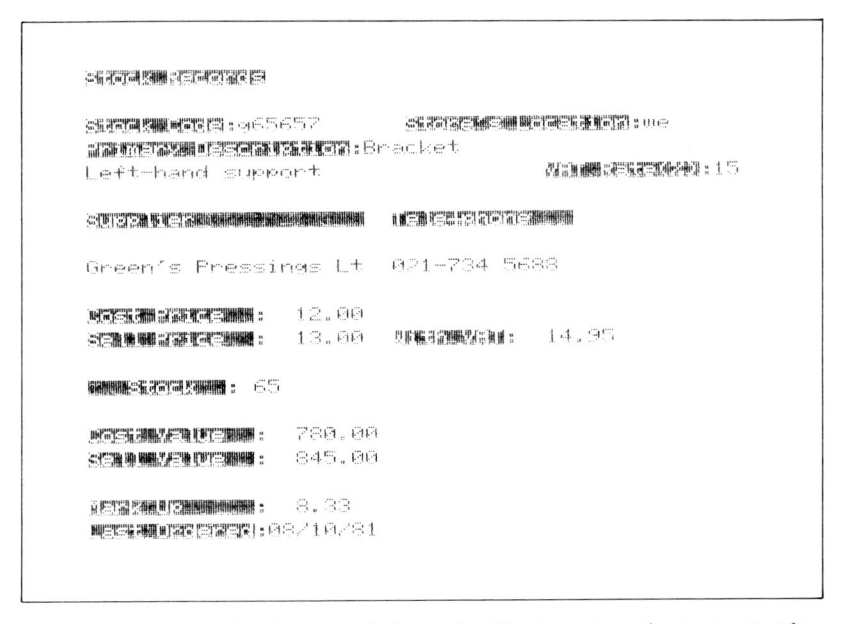

```
STOCK RECORD

STOCK No: 465657              STOCK DESCRIPTION: ...
MATERIAL DESCRIPTION: Bracket
Left-hand support                          RE-ORDER:15

SUPPLIER                      TELEPHONE
Green's Pressings Lt          021-734 5688

COST/UNIT:     12.00
SELL/UNIT:     13.00          MARGIN:   14.95

IN STOCK:      65

COST VALUE:   780.00
SELL VALUE:   845.00

PERCENTAGE:     8.33
LAST UPDATED:08/10/81
```

Figure 6.4 Example of a record from the file Inventory featuring 'within record' calculations (record length 190 bytes).

automatic, proportional reduction in the Cost Value and Sell Value figures.

Whilst the calculations which can be performed within a record are not too sophisticated, the following operations are usually available in packages where this facility is provided:

the four standard operators: (+) add or plus, (−) subtract or minus, (/) divide and (*) multiply,

percentage (%) calculates the percentage one field represents of another field,

integer part , calculates the integer value of a data field,

monetary, performs rounding on a numeric field to two decimal places.

Password access

If the data to be held on file are confidential, when the data disk is formatted to accept data records, a few packages provide a *password* facility to gain access to the file. This password, which is usually a short alphanumeric field, should not appear on the computer screen when it is keyed in. When creating a password, it is sensible to use an easily remembered set of characters since, although passwords can be changed, one still needs the original password to access this particular facility.

Sorting and indexing

In general, within the main data file, records will be held sequentially in the order they were entered into that file: in other words, the records are held unsorted.

When it is necessary to sort records, one way is simply to create a small *index file* of key fields stored in the order required. Since each record is, from the package's point of view, identified and accessed by its key field, this is clearly much more economic in storage terms than creating another complete data file with the records sorted. The index file occupies only a small fraction of the storage space required for the related data file. The creation of such an index file called Houseprice is shown diagram-matically in figure 6.5 and indicates that the key fields (reference numbers) of the records in the data file Houselist are held in the Houseprice index file in descending order of the price field.

Such sorted index files can be based on any field or combination of fields within a record. Where the field being used is alphanumeric, sorting is performed alphabetically. When the value of a field within a particular record is changed and that field has been used previously to create an index file, should the change of value change the sorted order a well designed package will automatically change the order of the index file. New records added to the file can be similarly accommodated.

An example of indexing on a combination of fields is shown in figure 6.6 where a small file of personnel records with the record structure shown as in figure 6.2 is shown initially unsorted and then linked to an index file created on a combination of three fields namely COMPANY + DIVISION + DEPARTMENT. Examination of

112 *General purpose applications packages*

MAIN or DATA FILE held sequentially in order of record entry (UNSORTED)

INDEX FILE of key fields sorted in descending order of price (SORTED)

key field

price field

1008	£20,000
1007	£25,000
1006	£60,000
1005	£40,000
1004	£30,000
1003	£25,000
1002	£80,000
1001	£40,000

1000 £50,000
Address: ═══
Bedrooms: ═══
Reception: ═══
Rates: ─────

MAIN or DATA FILE
HOUSE LIST

1008	£20,000
1007	£25,000
1003	£25,000
1004	£30,000
1005	£40,000
1001	£40,000
1000	£50,000
1006	£60,000
1002	£80,000

INDEX FILE
HOUSE PRICE

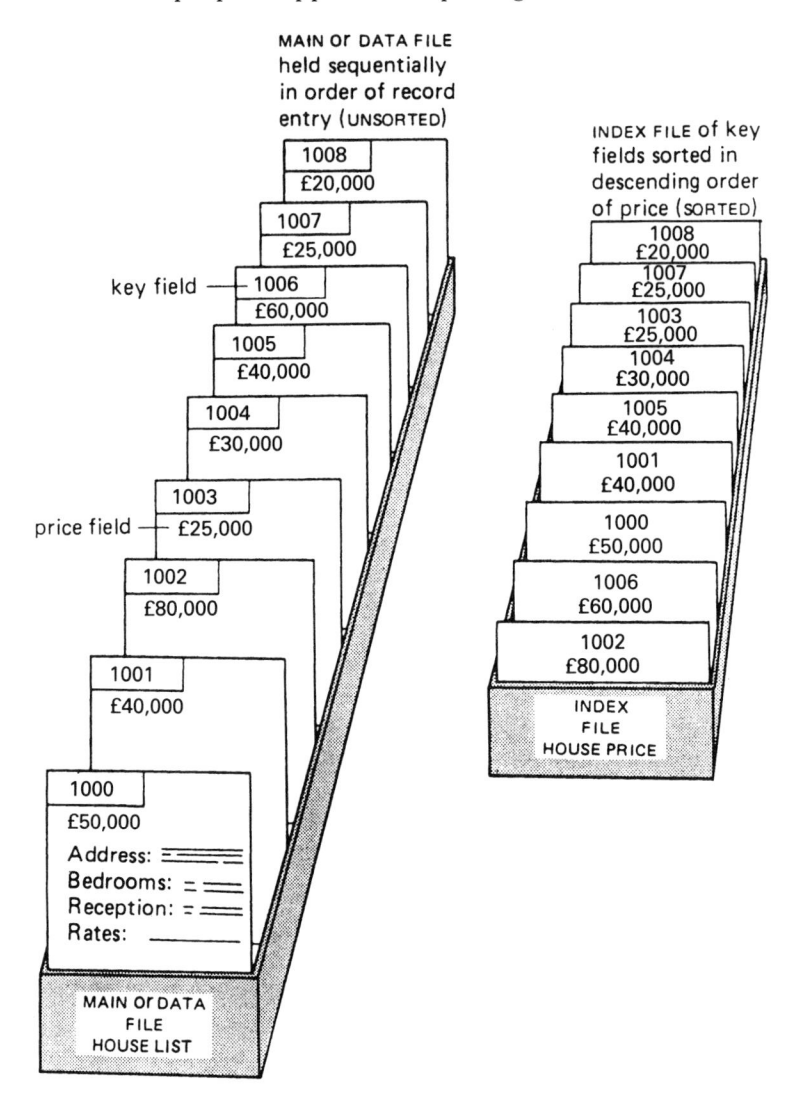

Figure 6.5 Diagrammatic representation of an unsorted data file and a sorted index file.

this example indicates that the records once indexed have been initially sorted alphabetically by COMPANY, then within COMPANY alphabetically by DIVISION and finally within DIVISION alphabetically by DEPARTMENT.

```
FILE OF EMPLOYEES LISTED UN-INDEXED ie AS ENTERED
==================================================

RECORD  COMPANY     DIV.     DEPT.   NAME          SALARY
======  =======     ====     =====   ====          ======
00001   UK MICRO    HOME     MKTG    JONES W       18000
00002   EURO MICRO  EXPORT   PROD    HALL P        16500
00003   UK MICRO    EXPORT   R & D   BRYANT P      16000
00004   EURO MICRO  HOME     PROD    YOUNG F       12000
00005   EURO MICRO  EXPORT   MKTG    SMITH F       17500
00006   UK MICRO    EXPORT   PROD    ABRAHAMS G    14300
00007   UK MICRO    HOME     MKTG    BROWN T       16570
00008   EURO MICRO  EXPORT   R & D   SQUIRES F     17400
00009   UK MICRO    EXPORT   MKTG    LEWIS C       18000
00010   EURO MICRO  HOME     PROD    GRANT W       15000
00011   EURO MICRO  EXPORT   MKTG    LOESER G      12679
00012   UK MICRO    EXPORT   PROD    DAVIS J A     12670
00013   EURO MICRO  HOME     R & D   BUNNAG A      19000
00014   EURO MICRO  HOME     R & D   BROWN R F     14678


RECORDS IN FILE ARE INDEXED ON  ----> COMPANY + DIVISION + DEPARTMENT
---------------------------------------------------------------------

RECORD  COMPANY     DIV.     DEPT.   NAME          SALARY
======  =======     ====     =====   ====          ======
00005   EURO MICRO  EXPORT   MKTG    SMITH F       17500
00011   EURO MICRO  EXPORT   MKTG    LOESER G      12679
00002   EURO MICRO  EXPORT   PROD    HALL P        16500
00008   EURO MICRO  EXPORT   R & D   SQUIRES F     17400
00014   EURO MICRO  EXPORT   R & D   BROWN R F     14678
00004   EURO MICRO  HOME     PROD    YOUNG F       12000
00010   EURO MICRO  HOME     PROD    GRANT W       15000
00013   EURO MICRO  HOME     R & D   BUNNAG A      19000
00009   UK MICRO    EXPORT   MKTG    LEWIS C       18000
00006   UK MICRO    EXPORT   PROD    ABRAHAMS G    14300
00012   UK MICRO    EXPORT   PROD    DAVIS J A     12670
00003   UK MICRO    EXPORT   R & D   BRYANT P      16000
00001   UK MICRO    HOME     MKTG    JONES W       18000
00007   UK MICRO    HOME     MKTG    BROWN T       16570
```

Figure 6.6 *Small personnel database file shown both unindexed and indexed by COMPANY + DIVISION + DEPARTMENT.*

The ability to sort and index is perhaps the most powerful feature of a microcomputer when compared with its manual equivalent.

Searching for specified records

After the creation of the data file, all database management and information retrieval packages allow the user to search through the data file to select records. This can be done either by 'nudging' or 'skipping' manually through sorted or unsorted files or by selecting records which meet either a single criterion or multiple criteria.

Search criteria can be set up using logical AND, NOT and OR functions together with criteria such as those shown in table 6.1.

Search criteria, once created, can sometimes be named and stored

114 *General purpose applications packages*

as a search criteria file. This saves the user setting them on each occasion which can be an advantage if the same ones are likely to be used again and again.

Records in a data file can be searched unsorted or sorted. If a sorted search is wanted, there must already be a named index file.

When searching for certain records in a data file, the user can typically:

print all records meeting the search criterion,

view all records meeting the search criterion,

view all records meeting the search criterion and print only those selected by the user.

Figures 6.7a and 6.7b show the results of two searches conducted on the Houselist file. Figure 6.7a uses the simple criterion of searching for any houses on file before the date 09/07/85 – the type of criterion an estate agent might well use to identify houses which had been on his books for a long time. In this case a sorted index file was not used, the unsorted data file was searched, although the records will, of course, be shown in ascending order of date accepted simply because the records were originally entered and, therefore, stored in that order.

Table 6.1 Search criteria

	Alphanumeric/key	Numeric/value	Date
Equal to, e.g.	= 'Lapworth'	= 100	= 12/11/85
Greater than, e.g.	> 'Lapworth'	> 100	> 12/11/85
Less than, e.g.	< 'Lapworth'	< 100	< 12/11/85
Greater than (after for alphanumeric) or equal to, e.g.	⩾ 'Lapworth'	⩾ 100	⩾ 12/11/85
Less than (before for alphanumeric) or equal to, e.g.	⩽ 'Lapworth'	⩽ 100	⩽ 12/11/85

The occurrence of a particular character in a particular position in a field can also be used. For example, + + + 11 can be used to identify records with a November date within a DD/MM/YY date field (since the 11 field, coincides with the MM field, uniquely identifies the month of November).

Flexible database packages 115

Figure 6.7b is the result of a search through the same Houselist file but in this case sorted on the field Asking Price. In this case the two records that have been found meet the criterion that the Asking Price should be greater than £80,000 and that the District is (equal to) Lapworth. Such a search criterion could be used to match houses to a relatively affluent prospective purchaser! Since the sorted index file was used the houses appear in ascending order of asking price.

Report writing

So far in this chapter we have discussed the design of a record, the creation of a data file of many records and the subsequent management of those records. In addition to these *record handling* facilities, many database management and information retrieval packages also offer a *report writing* facility.

A report is designed to extract information from particular fields on either all or selected records within a data file and to present that information as a printed report. Where numerical data are extracted from records, it is also possible to perform simple *within report' calculations* on those data in much the same way as for 'within record' calculations (see page 109). The design of the printed report has to be built up by the user and will generally be stored as a *report print control file* for subsequent use. For most reports it will be necessary to extract data from sorted records, hence a report print control file will generally be associated with a particular index file.

Designing the report

When building up the design of a printed report, most database management and information retrieval packages break the report into four elements which are:

Page controls. These specify headings, date, etc., which will appear on every page of the report and also indicate whether pages will be sequentially numbered or not.

Record controls. These specify which record data fields are to be extracted from records within the data file and give instructions as to where, on the page of the report, such fields are to be printed. If

116 *General purpose applications packages*

```
11/10/85  Houses on file since before 09/07/85

Address             :567 Warwick Road
District            :Solihull Wood
Asking Price        : 45000    Date accepted :09/06/85
Reception : 2                 Bedrooms  : 3
Bathrooms : 1                 Garage spaces: 0
Detached or semi   :Semi
Garden(small/medium/large):Small
Annual rates  :412
Reference No.  :S1008   Comments :Older terraced property
----------------------------------------------------------
Address             :65 Bermuda Avenue
District            :Sheldon
Asking Price        : 45000    Date accepted :08/07/85
Reception : 2                 Bedrooms  : 3
Bathrooms : 1                 Garage spaces: 0
Detached or semi   :Semi
Garden(small/medium/large):Small
Annual rates  :389
Reference No.  :S1012   Comments :Suitable first time buyer
----------------------------------------------------------
```

Figures 6.7a Example of a record search within an unsorted Houselist file for houses meeting a single criterion of date.

any calculations are to be performed on numeric or value fields, the print control file must include a specification of those calculations, together with instructions as to where the results of those calculations are to be printed.

Subtotal controls. Where subtotals are to be accumulated, the report print control file must specify which numeric or value fields

```
11/10/85  Houses above 50000 in Lapworth in price order

Address            :Greenways - Old Warwick Road
District           :Lapworth
Asking Price       : 86000    Date accepted :09/08/85
Reception : 3                Bedrooms    : 4
Bathrooms : 2                Garage spaces: 3
Detached or semi   :Det
Garden(small/medium/large):Large
Annual rates       :865
Reference No.      :S1005   Comments :Rural outlook
-----------------------------------------------------------
Address            :Blenheim - Copsewood Road
District           :Lapworth
Asking Price       : 98000    Date accepted :09/08/85
Reception : 3                Bedrooms    : 4
Bathrooms : 2                Garage spaces: 3
Detached or semi   :Det
Garden(small/medium/large):Large
Annual rates       :989
Reference No.      :S1010   Comments :Gentleman's Residence
-----------------------------------------------------------
```

Figure 6.7b Example of a record search within the Houselist file sorted by value for houses meeting two specified criteria of price and location.

are to be accumulated. Subtotals are usually printed and then set equal to zero when the specified index field changes. Subtotals, therefore, can only be used in reports associated with a sorted data file. Any printing requirements such as the heading SUBTOTAL must also be specified. Because the subtotal control is triggered by a change occurring in a specified field, this facility can be used most effectively to *separate sections* of a report, either by printing a separation line of, say, hyphens or even more simply by producing a line space.

Total controls. Where totals are to be accumulated for all records appearing in the printed report, the numeric or value data field to be accumulated must be specified together with any printing requirements, such as TOTAL.

Examples of reports

To illustrate these various facilities as they could appear in printed reports, several examples are reproduced in figures 6.8 to 6.10 together with comments on which facilities have been used and how.

Figure 6.8 shows a three-page report extracted from a telephone extension file. In this example the pages have been shortened to form a booklet and can accommodate only a maximum of 23 names per page. The title, column headings and date of issue are repeated on every page and pages are numbered sequentially. While there are no subtotal calculations, because the records are now sorted on the field DEPARTMENT, the subtotal control facility has been used to print a separation line of hyphens each time the DEPARTMENT field changes.

The sales commission example shown in figure 6.9 illustrates nearly all the facilities available in a report print from a database management and information retrieval package. In this example three fields are extracted from each record (namely Sales Rep, Total and NUMBER) whose format is shown in figure 6.10. The fourth figure to be printed per record (i.e., Commission) is calculated automatically as 10 per cent of the Total field. Thus the subtotals represent the commission earned by each sales representative and the total the overall commission to be paid. The report presupposes records are sorted alphabetically by sales representatives.

Although not apparent in the printed report itself, another facility that has been used is a search criterion specifying that only quotations with an acceptance date later than 05/09/85 be included. This obviously will ensure that no quotations accepted before that date, for which commission has already been paid, or quotations which have yet to be accepted are included in the report. The quotation record shown in figure 6.10 (to indicate the type of record on which the report was based) appears as the first commission due to sales reresentative FIN since the acceptance date for this quote was 20/10/81.

```
Page    1 TELEPHONE EXTENSIONS --- DEPARTMENT ORDER
10/11/85
        NAME                DEPARTMENT          EXTENSION
==================================================================
GORDON James G              Administration         721
PRENTICE Peter G            Administration         777
DIXON Edward J              Administration         707
LAWRENCE Jane (Mrs)         Administration         747
EDWARDS David S             Administration         721
HALLAM Geoffrey H           Administration         732
GABOR Peter                 Administration         721
GIBBS Neal F                Administration         732
------------------------------------------------------------------
GRIMLEY Edward J            Inspection             606
HALL Norman                 Inspection             632
JONES Ann (Mrs)             Inspection             607
GREGORY David               Inspection             654
ANDREWS Mark E              Inspection             654
------------------------------------------------------------------
HARTLEY Jennifer(Ms)        Marketing              490
WEBB Kenneth E              Marketing              454
BURTON Helen (Miss)         Marketing              421
CALE Ronald                 Marketing              444
LEWIS Colin D               Marketing              421
------------------------------------------------------------------
SANDERSON Andrew G          Production             387
JOHNSON Edward K            Production             365
        Page    2 TELEPHONE EXTENSIONS --- DEPARTMENT ORDER
        10/11/85
                NAME                DEPARTMENT          EXTENSION
        ==========================================================
        ISLIP John D                Production         307
        HARRIS David S              Production         305
        PHIPPS Gordon L             Production         305
        LING Maurice                Production         304
        ANTONY Barry                Production         333
        MORRIS Julian D             Production         303
        BENNETT David               Production         367
        JOHNSON Anne (Miss)         Production         375
        BURCHER Peter               Production         397
        NICHOLSON Garth H           Production         364
        WILLIAMS Graham J           Production         305
        ----------------------------------------------------------
        LANGLEY Edward              Production Planning    521
        MACMILLAN Brian L           Production Planning    532
        TAYLOR Brian S              Production Planning    555
        MACGREGOR John              Production Planning    521
        WILSON Brian H              Production Planning    532
        ----------------------------------------------------------
        LIVINGSTONE John D          Purchasing         276
        FREER Gill (Miss)           Purchasing         289
        WARING Philip A             Purchasing         207
        SMITH James J               Purchasing         264
        POWELL Graham J             Purchasing         234
                Page    3 TELEPHONE EXTENSIONS --- DEPARTMENT ORDER
                10/11/85
                        NAME                DEPARTMENT          EXTENSION
                ==================================================================
                SKINNER Jane (Ms)           Purchasing         254
                HIPKISS Jenny (Mrs)         Purchasing         231
                ------------------------------------------------------------------
                NANSEN Graham F             Sales              174
                BROWN John G                Sales              165
                DAVIES Sharon (Miss)        Sales              123
                GRENVILLE Alice (Ms)        Sales              109
                OAKLEY Mark F               Sales              109
                GRAY Anthony F              Sales              121
                BUCKLE Sandra (Mrs)         Sales              109
                ------------------------------------------------------------------
```

Figure 6.8 Example of a printed report from a telephone extension file, sorted on the field DEPARTMENT and incorporating page headings and separation lines between departments.

```
05/11/85

SALES REP'S COMMISSION FOR LAST 2 MONTHS


SALES REP    TOTAL    INV.NO.   COMMISSION
-----------------------------------------------


DGT          895.00      2          89.50
DGT         2205.00      9         220.50
DGT         2205.00      9         220.50

                      Sub Total    530.50

FIN         2611.10      5         261.11
FIN          105.00     10          10.50

                      Sub Total    271.61

FNL           34.90      6           3.49
FNL          175.85      8          17.59
FNL            8.11     11            .81
FNL         2144.65      3         214.47

                      Sub Total    236.36

GHS         2058.30      7         205.83
GHS          142.80      4          14.28

                      Sub Total    220.11


                        TOTAL     2171.48
```

Figure 6.9 Example of a printed report, sorted with commission calculated for each record, subtotalled for each representative and totalled for overall commission to be paid.

Flexible database packages 121

```
                   QUOTATION
   NUMBER :0005              DATE :17/09/85
   ---------------------------------------------
   From,                For,
   Bloggs & Co. Ltd.    CMS Ltd
   Southern Avenue      20 Universe Rd
   Birmingham B4 1ST    Bromley, Kent
   ---------------------------------------------
   QTY      DESCRIPTION        PRICE
       1    8032 Computer      895.00     895.00
       1    8050 Dual Disc Driv 895.00    895.00
       1    Aculab 1 Interface   90.00     90.00
       1    Anadex Printer DP95 999.00    999.00
                                          ----------
                             Sub Total    2879.00
                       10  %Discount       287.90
   Sales Rep              Carriage         20.00
   FIN
                             Total        2611.10
   Date Accepted             VAT           391.66
   20/10/81            INVOICE TOTAL      3002.76
   ---------------------------------------------
```

Figure 6.10 Example of a record from a quotations file (record length 508 bytes).

Other facilities

Global or selective record transactions

Another facility available on many database management and information retrieval packages is the ability to alter numeric or value fields on all, or selected, records. Thus, for example, all *price fields* on all records could be increased (or, less likely, decreased) by 10 per cent. An example of this is shown in figure 6.11 using the package dBASE II and the keyed in instruction:

   REPLACE ALL PRICE WITH PRICE*1.1

where ALL means all records and PRICE is the field to be changed.

A further sophistication offered by this package, also illustrated is *selective* transactions. The instruction:

122 General purpose applications packages

```
                    PRICE LIST FOR FIVE AND EIGHT INCH FLOPPY DISKS

          SIZE       DENSITY      SIDED      CODE:NO      PRICE

          FIVE INCH    SINGLE     SINGLE     M11A411X      1.50
          FIVE INCH    DOUBLE     SINGLE     M13A411X      1.66
          FIVE INCH    DOUBLE     DOUBLE     M14A411X      1.82
          FIVE INCH    DOUBLE     SINGLE     M15A411X      1.50
          FIVE INCH    DOUBLE     DOUBLE     M16A411X      1.63
          EIGHT INCH   SINGLE     SINGLE     F11A211X      1.50
          EIGHT INCH   DOUBLE     SINGLE     F13A211X      1.84
          EIGHT INCH   SINGLE     DOUBLE     F12A211X      1.91
          EIGHT INCH   DOUBLE     DOUBLE     F14A211X      2.00

. REPLACE ALL PRICE WITH PRICE*1.1
00009 REPLACEMENT(S)
. REPORT FORM DISKPRICE

                    PRICE LIST FOR FIVE AND EIGHT INCH FLOPPY DISKS

          SIZE       DENSITY      SIDED      CODE:NO      PRICE

          FIVE INCH    SINGLE     SINGLE     M11A411X      1.65
          FIVE INCH    DOUBLE     SINGLE     M13A411X      1.82
          FIVE INCH    DOUBLE     DOUBLE     M14A411X      2.00
          FIVE INCH    DOUBLE     SINGLE     M15A411X      1.65
          FIVE INCH    DOUBLE     DOUBLE     M16A411X      1.79
          EIGHT INCH   SINGLE     SINGLE     F11A211X      1.65
          EIGHT INCH   DOUBLE     SINGLE     F13A211X      2.02
          EIGHT INCH   SINGLE     DOUBLE     F12A211X      2.10
          EIGHT INCH   DOUBLE     DOUBLE     F14A211X      2.20

. REPLACE FOR SIZE="EIGHT INCH" PRICE WITH PRICE+.10
00004 REPLACEMENT(S)
. REPORT FORM DISKPRICE

                    PRICE LIST FOR FIVE AND EIGHT INCH FLOPPY DISKS

          SIZE       DENSITY      SIDED      CODE:NO      PRICE

          FIVE INCH    SINGLE     SINGLE     M11A411X      1.65
          FIVE INCH    DOUBLE     SINGLE     M13A411X      1.82
          FIVE INCH    DOUBLE     DOUBLE     M14A411X      2.00
          FIVE INCH    DOUBLE     SINGLE     M15A411X      1.65
          FIVE INCH    DOUBLE     DOUBLE     M16A411X      1.79
          EIGHT INCH   SINGLE     SINGLE     F11A211X      1.75
          EIGHT INCH   DOUBLE     SINGLE     F13A211X      2.12
          EIGHT INCH   SINGLE     DOUBLE     F12A211X      2.20
          EIGHT INCH   DOUBLE     DOUBLE     F14A211X      2.30
```

Figure 6.11 Example of non-selective and selective transactions on record fields.

REPLACE FOR SIZE = 'EIGHT INCH' PRICE WITH PRICE + .10

increases the price of only the 8 inch disks by a further 10p.

Macroprogramming

A few database management and information retrieval packages offer a very powerful facility known as macroprogramming, which allows the user to write programs made up of many instructions, each of which would normally have to be an individually keyed in instruction. Hence the instruction:

REPLACE ALL PRICE WITH PRICE*1.1

which was keyed into the computer to produce part of figure 6.11 although one instruction at the macro level would, however, be automatically translated into many instructions in a lower level language.

This macroprogramming facility is a powerful tool which can be used to design bespoke database applications much more rapidly than by using a normal, lower level language such as BASIC. The advantage is illustrated in the following example using the dBASE II macroprogramming facility.

Consider the following four-instruction program:

USE DFILE INDEX DFIND
ERASE
REPLACE ALL PRICE WITH PRICE*1.1
DISPLAY ALL FOR PRICE > 10.00 .AND. PRICE < 100

This simple little program instructs the computer to use a database file (DFILE) whose records are sorted in alphabetic order on a field specified by an index file (DFIND) and then proceeds to clear the VDU screen, increase all the price fields in all records by 10 per cent and then display on the screen all those records whose resultant price field is greater than 10 and less than 100. To write a program in BASIC to achieve the same result would require perhaps 30 instructions as opposed to the four used here.

Figure 6.12 illustrates the type of database system that can be designed using a macro system. In this particular example, which is ranged to maintain a company's telephone extension list, the user is always referred back to a simple four-option menu which allows the user to:

```
              DO MENU        DIRECTORY MAINTENANCE
                              *** MAIN    MENU ***

                              0 - LIST DIRECTORY
                              1 - ADD NEW RECORDS
                              2 - DELETE CURRENT RECORDS
                              3 - ALTER EXISTING RECORDS


                                  WAITING INSTRUCTION


          WAITING 0

          00013  DAVISON G H        ACCOUNTS      721
          00017  WILLIAMS G S       ACCOUNTS      649
          00019  SMITH Y (MISS)     ACCOUNTS      407
          00006  LEWIS C D          INSPECTION    723
          00018  SMITH D H          INSPECTION    640
          00010  JAMESON F T        PERSONNEL     653
          00021  CHAMBERS J J       PERSONNEL     657
          00001  BROWN R G          PRODUCTION    345
          00014  ASHID T F          PRODUCTION    555
          00015  PIPER T F          PRODUCTION    921
          00016  SMITH F S          PRODUCTION    555
          00024  SINDEN D F         PRODUCTION    290
          00025  EVERSFIELD D S     PRODUCTION    555
          00009  RANKIN G H         PURCHASING    386
          00012  BROWNLY   A        PURCHASING    432
          00022  BOLT    A          REGISTRY      412


          WAITING 1
           Enter 0 to exit

          Enter SURNAME I I:JAMES D F

          Enter DEPARTMENT:PERSONNEL

          Enter EXTENSION NO.:274


          Are all fields correct?:Y
```

Figure 6.12 Printout from a database macroprogram menu (operator's responses underlined).

WAITING 2
   Enter 0 to exit

      Enter 1 to delete a NAMED record
      Enter 2 to delete all records
      sharing a single EXTENSION number

WAITING 2
EXTENSION NUMBER to be deleted:555

00014   ASHID T F   PRODUCTION   555
00016   SMITH F S   PRODUCTION   555
00025   EVERSFIELD D S   PRODUCTION   555
DELETE?:Y

WAITING 3
   Enter 0 to exit

Enter SURNAME of persons
record to be changed:BROWN

These are all the records with that SURNAME
00001   BROWN R G   PRODUCTION   345
00012   BROWNLY G A   PURCHASING   432

Enter NUMBER of record
to be altered if MORE than one, OR
if ONLY one record listed, key in
that records number
:12

00012   BROWNLY G A   PURCHASING   432

Which FIELD do you want to alter
DEPARTMENT - D or EXTENSION - E?
WAITING E
New EXTENSION number:423

The new record is now as shown below

00012   BROWNLY G A   PURCHASING   423

WAITING 0

00013   DAVISON G H   ACCOUNTS   721
00017   WILLIAMS G S   ACCOUNTS   649
00019   SMITH Y (MISS)   ACCOUNTS   407
00006   LEWIS C D   INSPECTION   723
00018   SMITH D H   INSPECTION   640
00010   JAMESON F T   PERSONNEL   653
00021   CHAMBERS J J   PERSONNEL   657
00026   JAMES D F   PERSONNEL   274
00001   BROWN R G   PRODUCTION   345
00015   PIPER T F   PRODUCTION   921
00024   SINDEN D F   PRODUCTION   290
00009   RANKIN G H   PURCHASING   386
00012   BROWNLY G A   PURCHASING   423
00022   BOLTON A   REGISTRY   412

126 *General purpose applications packages*

  0 list the directory

  1 add new records to the directory

  2 delete records from the directory

  3 alter existing records in the directory

Throughout the example, the operator's responses are underlined. The initial response, 0, produces a listing of the current records. The next reponse, 1, allows the user to add a record for a D. F. James who has joined the PERSONNEL department and has been allocated extension number 274.

To delete all the records associated with extension 555, the operator keys in '2' to access the delete records facility and a subsequent '2' to indicate it is records linked to an EXTENSION (rather than a NAMED person) that are to be deleted. The macroprogram then requests the EXTENSION NUMBER and, given the response 555, identifies all the records associated with that extention and deletes them when a confirmatory Y is keyed in by the operator.

To alter an existing record, the operator responds to the menu with 3 and inadvertently keys in BROWN rather than the surname required which is BROWNLY. Since that search criterion finds two records, the operator can identify the particular record required by keying in its number, 12. To reassure the operator, the selected record is displayed and the field to be changed requested. In this case the EXTENSION number is changed from 432 to 423 and the altered record displayed. A final response of 0 relists the directory and confirms that all the alterations/deletions/additions have been made correctly and that records have been kept in departmental alphabetic order.

The macroprogram to achieve this directory maintenance system consists of only some 60 instructions.

Conclusion

The facilities of database management and information retrieval packages illustrated in this chapter are typical of many such packages. Some do have fewer facilities; and only a few allow the user to write macroprograms where instructions like CREATE (create a file), SORT, APPEND, etc., can be used within a program

Flexible database packages 127

in much the same way as the much simpler statements are used in a BASIC program. This macroprogramming facility offers exciting possibilities for management applications. However, they are normally the province of the professional systems analyst or programmer and only occasionally that of the enthusiastic manager.

Database management and information retrieval packages form the basis of many applications of microcomputers. The flexible type of proprietary package discussed here could be used far more widely were it not for the average user's preconceived fear that the design procedure involved is too complex. It is hoped that this chapter has, at least partially, dispelled that fear.

Before deciding to buy a flexible form of database management and information retrieval package, as opposed to a package tailored to a specific application consider the following:

> is the application so specific as to require a bespoke system designed around a flexible package? For most stock control, sales/purchase ledger and payroll applications a specially designed, proprietary package is usually more appropriate;

> are there further applications to which such a flexible package could be put to make it more cost effective?

More specifically:

> can the data stored on records within a file remain confidential, i.e., is there a password control?

> is the key field unique or non-unique? The former is preferable for efficiency, the latter if personnel records, etc., based on surnames are to be used;

> can the number of records within a file be specified and is the maximum number of records per file acceptable for the particular application?

> if a lot of information has to be stored per record, how many bytes (characters) per record can be stored, and how much information can sensibly be stored on the first screen before one has to resort to a multiple screen record?

> is a report printing facility available and what range of facilities does it offer? To reduce the purchase price for users not requiring report printing, some packages are offered without a report generator facility.

7

Integrated business packages

When it was originally launched, Lotus 1-2-3 was hailed by microcomputer pundits as the first widely available 'integrated' package. However, this package, an all-time best seller, was conceived essentially as a spreadsheet with added graphics and limited database facilities and, in retrospect, would now be regarded as a 'super' spreadsheet rather than as a truly integrated business package.

The concept of integration – advantages and disadvantages

As can be seen in figure 7.1, packages which now claim to be integrated business packages attempt in various ways to integrate the four principal microcomputer business functions or elements. These are word processing, spreadsheet, database and graphics to which some also add other facilities such as a personal diary, communications, terminal emulation plus file-transfer, etc.

Since it is generally agreed that the market response to integrated business packages has not been as ecstatic as their sponsoring software houses might have hoped and certainly has not matched the unit sales of 'super' spreadsheets, it might be sensible at this stage to detail some of the advantages and disadvantages of this form of business package.

1. An integrated package which offers the four elements of word processing, spreadsheet, database and graphics will generally be cheaper than four separate, stand-alone packages offering these self-same facilities. However, integrated business packages are not that cheap and unless the potential user definitely requires all four elements, fewer stand-alone or separate packages can indeed be cheaper.

INTEGRATED BUSINESS PACKAGE

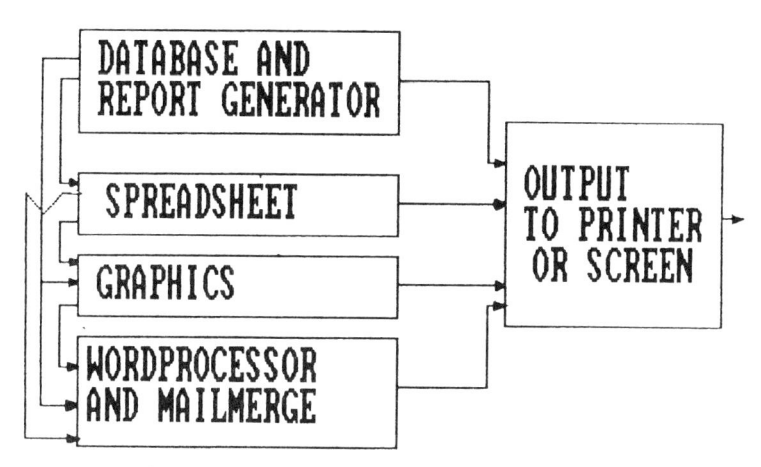

```
┌─────────────────────────┐
│ DATABASE AND            │
│ REPORT GENERATOR        │──┐
└─────────────────────────┘  │   ┌──────────────┐
┌─────────────────────────┐  │   │ OUTPUT       │
│ SPREADSHEET             │──┼──▶│ TO PRINTER   │──▶
└─────────────────────────┘  │   │ OR SCREEN    │
┌─────────────────────────┐  │   └──────────────┘
│ GRAPHICS                │──┤
└─────────────────────────┘  │
┌─────────────────────────┐  │
│ WORDPROCESSOR           │──┘
│ AND MAILMERGE           │
└─────────────────────────┘
```

Figure 7.1 Linking word processing, spreadsheet, database and graphics within an integrated business package.

    Integrated business packages which are 'disk based' (as opposed to RAM based) and achieve integration between the various elements via the medium of static disk files, can generally be purchased as several individual packages where each package represents one of the constituent elements. This package structure allows a user to purchase individual elements progressively although there is a cost advantage when all four are purchased simultaneously.

    RAM based packages, which can only be purchased complete, do, however, have the advantage that they can display the output of more than one of the integrated elements simultaneously whereas 'disk based' packages can only display one at a time.

2 Although none of their originators would admit to the fact, integrated business packages are not easy to use and certainly the full potential of these packages can generally only be realized by attending a training course. The fact that such courses, with the necessary accommodation, can cost twice as much as the price of the package itself has certainly been one of the reasons that integrated packages have not proved to be as popular as many had hoped.

3. Because the programs required to perform all four elements within an integrated business package are collectively large, such packages may require a minimum of 512 kbytes of internal memory to operate satisfactorily and whilst most operate with a twin floppy disk drive format, some only operate with a minimum of 5 Mbytes of hard-disk and are, therefore, not covered in this book.

4. One of the obvious advantages of an integrated package is that the screen format, command structure and documentation presented to the user can be made uniform (i.e., a common 'face' is presented). This standardization should make it much easier for the user to move between the various integrated elements and thus cut down the amount of learning required to use all elements for those users starting from scratch. However, a possible disadvantage of an integrated business package could be that the facilities offered by individual elements may not be as extensive as those contained within a specialized package concentrating on one element alone. Additionally, not all the elements within an integrated business package may be equally acceptable to an individual user.

5. Since integrated business packages were introduced to the market, and thus highlighted the assumed need of users to be able to integrate between different elements, several recently developed packages have now been produced which allow the simple transfer of files between existing stand-alone packages. This alternative approach allows users to stay with their favourite packages whilst enjoying the benefit of a relatively high degree of integration.

   Products such as GEM, Topview, The Integrator and Windows claim to fill this role.

6. Most integrated business packages, in addition to offering the four elements of word processing, spreadsheet, database and graphics, also offer communications and a macroprogramming facility with which relatively complex business systems can be designed. To take advantage of these facilities, a high level a programming ability on the part of the user is generally required. It is in this area – where third-party software houses are increasingly developing relatively complex business systems for their clients using the powerful facilities offered by an integrated business package – that many feel such packages are most suited.

Integration from a user's point of view

In discussing the potential use of an integrated package it might be most sensible to consider a possible business or management application which would involve all four elements of word processing, spreadsheet, database and graphics.

Of the four elements included in a typical integrated package, it is fairly clear that word processing is the element to which the other three would pass information whereas the word processing element would rarely be required to pass information to the other three. Additionally, transfers of information might also occur from the database element to either the spreadsheet or graphics elements and the spreadsheet element would certainly pass information to the graphics element, these two being now combined in most stand-alone spreadsheet packages.

A business application which might make use of all four elements could conceivably be:

a A customer database which could provide information on numbers of customers by product type (using a report generator with subtotalling – see page 115) and additionally provide the information required for the mailmerging facility of the word processing element (see page 78).

b Subtotal information on customer and product types passed to a spreadsheet for management to experiment with various marketing and sales strategies until a satisfactory strategy is evolved.

c Information passed from the spreadsheet to the graphics element to produce bar or pie-charts of the chosen strategy.

d Information (in the form of charts derived from the chosen strategy evolved using the spreadsheet fed with information from the database) passed from the graphics element to the word processor.

e Word processor used to create final report and include charts passed from the graphics element. Supplementary information passed from both the database and spreadsheets elements to the word processor for inclusion in an Appendix of the report thus substantiating the charts included in the main section of the report.

This hypothetical process could appear in the way shown in figure 7.2.

Disk based and RAM based integrated business packages

Broadly speaking, integrated business packages can be divided into two categories, namely disk based and RAM (i.e., internal memory) based.

Disk based integrated packages such as Xchange, OpenAccess and Smart provide integration of the four computing elements of word processing, spreadsheet, database and graphics via the medium of disk files. Thus having developed, for example, a spreadsheet from which it is now required to produce a graph, the spreadsheet 'exports' a named file to disk in a form in which that file can then be 'imported' to the graphics element of the package.

This process is illustrated here using a popular disk based integrated package. In figure 7.3 a simple spreadsheet is about to be exported to disk – in a form acceptable to the associated graphics element of the integrated business package – as a file 'fcst'. Subsequently, in figure 7.4, this file 'fcst' has been imported from disk by the graphics element and displayed as a line graph which has been automatically scaled and provided with an interpretive key.

Disk based integrated packages, whilst much slower in operation than RAM based packages and unable to display the results produced by two elements simultaneously, do have the advantage that they require less internal memory and do not usually impose restrictions on the size of the files involved, other than that imposed by overall disk capacity. Because each element of a disk based integrated business package uses the medium of disk files to communicate, such packages can generally 'stand alone' and can be purchased complete or as individual, constituent elements.

RAM based integrated business packages, whilst using disk as a permanent store for data, retain as many of the system's program elements in RAM (internal memory) as can be accommodated. Thus the RAM based integrated packages Symphony and Framework both require a minimum of 340 and 512 kbytes respectively of internal memory and offer greater operational speed than disk based packages. Another feature of such RAM based packages is that the results of two or more processes can be displayed simultaneously, whereas disk based systems can only usually display one at a time. However, since the provision of RAM is finite and is also required for operating system programs and data, the facilities offered within each individual element of such a RAM

APPLICATION OF AN INTEGRATED BUSINESS PACKAGE

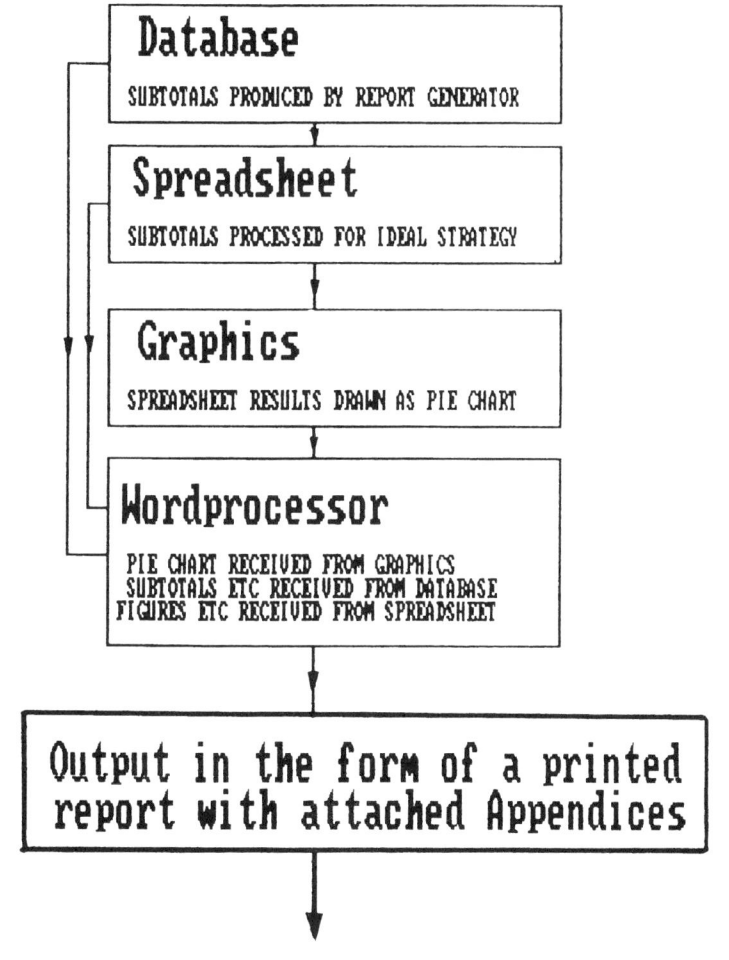

Database
SUBTOTALS PRODUCED BY REPORT GENERATOR

Spreadsheet
SUBTOTALS PROCESSED FOR IDEAL STRATEGY

Graphics
SPREADSHEET RESULTS DRAWN AS PIE CHART

Wordprocessor
PIE CHART RECEIVED FROM GRAPHICS
SUBTOTALS ETC RECEIVED FROM DATABASE
FIGURES ETC RECEIVED FROM SPREADSHEET

Output in the form of a printed report with attached Appendices

Figure 7.2 Hypothetical business example using all four elements of an integrated business package.

134 *General purpose applications packages*

```
┌─────────────────────────────────────────────────────────────┐
│ EXPORT to a file on disk                                    │
│      Type file name and press ←┘                            │
│      or press ? for a list of files.                        │
├─────────────────────────────────────────────────────────────┤
│      A    :  B   :  C   :  D   :  E   :  F   :  G          │
│ 1 Period      1      2      3      4      5      6         │
│ 2                                                           │
│ 3 Demand    240    450    342     45    560    450         │
│ 4                                                           │
│ 5 Forecast  200    208    256    274    228    294         │
│ 6                                                           │
│ 7                                                           │
│ 8                                                           │
│ 9                                                           │
│ 10                                                          │
│ 11                                                          │
│ 12                                                          │
│ 13                                                          │
│ 14                                                          │
│ 15                                                          │
│ files:export to easel,range A1:G5                           │
│                                                             │
│ CELL C5      GRID USED A1:G5     TASK a                     │
│ CONTENTS 0.8*B5+0.2*B3                                      │
└─────────────────────────────────────────────────────────────┘
  command> Files: export to fcst▮
  ▓▓▓▓▓▓▓ demand ▓▓▓▓▓▓▓▓▓▓▓▓▓ 1 ▓▓▓▓▓▓▓▓▓▓▓▓▓▓▓▓▓▓
```

Figure 7.3 Simple spreadsheet about to be exported as a file 'fcst' for subsequent importing by the associated graphics element of a disk based integrated business package.

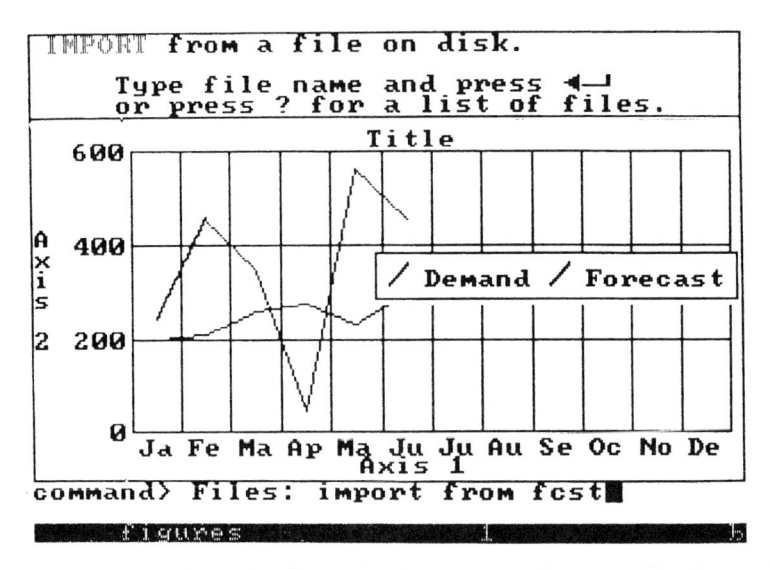

```
┌─────────────────────────────────────────────────────────────┐
│ IMPORT from a file on disk.                                 │
│      Type file name and press ←┘                            │
│      or press ? for a list of files.                        │
├─────────────────────────────────────────────────────────────┤
│                          Title                              │
│      600 ┬──┬──┬──┬──┬──┬──┬──┬──┬──┬──┬──┐                │
│          │  │  │  │  │  │  │  │  │  │  │  │                │
│      A   │  │  │  │  │ /\  │  │  │  │  │                   │
│      x  400├──┼──┼──┼──┼─/\┼──┼──┼──┼──┼──┼──┤             │
│      i   │  │  / \│  │/  \│  │  │  │  │  │                 │
│      s   │  │ /   \ /│    │ / Demand  / Forecast          │
│          │  │/     \│    │/                                │
│      2  200├──┼─────┼────\┼──┼──┼──┼──┼──┼──┼──┤           │
│          │  │      │     \│  │  │  │  │  │  │              │
│          │  │      │      \  │  │  │  │  │  │              │
│          │  │      │       │ │  │  │  │  │  │              │
│        0 └──┴──────┴───────┴─┴──┴──┴──┴──┴──┴──┘           │
│           Ja Fe Ma Ap Ma Ju Ju Au Se Oc No De              │
│                        Axis 1                              │
└─────────────────────────────────────────────────────────────┘
  command> Files: import from fcst▮
  ▓▓▓▓▓▓▓ figures ▓▓▓▓▓▓▓▓▓▓▓▓▓ 1 ▓▓▓▓▓▓▓▓▓▓▓▓▓▓▓
```

Figure 7.4 Graphics display of 'fcst' imported as a file from the spreadsheet element of a disk based integrated business package.

based integrated business package may be restricted relative to those which are disk based. In particular, the data associated with each application (often referred to as a window or frame) will often be limited in size, to 32 kbytes for instance. Whilst such windows or frames can be strung together for larger applications, such restrictions can be inconvenient, for word processing in particular.

However, the ability to display simultaneously the information derived from more than one element of an integrated package is a distinct advantage of the RAM based system, and the proponents of this type of package would argue that it represents the only form of true integration. This ability is demonstrated in figure 7.5 where the results of a simple spreadsheet are displayed simultaneously with its associated graph. Figure 7.6 takes this process one step further by demonstrating a RAM based integrated package's ability to display the results of more than two elements. In this example the spreadsheet and graph of figure 7.5 have been moved and reduced in size, the spreadsheet has been modified (note the increase from 100 to 1200 of the Design costs in March), the graph has been recalculated to reflect this change (note the increase in the size of the bar representing Design in March) and a word processed explanation has been incorporated in the space created by moving and reducing the size of the spreadsheet and graph.

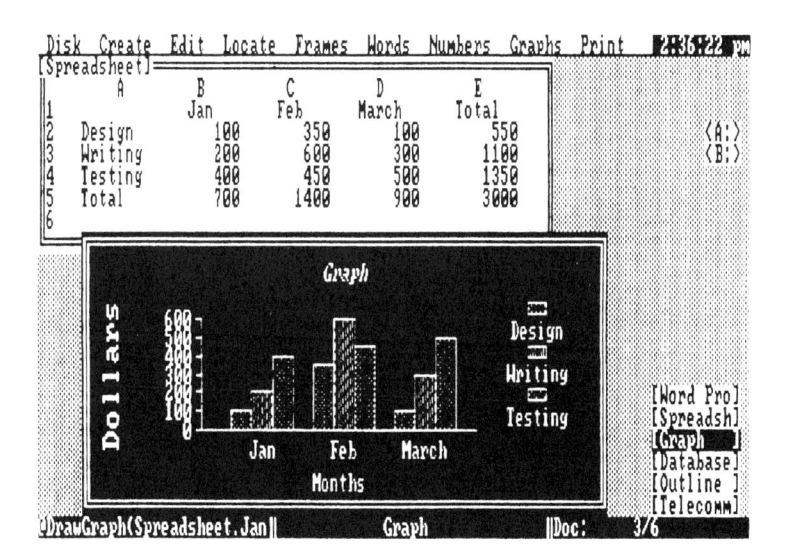

Figure 7.5 A simple spreadsheet and its associated graph displayed simultaneously using a RAM based integrated business package.

136 *General purpose applications packages*

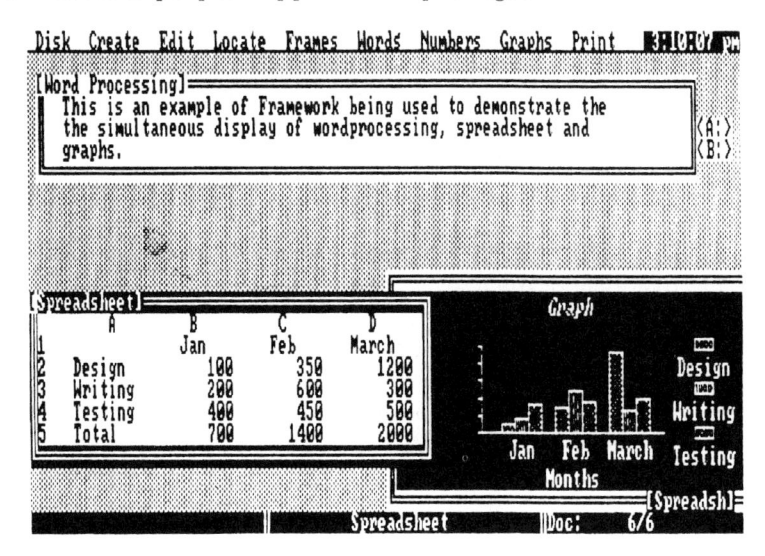

Figure 7.6 Modified spreadsheet and its associated, recalculated graph together with an additional word processed explanation.

Conclusion

Integrated business packages offer, in various forms, the four principal microcomputer functions required by the manager or business user. The four elements always offered within such integrated packages are word processing (for more detailed information on word processing see chapter 4), spreadsheet (chapter 5), database (chapter 6) and graphics.

Integrated packages can either be disk or RAM based, and each form has some relative advantages. Because they offer so many computing facilities, integrated business packages are not easy to use and attendance at a training course may well be necessary for the manager or business user to take full advantage of the facilities offered.

Section C

The Three Most Popular Business Packages

8 Payroll
9 Sales, purchase and nominal ledger
10 Stock control

8

Payroll

Payroll packages

Although stock control packages (see chapter 10) represent the largest area of application in terms of variety of packages, when one turns to consider actual installations, payroll packages predominate. The implication is that, although there are slightly fewer payroll packages on the market, those which are successful are used at a larger number of sites. Since every company must pay its employees, although it may not necessarily hold stock, this is hardly surprising.

One factor that distinguishes payroll from all other packages is that failure of the system must be avoided at all costs. A failure of stock control system might cause chaos for a period of time, and perhaps even precipitate an additional stocktake, but a failure to pay employees would be a major disaster. Thus, the successful payroll packages tend to be those written by the larger software houses such as Tridata Micros, TABS, Graffcom, Peachtree, Microtrend, Holland Auto, Compact, OMICRON etc., who, because of their size, can offer a reasonable guarantee of continued support. This, in practice, mainly means that staff are available to answer queries (over the phone) in an emergency. Such support is absolutely essential for a payroll package, not only for the occasional difficulty but also to ensure that the system is updated in line with any legislative changes, some of which usually occur every year. Recent examples of changes which will result or have already resulted in alterations of payment procedures are:

    April 1983   petrol expenses for company owned cars/sick pay
    Jan. 1984   major clearing banks stopped accepting printed bank giros, so they either have to be 'machine

readable', transmitted electronically over telephone lines or recorded on disk to a format acceptable to the banks.

A software *support contract* or *'update agreement'* ensures that any such changes will be incorporated in the payroll package, usually in the form of a new program disk delivered a few weeks before the changes have to be implemented.

Software support contracts are rare outside the payroll field; within it they are almost universal and relatively cheap at about £200 per annum.

The more successful payroll packages now available in the UK market have certainly all been around for five years of so. Hence, through an evolutionary process of development stimulated by customer feedback, such packages should now be able to cope with the majority of idiosyncrasies of most payments systems. However, if a feature of a company's payment system is so unusual that no microcomputer payroll package can deal with it, the sensible course is to change that feature rather than get involved in the necessarily great expense of a bespoke payroll package. At a cost of approximately £300, the advantages of a standard, proprietary payroll package are such that several companies, even with as few as five employees, are more than satisfied with their purchase.

In brief, a typical payroll package should be able to:

deal with hourly, weekly, two, three and four weekly and monthly paid staff;

produce pay advice slips for all employees and also bank giros if required. (Automatic printing of cheques is not usually a feature of microcomputer payroll packages, mainly because the pre-printed cheque stationery has to be obtained from security-approved printers, who often insist on a minium quantity of 2,000. Accounting for each individual cheque form is also a problem and, since the average number of employees on a microcomputer payroll system is small (see below), it is generally much more practical to print a cheque list and then raise cheques manually);

cope with all PAYE tax deductions, national insurance contributions, pension and other specified deductions and also non-taxable allowances;

produce departmental analysis of payments made in both the current period and year-to-date;

produce information for, and be able to print that information in a format suitable for, year-end tax forms such as P60s, P11s and P35(CS)s.

if an integrated ledger system is operated, produce balance postings to the PAYE, national insurance, cash at bank and wages accounts of the nominal ledger

The payroll package used to illustrate this chapter is the Gilt Edge payroll package written by Fast Software Products, Birmingham. Over a thousand copies of this package have been installed on a wide range of microcomputer installations throughout the UK. With a range of from 5 to 1,400 employees per installation, but with an average of 50, this one package is therefore processing payment information for more than 50,000 people. The package is menu driven and the principal options (called programs here) are accessed through the main menu which is shown in figure 8.1.

```
VERSION AD.08                P A Y R O L L                      29/04/81
                             -------------

         1) CREATE/AMEND EMPLOYEE DATA      9) PRINT ANALYSIS TOTALS

         2) CLEAR B.T.G. DETAILS           10) END OF YEAR PROCEDURES

         3) BUILD UP TO GROSS              11) BLANKET CHANGES

         4) GROSS TO NET CALCULATION       12) AMEND SYSTEM PARAMETERS

         5) PRINT PAYSLIPS                 13) AMEND TOTALS

         6) PRINT COIN ANALYSIS            14) LIST EMPLOYEE NUMBERS

         7) PRINT CHEQUE'S LIST            15) RESET SYSTEM DATE

         8) PRINT BANK GIROS               16) END PAYROLL RUN

                        Select Program No.(1-16):..

     Copyright TRIDATA MICROS LTD/1980/81          Telephone 021 622 6085
```

Figure 8.1 Payroll package's main menu.

Setting up a payroll system

Set up employer information (amend system parameters – program 12)

When installing a payroll system initially the user provides basic information as to the company's address, tax district, tax reference number, bank, etc. This information and any changes to either PAYE or national insurance (NI) tables can be made using program 12 of the main menu. The system will itself provide the PAYE and NI information details currently in force and these will require altering only if and when legislative changes are enacted.

In this package employer's data, PAYE data and NI data are displayed on three separate screens as shown in figure 8.2.

Note particularly on screen 1:

> field 9 – *highest note* ($) refers to the highest note denomination in pounds sterling that can be used in cash net payments. Values can be £20, £10, £5 or £1. (Because many printers are manufactured abroad, the $ sign, or sometimes the # (hash) sign, is often used to represent the £ sign);

> field 10 – *net pay adjustment amount* indicates the smallest multiple amount that can be used in cash net payments, e.g. if 50p is entered (as here) then net pay will be made up to the next 50p and the difference carried forward as a debit to the following period. The maximum adjustment amount is £1.00;

> fields 11 to 14 – *overtime rates* 1 to 4 refer to the four overtime rates which can be used in the build-up-to-gross procedure (BTG, see below) if overtime hours are booked for employees, e.g. 1.5000 is time-and-a-half.

This option of setting up employer information is normally only used when setting up the payroll system and whenever legislative changes alter PAYE or NI parameters.

```
PAYROLL PARAMETER FILE MAINTENANCE          AMEND              1/04/81

          EMPLOYER'S DATA                              Screen 1 of 3

1) Employer's Name : J.B. SMITH & SONS LTD.
2) Address Line 1  : 156-160 COVENTRY ROAD
3) Address Line 2  : ERDINGTON
4) Address Line 3  : BIRMINGHAM B5 6BS
5) Tax District    : BIRMINGHAM 10
6) Tax Ref No      : 72/T680

7) Std Works Hours : 40.00         8) Std Staff Hours : 35.00
9) Highest Note($) : 10            10)Net Pay Adj Amt : 0.50

11)Overtime Rate 1 : 1.0000        12)Overtime Rate 2 : 1.2500
13)Overtime Rate 3 : 1.3330        14)Overtime Rate 4 : 1.5000

15) Bank Name      : NATIONAL WESTMINSTER
16) Address Line 1 : LAW COURTS BRANCH
17) Address Line 2 : DALE END

          P.A.Y.E. DATA                                Screen 2 of 3

BAND    RATE        LIMIT         BAND    RATE        LIMIT
 1  20) 30.00%  32) 11250          7  26) 60.00%  38) 90000

 2  21) 40.00%  33)  2000          8  27) 60.00%  39) 90000

 3  22) 45.00%  34)  3500          9  28) 60.00%  40) 90000

 4  23) 50.00%  35)  5500         10  29) 60.00%  41) 90000

 5  24) 55.00%  36)  5500         11  30) 60.00%  42) 90000

 6  25) 60.00%  37) 90000         12  31) 60.00%  43) 90000


44) Basic Rate Band No. :  1

          N.I. DATA                                    Screen 3 of 3

EMPLOYEE'S RATES                    EMPLOYER'S RATES
RATE     NORMAL     REDUCED         RATE     NORMAL     REDUCED

 A   50)  7.75%  55)  7.75%          A   60) 13.70%  65) 13.70%

 B   51)  2.75%  56)  2.75%          B   61) 13.70%  66) 13.70%

 C   52)  0.00%  57)  0.00%          C   62) 13.70%  67) 13.70%

 D   53)  7.75%  58)  5.25%          D   63) 13.70%  68)  9.20%

 E   54)  2.75%  59)  2.75%          E   64) 13.70%  69)  9.20%

70) N.I. Lower Limit: 1404.00       71) N.I. Upper Limit:10400.00
```

Figure 8.2   Employer, PAYE and NI data.

Create/amend employee data (program 1)

This program is used initially to create employee records and subsequently to create additional records for the new employees. The program can also be used to amend employee records, although financial information can only be altered if the program 'clear BTG details' has been run. The create/amend program can also be used to access an employee record purely for information.

Each employee must be allocated an *employee number* which becomes the unique key code through which employee records are identified. The format of the employee number is DD.NNN where:

DD = department number in the range 0–35 (99 on some machines)

NNN = a three digit number in the range 001–250 (700 on Tandy model II) (e.g. 0.083 is employee 83 in department 0)

Figure 8.3 shows an employee record for F. T. Morris code number 1.003, a monthly paid employee, whose bank details are included as payments to be made by bank/giro (B/G). The employee record is divided into three screens: *basic information, to-date-totals* and *other information*. Detailed points of interest to note from figure 8.3 are as follows:

On screen 1 – basic information

field 7 – *pension option*, which specifies the type of company pension deduction. The eight pension options available in this particular package are:

- 0 = no company pension;
- 1 = contracted in where the deduction is an amount (N/A – not allowable for tax);
- 2 = contracted in where the deduction is a percentage (N/A);
- 3 = contracted out where the deduction is an amount (allowable);
- 4 = contracted out where the deduction is a percentage (allowable);
- 5 = contracted in where the deduction is an amount and allowable against tax;
- 6 = contracted in where the deduction is a percentage and allowable against tax;

```
PAYROLL EMPLOYEE DATA FILE MAINTENANCE         AMEND              1/04/81

   EMPLOYEE NO. :   3          BASIC INFORMATION         Screen 1 of 3

    1) Initials      : F T
    2) Surname       : MORRIS
    3) N.I. Number   : AS998763A    BANK/GIRO DETAILS
    4) N.I. Code     : D            -----------------
    5) Tax Code      : 400H
    6) Wk1/Mth1 Basis: N       17) Bank Code :   80-98-65
    7) Pension Option:   4     18) Account No :  43542312
    8) Employee Type : MNTHLY  19) Ac Name: F T MORRIS
    9) Std. Weeks Hrs:  35.00  20) Bank    : LLOYDS
   10) Payment By    : B/G     21) Branch  : SOLIHULL
   11) Basic Salary  : 9990.00
   12) Department No.:   1
   13) Paid To Period:   0
   14) Start Date    : 9/08/77
   15) Leaving Date  :
   16) Birth Date    : 12/12/43


   EMPLOYEE NO. :   3           TO DATE TOTALS           Screen 2 of 3

       PREVIOUS EMPLOYMENT          NATIONAL INSURANCE CONTRIBUTIONS
       -------------------          --------------------------------

   30) Gross Pay :    0.00         EMPLOYEE'S    EMPLOYEE'S    EMPLOYER'S
   31) P.A.Y.E.  :    0.00                        C/O RATE
                              A  36)  0.00   37)   0.00   38)   0.00
       THIS EMPLOYMENT
       ---------------        B  39)  0.00   40)   0.00   41)   0.00
   32) Gross Pay :    0.00
   33) P.A.Y.E.  :    0.00    C  42)  0.00   43)   0.00   44)   0.00

       PENSION CONTRIBUTIONS  D  45)  0.00   46)   0.00   47)   0.00
       ---------------------
   34) Employee :     0.00    E  48)  0.00   49)   0.00   50)   0.00
   35) Employer :     0.00


   EMPLOYEE NO. :   3          OTHER INFORMATION         Screen 3 of 3

       EMPLOYEE'S DEDUCTIONS         EMPLOYER'S DEDUCTIONS
       ---------------------         ---------------------

   60) Pension Amt :    0.00     62) Pension Amt :    0.00
   61) Pension %ge :    5.00     63) Pension %ge :   10.00

   64) Deduction 1 :    0.00
   65) Deduction 2 :    0.00              MISCELLANEOUS
   66) Other Dedns :    0.00              -------------
                                  68) Wk 53 Gross :    0.00
       ALLOWANCES                 69) Wk 53 Tax   :    0.00
       ----------                 70) Last Net Pay:    0.00
   67) Non-taxable :    0.00      71) Carried Fwd :    0.00
```

Figure 8.3   *Monthly paid employee record at start of tax year.*

7 = contracted out where the deduction is a percentage allowable against tax and only to be taken within NI limits;

8 = contracted in where the deduction is a percentage allowable against tax and only to be taken within NI limits;

Pension amounts and percentages are specified as fields 60 and 61 respectively for employees and 62 and 63 for employers;

field 8 – *employee type*, which can be:

0 = hourly;
1 = weekly;
2 = 2 weekly;
3 = 3 weekly;
4 = 4 weekly;
5 = monthly;

field 9 – *standard weekly hours*, which for hourly employees (type 0) has a maximum value of 60 and is used for setting standard weekly hours when these differ from the employer's normal working week, e.g. for part-timers;

field 10 – *payment method*, which offers three alternatives:

0 = cash;
1 = cheque (drawn up manually);
2* = bank/giro (printed on B/G forms);

An * in this field indicates that the employee's record has already been through a payroll run;

field 11 – *hourly rate* or *basic salary*, which specifies either the hourly rate (limited to £30) for hourly employees or annual salary (limited to £99,999) for salaried employees;

field 13 – *paid to period*, which indicates the week or month up to which the employee has been paid. Since this example is created at the start of the tax year this period is zero, as are all the to-date-totals on the second screen. All these later data fields would also be set to zero when running program 10 – *end-of-year procedures*.

On screen 2 – to-date-totals

fields 30 and 31 – *gross pay and PAYE*, which for new employees is entered from previous employment P45 forms;

fields 32 and 33 – *gross pay and PAYE*, which are respectively gross pay and tax to date for the current tax year in this employment;

fields 34 and 35 – *employee's and employer's pension contributions* to date this tax year;

fields 36 to 50 – *NI contributions*, which record contributions made by the employee (contracted in or out) and also employer contributions.

On screen 3 – other information

fields 60 and 62 – *pension amount*, which is a fixed amount contributed by the employee (60) or employer (62);

fields 61 and 63 – *pension percentage*, which is the percentage (of gross salary including bonus, etc.) contributed by the employee (61) and employer (63), 5 per cent and 10 per cent respectively here;

fields 64 to 66 – *deductions*, which are fixed amounts;

field 67 – *non-taxable*, which is a regular fixed payment that is non-taxable, e.g. car allowance;

fields 68 and 69 – *week 53 gross and tax*, which are automatically stored for use on P60 if period number is 53, 54 or 56;

field 71 – *carried forward*, which is an amount credited to any employee paid in cash to bring his or her net current pay up to a rounded amount. It is recoverable in the next pay period or upon leaving.

While it is obviously much easier to start a payroll system at the beginning of the tax year, since all cash figures are then zero, the system can be started up at any time by transferring the figures from the previous manual system.

When allocating employee numbers and creating records with this Gilt Edge payroll package, it is also possible to allocate numbers to blank records which can subsequently be used for new employees who join the company after the original payroll system has been established. Once the employee details have been created using program 1, a complete list of employees can be produced using program 14, which can also print a list of numbers only allocated to blank records. An example of a list for just five employees, in two departments, is shown in figure 8.4.

```
                    EMPLOYEE NO'S
J.B. SMITH & SONS LTD.                                    1/04/81


  NO.    NAME                              NO.    NAME

  0.001 G H    BROWN                       0.002 T B       SMITH

  1.003 F T    MORRIS                      0.004 R G       EVANS

  0.005 R S    HAMMER
```

Figure 8.4 Employee listing.

The facilities offered by the Gilt Edge payroll package will be illustrated via the payment records of these five employees whose basic details are shown in table 8.1.

Table 8.1 Payment records of the five employees

Name	Hourly, weekly or monthly	Method of payment	Annual salary or basic hourly rate
G. H. Brown	hourly	cash	£3.50
T. B. Smith	weekly	cheque	£5600.00
F. T. Morris	monthly	bank/giro	£9990.00
R. G. Evans	monthly	bank/giro	£7800.00
R. S. Hammer	hourly	cheque	£3.70

Payroll 149

Week-to-week and month-to-month payroll operations

Having created the necessary employer information (program 12) and all employee records (program 1), the payroll system is ready to become operational. The normal sequence of tasks before each pay day is given below.

Clear BTG details (program 2)

This program must be run before any processing for the new pay period can take place. Since this procedure will clear out any previously inserted build-up-to-gross information, such as overtime hours booked in the previous pay period, the period backup disk must be generated before running this program.

This procedure 're-initializes' all employee records by reinstating the basic salary (per period), for salaried staff, and, for hourly paid staff, *standard weekly hours* are reset to the standard for each employee. All other build-up fields are set to zero (or 'zeroized' to use US computer jargon).

This program can be run for individual departments or for all employees on the disk being processed. However, only employee records which have been processed through a previous payroll run will be cleared.

Build up to gross (program 3)

This procedure is used to introduce any relevant data which changes from one pay period to the next. It is, therefore, principally used for booking overtime hours, recording leavers, paying bonuses, and holiday pay in advance.

When this program is used, the particular employee must be specified using the employee number, and then the *build-up-to-gross* details appear as is shown in figure 8.5 for G. H. Brown, an hourly paid employee. Note particularly:

> field 1 – *basic hours*, which records the basic number of hours for hourly paid employees and salary for all other employees;
>
> fields 2 to 5 – *overtime hours*, which records the number of hours of overtime at rates previously specified under employer's data and which are repeated on the second line of the screen;

field 6 – *unpaid hours*, which records number of hours laid off without pay;

field 7 – *leaving date*, which records the date an employee leaves and ensures that the next payslip is the last. The only time a leaver's record is processed again after that is at the end of the tax year;

field 8 – *holiday weeks*, which records the number of weeks for which holiday pay is being paid in advance. The system advances the tax period and apportions NI contributions over the number of weeks advanced. *Total holiday pay* (field 16) must be specified as the system does not calculate this amount. (This holiday procedure does not apply to monthly paid employees);

fields 9 to 12 – *bonus, commission, other pay 1* and *other pay 2*, which record additional payments made for this period;

field 13 – *NI benefit*, which records the amount received from the DHSS if the employee is absent through illness. This figure is, of course, deducted from the gross pay;

field 14 – *non-taxable 2*, which records an amount paid for this period which is not subject to tax, e.g. clothing allowance, etc.;

field 15 – *temporary deduction*, which records an amount deducted for this pay period only, e.g. cost of breakages;

field 16 – *holiday pay*, which records the amount paid in advance for holidays.

In practice, if hourly workers are not working overtime, the BTG procedure is normally only used for holidays and leavers. For companies employing only monthly staff the procedure is, therefore, rarely used.

On the BTG details screen, any field can be changed by specifying the field number. In the example shown in figure 8.5, the only field that has been changed is field 5 which records that G. H. Brown has worked ten hours overtime at time-and-a-half (+ O/T4).

Gross-to-net calculation (program 4)

This program, by taking gross pay figures and performing national insurance and tax calculations, produces net pay figures. As such it represents the greatest saving of a microcomputer-based payroll

```
PAYROLL BUILD UP TO GROSS                                    5/05/81
        O/T 1= 1.0000    O/T 2= 1.2500    O/T 3= 1.3330    O/T 4= 1.5000

    NO.   1  G H  BROWN

    1) + BASIC HOURS:    40.00      9) + BONUS        :   0.00

    2) - O/T 1 HOURS:     0.00     10) + COMMISSION   :   0.00

    3) + O/T 2 HOURS:     0.00     11) + OTHER PAY 1: :   0.00

    4) + O/T 3 HOURS:     0.00     12) + OTHER PAY 2: :   0.00

    5) + O/T 4 HOURS:    10.00     13) - N.I.BENEFIT: :   0.00

    6) - UNPD  HOURS:     0.00     14) + NON/TAX 2    :   0.00

    7)   LEAVING  ET :       0     15) - TEMP DEDN    :   0.00

    8)   HOL WEEKS  :        0     16) + HOLIDAY PAY: :   0.00
```

Figure 8.5 Build up to gross details.

system compared to a manually operated system. In the Gilt Edge payroll packages, employees are processed together depending on their type (all hourly, all weekly, all monthly etc.).

When processing monthly employees immediately after weekly, the user should remember that period (month) in the former case will be different from period (week) in the latter.

This gross-to-net procedure is completely automatic. To indicate progress, as an employee record is about to be updated, the computer flashes up that employee's number on the screen. To give some estimate of the speed with which pay details can be processed, the gross-to-net calculation program typically takes approximately one hour to update all the information on one disk containing data for 250 employees.

Print payslips (program 5)

This program is used to print payslips either for individual employees or for all employees. Departments are processed sequentially and departmental total payslips and overall total payslips are also produced.

For this procedure special pre-printed pay advice stationery has

152 *Most popular business packages*

to be loaded into the printer equipped with a facility for correctly aligning this stationery. This feature is illustrated in figure 8.6 where the pay advice slip for hourly paid employee G. H. Brown is preceded by an alignment slip. Since this employee's basic hourly rate for a 40 hour week is £3.50, adding a further ten hours at time-and-a-half, his gross earnings are the equivalent of 55 hours at £3.50, that is, £192.50.

Print coin analysis (program 6)

This procedure produces a coin analysis report showing the breakdown of each employee's net pay for selected coin denominations which have previously been specified as system parameters. Any employee paid in cash and whose record has already been processed by a gross-to-net calculation procedure will be included in this report. The printing is automatic and the report can be

TAX CODE	N.I. No.	TABLE LETTER		PAY ADVICE					NAME		
XXXXXXXXXXXXXXXXXXXXX									XXXXXXXXXXXXXXXXXXXXXXX		
DATE	STD HOURS	O/T 1 HOURS	O/T 2 HOURS	O/T 3 HOURS	O/T 4 HOURS	UNPAID HRS	DEPT	PERS. No.		PERIOD No	
BASIC PAY	OVERTIME PAY	BONUS	COMMISSION	OTHER PAY 1	OTHER PAY 2	N.I. BENEFIT	HOLIDAY PAY			GROSS PAY	
PENSION	NET GROSS PAY	TAX	N.I.	N.I. (C/O)	STD. DEDN. 1	STD. DEDN. 2	OTHER DEDNS	TEMP DEDN		TOTAL DEDNS	
PENSION T/D	GROSS T/D	TAX T/D	N.I. T/D	N.I. (C/O) T/D	FREE PAY	TAXABLE GROSS		NON-TAXABLE 1		NON-TAXABLE 2	
EMPLOYER'S N.I.	EMPLY RS N.I. T/D					NET PAY	B/FWD	C/FWD		PAYABLE NET	
TAX CODE	N.I. No.	TABLE LETTER		PAY ADVICE					NAME		
200L	AA6453321A	A							G H BROWN		
DATE	STD HOURS	O/T 1 HOURS	O/T 2 HOURS	O/T 3 HOURS	O/T 4 HOURS	UNPAID HRS	DEPT	PERS. No.		PERIOD No	
5/05/81	40.00	0.00	0.00	0.00	10.00	0.00	0	1		5	
BASIC PAY	OVERTIME PAY	BONUS	COMMISSION	OTHER PAY 1	OTHER PAY 2	N.I. BENEFIT	HOLIDAY PAY			GROSS PAY	
140.00	52.50	0.00	0.00	0.00	0.00	0.00	0.00			192.50	
PENSION	NET GROSS PAY	TAX	N.I.	N.I. (C/O)	STD. DEDN. 1	STD. DEDN. 2	OTHER DEDNS	TEMP DEDN		TOTAL DEDNS	
0.00	192.50	46.20	14.92	0.00	1.00	0.50	0.00	0.00		62.62	
PENSION T/D	GROSS T/D	TAX T/D	N.I. T/D	N.I. (C/O) T/D	FREE PAY	TAXABLE GROSS		NON-TAXABLE 1		NON-TAXABLE 2	
0.00	752.30	167.70	58.32	0.00	193.25	559.00		2.00		0.00	
EMPLOYER'S N.I.	EMPLY RS N.I. T/D					NET PAY	B/FWD	C/FWD		PAYABLE NET	
26.37	103.09					3.5000 131.88	0.40	0.01		131.50	

Figure 8.6 Alignment payslip together with payslip recording overtime payment.

Payroll 153

printed either by department or for all departments. Totals indicate the amounts of each note or coin required from the bank.

Figure 8.7 shows a very short coin analysis report simply for the purposes of illustration. In this case it can be seen that the net payment of £131.50 has been broken down into 13 × £10, 1 × £1, and 1 × 50p. Since G. H. Brown is the only employee paid in cash in this small hypothetical company, the total figure does not vary, but in a department of some 30 employees paid by cash the time saved by this automatic coin analysis procedure compared with a manual breakdown would be considerable.

Print cheques list (program 7)

This program produces a list of all employees who are paid by cheque, together with their net pay figure. A blank column is provided to record the identification numbers of the cheques which

		COIN ANALYSIS							
J.B. SMITH & SONS LTD.						5/05/81			PAGE 1
NO	NAME	NET PAY	10'S	5'S	1'S	50P	10P	5P	2P	1P
0.001	G H BROWN	131.50	13		1	1				
TOTAL		131.50	13	0	1	1	0	0	0	0

Figure 8.7 *Coin analysis for cash payments.*

		CHEQUE PAYMENTS	
J.B. SMITH & SONS LTD.			29/04/81 PAGE 1
NO	NAME	AMOUNT	CHEQUE NO.
0.003	T B SMITH	96.99	
0.005	R S HAMMER	103.83	
TOTAL		200.82	

Figure 8.8 *Listing of payments to be made by cheque.*

154 *Most popular business packages*

will have to be drawn up manually. Once started, the printing of this report is automatic, and it can be printed either by department or for all departments. Departmental and overall totals are also printed.

Figure 8.8 shows a cheque payment list for the two employees, T. B. Smith and R. S. Hammer, who have opted to be paid by cheque.

Update employee record

Before we move on to the third method of payment, namely by bank giro (B/G) (program 8), which in practice usually applies to monthly paid employees, it will be useful to examine in detail the records of one employee, F. T. Morris. Figure 8.3 showed F. T. Morris's payroll details at the *start of the tax year* and figure 8.9 shows the equivalent details at the *end of the first month* of that tax year and which have been produced by processing this employee's record through the gross-to-net calculation procedure.

Specific points to note on figure 8.9 are:

field 10 – an asterisk here indicates that this employee's record has been through a payroll run;

field 32 – *gross pay* for this month has been calculated as £9990/12 = £832.50 less 5 per cent pension contribution = £790.87;

field 33 – PAYE has been assessed at £136.50 on the basis that with a 400H tax code this employee can earn £334.90 tax free this period, leaving a taxable gross of (£790.87−£334.90) = £455.00 which at 30 per cent produces a £136.50 tax deduction;

field 34 – *pension contribution for the employee* is 5 per cent of gross pay, i.e. 5 per cent of £832.50 = £41.63;

field 35 – *pension contribution by the employer* for this employee is 10 per cent of gross pay, i.e. 10 per cent of £832.50 = £83.25;

field 45 – *employee's NI contribution*, evaluated as 7.75 per cent of NI lower limit of £1,404 annual (i.e. £117 monthly) plus contracted out rate evaluated as 5.25 per cent of balance of monthly gross pay of £832.50 after NI lower limit deduction of £117, i.e. 7.75 per cent of £117 + 5.25 per cent of (£832.50−£117) = £9.07 + £37.56 = £46.63;

```
PAYROLL EMPLOYEE DATA FILE MAINTENANCE        ENQUIRY            29/04/81

EMPLOYEE NO. :    3          BASIC INFORMATION            Screen 1 of 3

   1) Initials       : F T
   2) Surname        : MORRIS
   3) N.I. Number    : AS998763A      BANK/GIRO DETAILS
   4) N.I. Code      : D              -----------------
   5) Tax Code       : 400H
   6) Wk1/Mth1 Basis : N       17) Bank Code  :  80-98-65
   7) Pension Option :   4     18) Account No :  43542312
   8) Employee Type  : MNTHLY  19) Ac Name: F T MORRIS
   9) Std. Weeks Hrs :  35.00  20) Bank    : LLOYDS
  10) Payment By     : B/G*    21) Branch  : SOLIHULL
  11) Basic Salary   : 9990.00
  12) Department No. :   1
  13) Paid To Period :   1
  14) Start Date     : 9/08/77
  15) Leaving Date   :
  16) Birth Date     : 12/12/43

EMPLOYEE NO. :    3          TO DATE TOTALS               Screen 2 of 3

      PREVIOUS EMPLOYMENT            NATIONAL INSURANCE CONTRIBUTIONS
      -------------------            --------------------------------
  30) Gross Pay :     0.00         EMPLOYEE'S    EMPLOYEE'S    EMPLOYER'S
  31) P.A.Y.E. :      0.00                        C/O RATE
                                A  36)  0.00  37)  0.00  38)  0.00
      THIS EMPLOYMENT
      ---------------           B  39)  0.00  40)  0.00  41)  0.00
  32) Gross Pay :   790.87
  33) P.A.Y.E. :    136.50      C  42)  0.00  43)  0.00  44)  0.00

      PENSION CONTRIBUTIONS     D  45) 46.63  46) 37.58  47) 51.85
      ---------------------
  34) Employee :     41.63      E  48)  0.00  49)  0.00  50)  0.00
  35) Employer :     83.25

EMPLOYEE NO. :    3          OTHER INFORMATION            Screen 3 of 3

      EMPLOYEE'S DEDUCTIONS           EMPLOYER'S DEDUCTIONS
      ---------------------           ---------------------
  60) Pension Amt :   0.00       62) Pension Amt :   0.00
  61) Pension %ge :   5.00       63) Pension %ge :  10.00

  64) Deduction 1 :   0.00
  65) Deduction 2 :   0.00             MISCELLANEOUS
  66) Other Dedns :   0.00             -------------
                                   68) Wk 53 Gross :    0.00
      ALLOWANCES                   69) Wk 53 Tax   :    0.00
      ----------                   70) Last Net Pay:  607.74
  67) Non-taxable :   0.00         71) Carried Fwd :    0.00
```

Figure 8.9 *Monthly paid employee record at the end of the first month (compare figure 8.3).*

156 *Most popular business packages*

see figure 8.2 for NI details under D;

field 46 – *employee's contracted out rate* taken as £37.56, evaluated above;

field 47 – *employer's NI contribution* evaluated as 13.7 per cent of NI, lower limit of £1,404 annual (i.e. £117 monthly) plus contracted out rate evaluated as 9.2 per cent of balance of monthly gross pay of £832.50 after NI lower limit deduction, i.e. 13.7 per cent of £117 + 9.2 per cent of (£832.50 −£117) = £16.02 + £65.83 = £81.85;

field 70 – *last net pay* is evaluated simply as gross pay (£790.87) less PAYE payment (£136.50) less NI deduction (£46.63), i.e. £790.87−£136.50−£46.63 = £607.74.

The above discussion indicates how all the fields that have been updated using the gross-to-net calculation procedure have been evaluated. The pay advice slip resulting from figure 8.9 is shown as figure 8.10.

Print bank giros (program 8)

This program prints bank giro forms for employees paid by bank giro, and also produces a summary list of all such employees, their payment and the total payment made by bank giro. Both bank giro and summary list printing can be for employees in a specified department or for all employees.

Since special stationery is required for bank giro printing, if plain

Figure 8.10 *Pay advice slip for a monthly paid employee.*

```
                        BANK-GIRO SUMMARY
J.B. SMITH & SONS LTD.                                   29/04/81


    NO     NAME               AMOUNT

    1.003  F T MORRIS         607.74
    0.004  R G EVANS          516.95

    TOTAL                    1124.69
```

Figure 8.11 Bank giros with initial alignment.

paper is already in the printer when this program is to be used, it is sensible to print the summary first. Figure 8.11 shows the bank giro summary list for the two employees, F. T. Morris and R. G. Evans, who receive payments by this method.

As from January 1984, the major clearing banks have only accepted machine readable bank giros, so that those shown in figure 8.12 for Morris and Evans are no longer acceptable. A preferred alternative method is to transmit bank giro information electronically from microcomputer to bank via a modem over telephone lines or recorded on disk to an agreed format.

Print analysis totals (program 9)

This program allows the user to print various sets of analysis totals developed by the payroll system. It offers four options for analysis total printing which can be accessed via the analysis totals menu shown in figure 8.13.

As an indication of the type of information that is produced using this program, the year-to-date totals listing (option 3) for the five employees in two departments considered in this chapter is shown in figure 8.14.

The payroll cycle

The discussion so far has covered in detail the facilities offered by the Gilt Edge payroll package to provide a comprehensive week-to-week and month-to-month payroll system.

The sequence of activities required to complete a payroll cycle, which for 250 employees would represent approximately a morning's work for one person, are shown in figure 8.15.

bank giro credit

FROM

DATE

DESTINATION BRANCH CODE NUMBER	XXXXXXXX
£	
BANK	
BRANCH	
ACCOUNT	
BY ORDER OF	

bank giro credit

FROM NATIONAL WESTMINSTER
LAW COURTS BRANCH
DALE END

DATE 09/04/81

DESTINATION BRANCH CODE NUMBER	80-98-65
£	607.74
BANK	LLOYDS
BRANCH	SOLIHULL
ACCOUNT	F T MORRIS NO. 43542312
BY ORDER OF	J.B. SMITH & SONS LTD.

REFERENCE : 1.003

bank giro credit

FROM NATIONAL WESTMINSTER
LAW COURTS BRANCH
DALE END

DATE 09/04/81

DESTINATION BRANCH CODE NUMBER	09-08-76
£	516.95
BANK	NATIONAL WESTMINSTER
BRANCH	ERDINGTON
ACCOUNT	R G EVANS NO. 65433763
BY ORDER OF	J.B. SMITH & SONS LTD.

REFERENCE : 0.004

Figure 8.12 Print analysis totals menu.

```
PAYROLL              ANALYSIS TOTALS              29/04/81
                     ---------------


                  1  PERIOD TO DATE TOTALS

                  2  PERIOD END TOTALS

                  3  YEAR TO DATE TOTALS

                  4  YEAR END TOTALS

                  5  RETURN TO MENU



                     Select Option (1-5):.
```

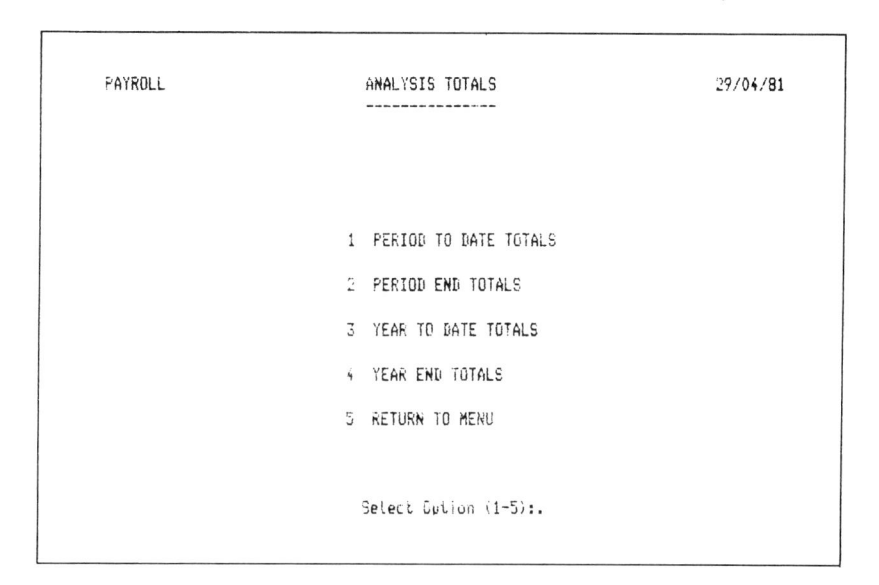

Figure 8.13 Year-to-date totals.

Should any incorrect entries be made during the payroll cycle, the resulting incorrect totals can be amended using program 13 – amend totals – which permits the user to amend either totals for the current period or year-to-date totals.

End-of-year procedures

End-of-year procedures (program 10)

At the end of the tax year it is necessary to produce certain payroll documentation, make a backup disk, and then to reset the system in readiness for the next tax year. Thus the end-of-year procedures program provides facilities to:

1 print P60 forms for all employees on pre-printed stationery;
2 print P35 (CS) documents on plain stationery;
3 perform the end-of-year 'cleardown' which will clear each employee record of 'active' data in preparation for the next tax year, delete leavers from the payroll file and release their employee numbers for re-allocation.

160 *Most popular business packages*

```
                    P A Y R O L L   A N A L Y S I S   T O T A L S
J.B. SMITH & SONS LTD.                                      5/05/91

  FINAL TOTALS     YEAR-TO-DATE TOTALS FOR PERIOD NO. - 2

                   STANDARD HOURS              540.00
                   OVERTIME HOURS @ RATE 1       0.00
                   OVERTIME HOURS @ RATE 2       0.00
                   OVERTIME HOURS @ RATE 3       0.00
                   OVERTIME HOURS @ RATE 4      10.00
                   UNPAID HOURS                  0.00

                   BASIC PAY OR SALARY         4835.76
                   OVERTIME PAY                  52.50
                   BONUS                          0.00
                   COMMISSION                     0.00
                   OTHER PAY 1                    0.00
                   OTHER PAY 2                    0.00
                   N.I. BENEFIT                   0.00
                   HOLIDAY PAY                    0.00

                   GROSS PAY                              4888.26

                   COMPANY PENSION              123.26
                   P.A.Y.E.                     610.20
                   EMPLOYEES N.I.               316.43
                   STANDARD DEDUCTION 1          20.00
                   STANDARD DEDUCTION 2           2.50
                   OTHER DEDUCTIONS               0.00
                   TEMPORARY DEDUCTION            0.00

                   TOTAL DEDUCTIONS                       1072.39

                   NON-TAXABLE 1                 47.00
                   NON-TAXABLE 2                  0.00

                   NON-TAXABLE PAY                          47.00

                   NET PAY                                3862.87

                   BROUGHT FORWARD (START OF PERIOD)  0.00
                   CARRIED FORWARD                0.02

                   EMPLOYER'S N.I.              557.31

                   EMPLOYER'S PENSION           206.00
```

Figure 8.14 *The payroll cycle.*

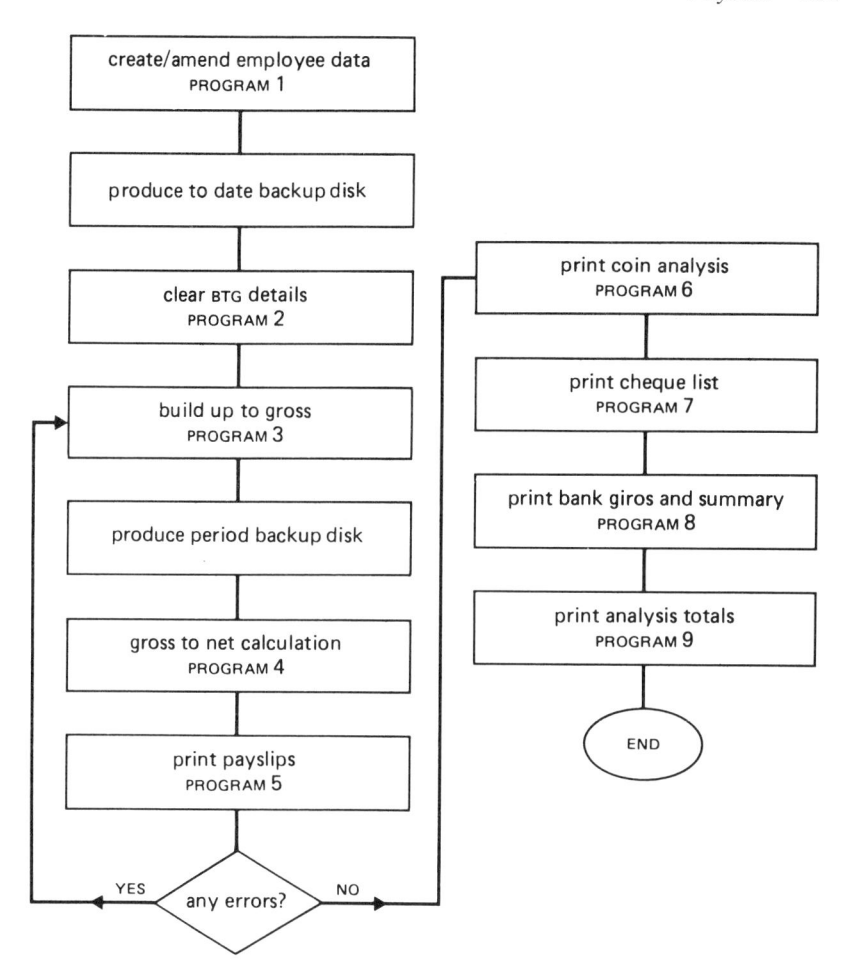

```
┌─────────────────────────────┐
│ create/amend employee data  │
│         PROGRAM 1           │
└──────────────┬──────────────┘
               │
┌──────────────▼──────────────┐
│ produce to date backup disk │
└──────────────┬──────────────┘
               │
┌──────────────▼──────────────┐
│     clear BTG details       │
│         PROGRAM 2           │
└──────────────┬──────────────┘
               │
┌──────────────▼──────────────┐          ┌─────────────────────────────┐
│     build up to gross       │          │     print coin analysis     │
│         PROGRAM 3           │          │         PROGRAM 6           │
└──────────────┬──────────────┘          └──────────────┬──────────────┘
```

Figure 8.15 *The payroll cycle.*

Blanket changes (program 11)

Although not strictly speaking an end-of-year procedure, blanket tax changes as issued by the Inland Revenue can be keyed in using this procedure. Such blanket changes are issued on P7X forms and will relate to suffix H,L,P and V tax codes. When the changes for these four tax code suffixes are entered, each employee's record whose code is to be amended is automatically updated and a report of the change also printed.

Conclusion

Payroll is an ideal application for a microcomputer for companies with up to 1,000 employees. Payroll calculations, although well specified, are reasonably intricate and extremely boring to perform manually. Equally, the amount of data that has to be stored for payroll is, in microcomputer terms, relatively small, so that records for up to 250 employees can be held on one 5¼ inch floppy disk.

Also, because most payroll functions are exactly specified, a microcomputer-based payroll system is very simple to implement and virtually mimics the equivalent manual system whilst operating much more quickly and efficiently.

These features, combined with the ability to produce printed reports and to print on pre-printed stationery, perhaps explain why there are more installations of payroll packages than any other single microcomputer applications package.

9

Sales, purchase and nominal ledger

Ledger systems

The 1981/82 survey of microcomputer applications packages available in the UK (figure 1.16) shows that 31 per cent of all packages deal with the areas of sales ledger (9 per cent), purchase ledger (9 per cent), general ledger (7 per cent) or integrated accounts (6 per cent). This preponderance of accounting packages is hardly surprising, since the efficient control of the money flowing into and out of a company is common to all business enterprises, even to companies that hold no stock whatsoever.

An integrated ledger package (that is, linked sales, purchase and nominal ledgers) can either stand alone or can itself be integrated with a stock control system. Where a package is designed to combine an integrated ledger system with stock control, the ledger system usually becomes a sub-system to the stock control system, simply because stock transactions normally occur every day, while the clearance of sales and purchase invoices is less frequent. Since the application of microcomputers to stock control is discussed fully in chapter 10, this chapter deals only with ledger systems.

In practice ledger packages can be operated as:

stand-alone sales ledger;

stand-alone purchase ledger;

sales and nominal ledger;

purchase and nominal ledger; or

integrated ledger (sales, purchase and nominal ledger);

stand-alone nominal ledger (occasionally used by such organizations as charities).

164 *Most popular business packages*

The above list is approximately ordered in descending order of usage, showing the stand-alone sales ledger as the most popular.

Function of the nominal ledger

Essentially the nominal ledger holds a series of nominal accounts – specifically nominated by the user – for recording the financial transactions of the company, the information thereafter being used as a basis for the preparation of financial statements. Typical categories of nominal accounts, which would apply to the majority of companies, are:

fixed assets;

current assets;

current liabilities;

long-term liabilities;

expenditure;

revenue;

trading account.

More specific nominal accounts, which could apply to a company involved in selling microcomputers, might be:

sales of hardware;

sales of software;

sales of supplies;

sales of books;

stock purchases etc.

A principal function of accounts in the nominal ledger is to maintain a financial record of the company's functions, for example, raising invoices to indicate indebtedness of customers via the sales ledger or to record liabilities for the receipt of goods and services from suppliers via the purchase ledger.

Thus, a simple *sales invoice* comprising:

a sales price of goods and services;

Sales, purchase and nominal ledger 165

VAT on the sales price;

carriage for the goods

would generate three separate credit entries to the following nominal revenue accounts held in the nominal ledger, namely:

sales of goods (which could be broken down further into sales of specific goods);

VAT on sales;

carriage on sales.

To achieve this allocation of funds to the nominal ledger, each item on the sales invoice needs to be identified with its respective nominal account.

At the same time as these individual nominal revenue accounts are credited, to maintain a balance, the nominal debtor account must be debited by the total value of the sales invoice.

A similar procedure applies to the processing of *purchase invoices received* from suppliers of goods and services. Debited entries are made to particular nominal expenditure accounts, such as:

purchase of goods and services;

VAT on purchases;

carriage on purchases

while simultaneously the nominal creditor account is credited with the total value of the purchase invoice to maintain the balance of the nominal ledger.

In addition to receiving money from the sales ledger and sending money to the purchase ledger, certain transactions occur *directly with the nominal ledger*, such as those concerning:

rent and rates;

light and heat;

capital;

auditing, etc.

These are often referred to as 'journal postings'.

The nominal ledger, therefore, integrates the sales and purchase ledgers and also maintains a record of all other financial transactions. Because a nominal ledger always operates a conventional 'double entry' method of accounting, it always maintains a balance between debits and credits.

Many companies operating a manual ledger system (particularly smaller companies) do not integrate their sales and purchase ledger with a nominal ledger simply because of the manual effort involved. Since the transference of information to a nominal ledger is so much simpler within a computerized system, many such companies are now tending to opt for integration with a nominal ledger when transferring from a manual system.

Function of the sales ledger

The sales ledger is essentially a file of all customers' accounts and as such maintains records of:

invoices sent to customers;

credit allowed to customers;

payments received from customers;

credit notes sent to customers (e.g. for goods damaged in transit, etc.);

discounts (to cope with optional discounts, etc.);

direct entries (to cover bad debts, etc.).

Some sales ledger packages assume that invoices are raised manually and that the sales ledger simply records the transaction specified by those already raised invoices. Increasingly, however, sales ledger packages are incorporating invoicing routines which allow the user to create invoices on the computer screen, to print a batch of them (with several copies if required) and to post information from those invoices to the respective accounts in the sales and nominal ledger.

As well as maintaining customer accounts, from which statements can be derived for printing and posting, the sales ledger can produce summaries of credit allowed to customers (*aged debtor reports*) and also an analysis of sales. It also has a controlling function since it provides the nominal ledger with debtor's figures.

Function of the purchase ledger

The purchase ledger is essentially a file of all suppliers' accounts and as such it maintains records of:

invoices received from suppliers;

credit allowed by suppliers;

payments to suppliers;

credit notes sent to customers (e.g., for goods damaged in transit, etc.).

As well as maintaining supplier accounts, from which statements can be derived to check customer statements sent by suppliers, the purchase ledger can produce summaries of credit allowed by suppliers (*aged creditor reports*) and also an analysis of purchases made.

Integrated ledger applications packages

A fully integrated ledger package combines the functions of sales, purchase and nominal ledgers. A diagrammatic representation of the files of records held by a microcomputer for such an integrated system, together with the transactions between the company and its customers and suppliers is shown in figure 9.1.

The particular integrated ledger package used in this chapter is known as GBS and was developed by Bytesoft Systems Limited of Leicester, a member of the Byteshop Group. GBS can either stand alone as in integrated ledger system or can be used as a ledger sub-system within an integrated stock and ledger package known as ISL. Both packages can be tailored to run on any microcomputer using CP/M, MS-DOS or PC-DOS operating systems.

On even a small, dual floppy disk microcomputer the capacity of GBS is:

400 sales or customer accounts;

2,000 open sales orders;

400 purchase or supplier accounts;

2,000 open purchase orders;

200 nominal ledger accounts.

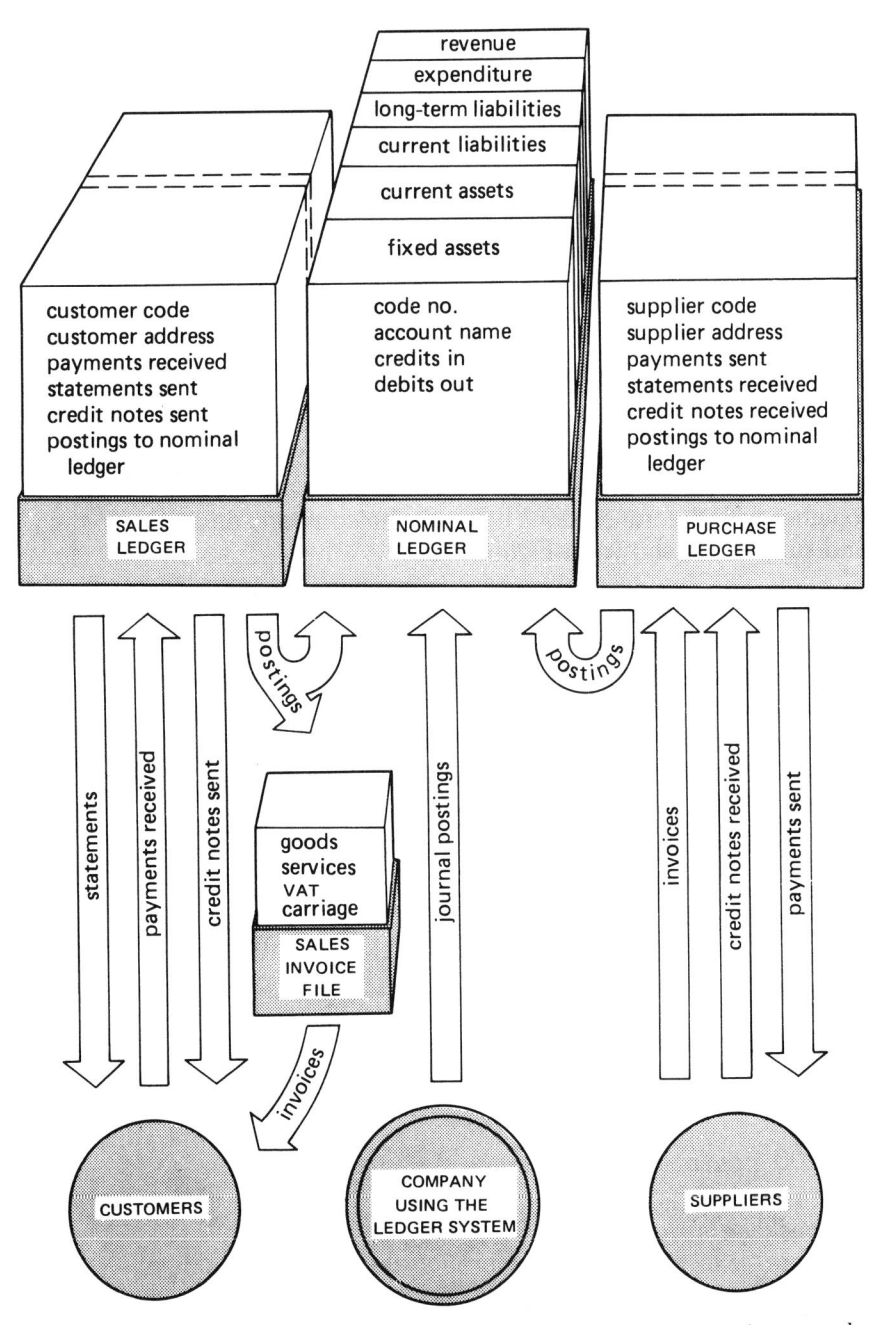

Figure 9.1 *Diagrammatic representation of a microcomputer integrated ledger system.*

The package is menu driven. The simplest way to explain its operation, therefore, is to move logically through the various options offered by the package via the four principal menus.

Main menu of the GBS integrated package

The main menu of the GBS integrated ledger applications package offers five options, namely:

1. nominal ledger (which in turn offers nominal ledger menu);
2. sales ledger (which in turn offers sales ledger menu);
3. purchase ledger (which in turn offers purchase ledger menu);
4. backup system files;
5. check system integrity.

On start-up the system requires the current date and then expects the user to check the system's integrity by selecting option 5. (Note: later versions perform this check automatically.)

Check system integrity (main menu, option 5)

This is one of the most important facilities of the system. It should be used at each start-up and the resulting system checkout print, an example of which is shown as figure 9.2, should be filed for information. In the case of a crash of the system, details from this checkout will be needed before the system can be resurrected. A software support contract for this package would stipulate that the user retain these checkouts, which are numbered serially to facilitate filing.

The system checkout takes about one minute to run and essentially checks the validity of all records and carries out certain book-keeping checks; for example, the 'total owing' balance of the sales ledger should equal the 'debtors' balance of the nominal ledger, and 'total owed' balance of the purchase ledger should equal the 'creditors' balance of the nominal ledger.

As figure 9.2 shows, the system checkout print indicates the percentage of each file already occupied by data and also the numbers of the last sales invoice, purchase invoice etc. This ensures that the user is aware at exactly what stage the last series of transactions occurred.

```
===========================================================
                  BYTESOFT GENERAL BUSINESS SYSTEM
              SYSTEM  CHECKOUT  No.  37

                    Bykeshop Commuterland
                    2b Railway Arches
                    Birmingham B5 4TD                18/10/81
===========================================================
                 All files are generation 7
Last Audit (Sales)           10    Last Invoice Audit (Sales)      10
Last journal transaction:    79
Nominal Ledger               49 recs.       60,783.08     49% full
Nominal statement file       64 recs.                     34% full
Last sales inv:            1213    Last sales cash receipt         5
Last sales credit note        0
Sales Ledger total           16 recs.       29,644.63     15% full
Sales Invoice File           15 recs.       29,644.63      3% full
===========================================================
                 SALES/NOMINAL SYSTEM IN BALANCE
===========================================================
Last Audit (Purchase)        12    Last Invoice Audit (Purchase)   12
Last purchase inv:          155    Last purchase cash receipt       5
Last purchase credit note     0
Purchase Ledger total        33 recs.        5,231.77     66% full
Purchase Invoice File        12 recs.        5,231.77      4% full
===========================================================
               PURCHASE/NOMINAL SYSTEM IN BALANCE
```

Figure 9.2 *Initial system checkout print.*

Backup system files (main menu, option 4)

This facility allows the user to produce backup disks regularly. When the backup disk has been produced, the user is advised to operate with the latest disk, the one just created. This helps cycle the disks rather than using one set continually until a fault occurs. It also ensures that if there have been any copying errors in the backing up procedure, they are detected at once (using the system checkout) rather than days later.

To help the user identify which disk is a backup disk and which an original, the backing up procedure – while otherwise producing an identical copy of data files – updates a *generation number* which uniquely identifies the newly backed-up disk and its sequence relative to other disks.

Following a backing up procedure, the older generation disk, which now becomes the main backup disk, should be safely stored some distance from the microcomputer installation.

The remaining options offered within the main menu, namely nominal ledger (option 1), sales ledger (option 2) and purchase edger (option 3) represent the major part of the package and each needs to be discussed in detail. Before proceeding to the discussion of the facilities offered by these three ledger systems, however, we must look at the important concept of the audit trail.

The audit trail

After each session of entering transactions into the integrated ledger package, an audit trail listing all invoices/credit notes/cash payments entered/journal postings made during the session should be produced. With the GBS package this audit trail is automatically printed whenever any transactions are made which affect the balance of the system. The audit trails are numbered and, like system checkouts, should be filed safely. On the next start-up of the system, the last invoice/credit note numbers will be displayed and these should be checked agains the most recent audit trail to prevent duplication of postings. The audit trail also displays the brought forward debtors' total, for comparison with the brought forward total of the previous audit trail.

If a user safely retains:

all backup disks;
all system checkout reports; and
all audit trails

the very worst that can happen, in the event of a system crash, is that the information posted during the session in which the crash occurred is lost.

Lest some readers think that the various steps being recommended to avoid disaster are excessive, it should be remembered that company auditors will require hard copy of all the company's transactions when they produce their annual audit.

Nominal ledger (main menu, option 1)

The nominal ledger option offers a menu with eleven further options which are:

1 enter journal transactions, print and post;
2 sort nominal ledger file;

3   list nominal ledger accounts;
4   maintain nominal ledger*;
5   list trial balance*;
6   list profit and loss account*;
7   list balance sheet*;
8   list VAT report;
9   change password*;
10 print nominal statements*;
11 end-of-month processing*;

print = print audit trail;

post = post to nominal accounts.

For security reasons many of the options (those marked with an asterisk) may only be accessed by use of a password. For additional security the password does not appear on the computer's screen when entered, and can be changed from time to time using option 9 which may itself only be accessed by the current password.

The various facilities offered by the nominal ledger are dealt with in the sequence in which they would normally be used.

Maintaining the nominal ledger (option 4)

This option allows the user to add new nominal accounts, with their associated codes, to the existing file (up to a maximum of 200) or to delete accounts which are no longer required. However, such accounts can only be deleted when their balance is zero.

The GSB package has six nominal accounts built permanently into the system which are:

```
100100    debtors;
100200    cash at bank;
100500    VAT on purchases;
200100    creditors;
200500    VAT on sales;
300100    capital.
```

Each nominal account is uniquely identified by its 6 digit code and these codes are organized in such a way that the first digit indicates the type of account, namely:

```
000000 – 099999    fixed assets;
```

Sales, purchase and nominal ledger

```
=================================================================
                     BYTESOFT NOMINAL LEDGER
                     NOMINAL ACCOUNTS

                     Bykeshop Commuterland
                     2b Railway Arches
   18/10/81          Birmingham B5 4TD                    Page  1
=================================================================
    1     000010   LEASE                 Fixed Assets
    2     000020   LEASE IMPROVEMENTS    Fixed Assets
    3     000030   FIXTURES & FITTINGS   Fixed Assets
    4     000040   OFFICE FURNITURE      Fixed Assets
    5     100010   STOCK OF WIDGETS      Current Assets
    6     100020   STOCK OF BOOKS        Current Assets
    7     100030   STOCK OF PAPER        Current Assets
    8     100100   DEBTORS               Current Assets
    9     100200   CASH AT BANK          Current Assets
   10     100500   VAT ON PURCHASES      Current Assets
   11     100600   RENT PAID IN ADVANCE  Current Assets
   12     100610   RATES, IN ADVANCE     Current Assets
   13     200100   CREDITORS             Current Liabilities
   14     200110   DEPOSITS TAKEN        Current Liabilities
   15     200500   VAT ON SALES          Current Liabilities
   16     200600   PROVISION, TELEPHONE  Current Liabilities
   17     200610   PROVISION, PROFESS.   Current Liabilities
   18     200620   PROVISION, ELECTRIC.  Current Liabilities
   19     200650   PROVISION INCOME TAX  Current Liabilities
   20     200700   STOCK SUSPENSE        Current Liabilities
   21     300010   CAPITAL               Longterm Liabilities
   22     300020   LOANS                 Longterm Liabilities
   23     400010   WAGES & SALARIES      Expenditure
   24     400020   EMPLOYERS' NHI        Expenditure
   25     400030   REPAIRS TO WIDGETS    Expenditure
   26     400040   COST OF SALES         Expenditure
   27     400050   INCOME TAX            Expenditure
   28     400070   PETTY CASH            Expenditure
   29     400100   ELECTRICITY           Expenditure
   30     400110   TELEPHONE             Expenditure
   31     400120   ADVERTISING           Expenditure
   32     400150   RENT                  Expenditure
   33     400160   RATES                 Expenditure
   34     400170   PROFESSIONAL          Expenditure
   35     400180   ENTERTAINING          Expenditure
   36     400200   DEPRECIATION          Expenditure
   37     500010   SALES, BROWN WIDGETS  Revenue
   38     500020   SALES, BLUE WIDGETS   Revenue
   39     500030   SALES, GREEN WIDGETS  Revenue
   40     500040   SALES, BOOKS          Revenue
   41     500050   SALES, PAPER ETC.     Revenue
   42     500100   HIRE OF WIDGETS       Revenue
   43     500110   REPAIRS OF WIDGETS    Revenue
   44     500500   DELIVERY              Revenue
   45     600010   P&L, BROUGHT FORWARD  Trading Account
   46     100620   PETTY CASH FLOAT      Current Assets
   47     200700   WORK IN PROGRESS      Current Liabilities
   48     500200   MR B CONTRACT         Revenue
   49     500210   MR J CONTRACT         Revenue
=================================================================
```

Figure 9.3 *Listing of the nominal accounts.*

100000 – 199999   current assets;
200000 – 299999   current liabilities;
300000 – 399999   long-term liabilities;
400000 – 499999   expenditure;
500000 – 599999   revenue (i.e. income).

In addition, the last 3 digits in each 6 digit code indicate whether that account is VAT rated:

000 – 899   VAT rated (including zero rated);
900 – 999   exempt from VAT.

Thus, for example, a nominal account code 100350 would represent a current asset which, if bought or sold, would be subject to VAT whereas code 400904 would represent an expense which is VAT exempt. It is necessary to distinguish between 'exempt' and 'zero rated'.

The purpose of this nominal account coding system is to enable the package to classify the nominal ledger accounts and determine whether they should appear in the balance sheet (option 7) or the profit and loss account (option 6) and also to determine whether a transaction should be entered into the VAT account, thus enabling the production of a VAT report on demand.

A listing of all nominal accounts and their respective codes can be produced using option 3 (see figure 9.3). Reference to such as listing is always necessary when operating the sales or purchase ledger.

Enter journal transactions (option 1)

This option is used to record the company's financial transactions which are not processed by either the sales or the purchase ledger. Once a suitable set of nominal accounts has been created, this option can be invoked to pay rent, electricity bills, clearing bills, or to record end-of-period adjustments such as depreciation of assets, accrual of rates and so on. This facility must NOT be used for paying suppliers' bills, which must be handled through the purchase ledger; similarly cash received from customers must be put through the sales ledger.

When this option is invoked, the system will list the last journal transactions entered, which should match the last journal transactions noted on the last audit trail.

Sales, purchase and nominal ledger 175

When making journal transactions direct to the nominal ledger, convention insists that *credits* are made to accounts that *give* and *debits* to accounts that *receive*. Hence, for a £250 payment of rent, the cash at bank account is credited with £250 which it then gives to the rent account which receives the £250 as a debit. For the payment of a number of cheques, a series of debits can first be allocated to the receiving accounts (rent, electricity, petty cash, etc.) and covered by a single credit to the donating account (cash at bank).

Debit and credit transactions to the nominal ledger must always balance out and, in fact, this GBS journal transaction option does not permit a batch of journal transactions to be entered unless they do balance. At the end of a batch of journal transactions, an audit trail is automatically printed and the individual transactions are posted to their respective nominal accounts. As added security, if a printer is not connected, or connected but not on-line to the computer, the system is designed not to proceed. It cannot, therefore, accept journal transactions that would have gone unrecorded on hard copy.

Sort nominal ledger file (option 2)

This option sorts nominal accounts into ascending order of the identifying 6 digit code. It is usually only exercised at the beginning, when setting up the accounts in the nominal ledger, but clearly the inclusion of a new account, or the deletion of an existing one, may mean the file needs to be re-sorted.

Readers may note that the nominal accounts listing (figure 9.3) indicates that four new accounts have recently been added to the end of the nominal ledger which have yet to be re-sorted. Nevertheless, the package will still operate correctly, whether the nominal accounts are sorted into categories or not.

List trial balance (option 5)

This option allows the user to obtain a listing, either on the screen or printer, of the balances of all the nominal accounts other than those with a zero balance. The nominal ledger will ALWAYS be in balance unless affected by some disaster such as a power failure or a corrupted disk.

Figure 9.4, which presents a trial balance from the nominal ledger, shows clearly the balance between the company's debts and credits.

Most popular business packages

```
===============================================================
                   BYTESOFT NOMINAL LEDGER
                   TRIAL  BALANCE

                  Bykeshop Commuterland
                  2b Railway Arches
18/10/81          Birmingham B5 4TD                     Page
===============================================================
Line  - Description        Debits      Credits
===============================================================
  1   LEASE            .   6,500.00.    .Fixed Assets
  3   FIXTURES & FITTINGS. 2,775.00.    .Fixed Assets
  5   STOCK OF WIDGETS .   1,733.80.    .Current Assets
  6   STOCK OF BOOKS   .   7,269.96.    .Current Assets
  7   STOCK OF PAPER   .   4,510.29.    .Current Assets
  8   DEBTORS          .  29,644.63.    .Current Assets
  9   CASH AT BANK     .                20,833.19.Current Assets
 10   VAT ON PURCHASES .   2,323.50.    .Current Assets
 11   RENT PAID IN ADVANCE.  500.00.    .Current Assets
 12   RATES, IN ADVANCE .    220.00.    .Current Assets
 13   CREDITORS        .                5,231.77.Current Liabilities
 14   DEPOSITS TAKEN   .     200.00.    .Current Liabilities
 15   VAT ON SALES     .      .         2,207.61.Current Liabilities
 16   PROVISION, TELEPHONE.  .             25.00.Current Liabilities
 17   PROVISION, PROFESS..   .              5.00.Current Liabilities
 18   PROVISION, ELECTRIC..  .             15.00.Current Liabilities
 19   PROVISION INCOME TAX.  .            129.60.Current Liabilities
 21   CAPITAL          .     .            100.00.Longterm Liabilities
 22   LOANS            .     .          9,900.00.Longterm Liabilities
 23   WAGES & SALARIES .     604.70.    .Expenditure
 24   EMPLOYERS' NHI   .      45.20.    .Expenditure
 25   REPAIRS TO WIDGETS .   102.10.    .Expenditure
 26   COST OF SALES    .   3,402.00.    .Expenditure
 28   PETTY CASH       .      35.70.    .Expenditure
 31   ADVERTISING      .      91.00.    .Expenditure
 32   RENT             .     120.00.    .Expenditure
 34   PROFESSIONAL     .      34.00.    .Expenditure
 35   ENTERTAINING     .      12.78.    .Expenditure
 37   SALES, BROWN WIDGETS.    .          127.10.Revenue
 38   SALES, BLUE WIDGETS .    .          123.88.Revenue
 39   SALES, GREEN WIDGETS.    .        1,097.02.Revenue
 40   SALES, BOOKS     .       .           69.60.Revenue
 41   SALES, PAPER ETC..       .          137.60.Revenue
 42   HIRE OF WIDGETS  .       .        2,434.00.Revenue
 43   REPAIRS OF WIDGETS .     .          112.00.Revenue
 44   DELIVERY         .       .           62.80.Revenue
 45   P&L, BROUGHT FORWARD.    .       17,391.91.Trading Account
 46   PETTY CASH FLOAT .      78.42.    .Current Assets
 47   WORK IN PROGRESS .     580.00.    .Current Liabilities
 48   MR B CONTRACT    .       .          780.00.Revenue
===============================================================
Totals:                  60,783.08   60,783.08
===============================================================
```

Figure 9.4 Trial balance listing from the nominal ledger.

Sales, purchase and nominal ledger 177

```
=================================================================
                        BYTESOFT NOMINAL LEDGER
                   Profit & Loss Account

                        Bykeshop Commuterland
                        2b Railway Arches
    18/10/81             Birmingham B5 4TD                Page  1
=================================================================
                        --------MTD--------    --------YTD--------
    Revenue                            %                        %
      SALES, BROWN WIDGETS    127.10   2.57      2123.10      5.78
      SALES, BLUE WIDGETS     123.88   2.51       625.88      1.70
      SALES, GREEN WIDGETS   1097.02  22.19      3523.02      9.60
      SALES, BOOKS             69.60   1.41      3157.60      8.60
      SALES, PAPER ETC.       137.60   2.78     15512.60     42.26
      HIRE OF WIDGETS        2434.00  49.23      8846.00     24.10
      REPAIRS OF WIDGETS      112.00   2.27      1600.20      4.36
      DELIVERY                 62.80   1.27       540.80      1.47
      MR B CONTRACT           780.00  15.78       780.00      2.12
                            --------            --------
                            4944.00 ** 100.00   36709.20    100.00
    Expenditure
      WAGES & SALARIES        604.70  12.23      2245.70      6.12
      EMPLOYERS' NHI           45.20    .91        88.80       .24
      REPAIRS TO WIDGETS      102.10   2.07       247.10       .67
      COST OF SALES          3402.00  68.81     14610.30     39.80
      INCOME TAX                 .00    .00       129.60       .35
      PETTY CASH               35.70    .72       164.49       .45
      ELECTRICITY                .00    .00       120.00       .33
      TELEPHONE                  .00    .00       150.00       .41
      ADVERTISING              91.00   1.84       261.00       .71
      RENT                    120.00   2.43       492.00      1.34
      RATES                      .00    .00        20.00       .05
      PROFESSIONAL             34.00    .69       204.00       .56
      ENTERTAINING             12.78    .26        12.78       .03
      DEPRECIATION               .00    .00        75.00       .20
                            --------            --------
                            4447.48 ** 89.96    18820.77     51.27
    Profit/Loss              496.52    10.04    17888.43     48.73
                            4944.00   100.00    36709.20    100.00
=================================================================
=================================================================
```

Figure 9.5 *Profit and loss account taken from revenue and expenditure accounts in the nominal ledger.*

List profit and loss account (option 6)

Assuming that the user of the GBS package has specified the nominal accounts intelligently and has observed the simple rules for classifying the nominal codes into revenue, expenditure, fixed assets, current assets, etc., this listing will provide a most useful first attempt at a profit and loss account. Of course, it is most unlikely that such a listing could represent the company's true

178 *Most popular business packages*

trading figures, since the company's accountant would almost certainly wish to make adjustments for accruals, depreciation and so on but such a listing does provide an excellent starting point.

The profit and loss account shown in figure 9.5 is drawn up from the revenue and expenditure accounts of the nominal ledger (see figure 9.3) and includes figures on a month-to-date (MTD) basis to indicate the current trading position, and a year-to-date (YTD) basis to indicate the overall yearly trading position. A useful feature of the printout is that percentages are evaluated.

List balance sheet (option 7)

Whereas the profit and loss account represents a company's trading position for a specific period and is based on revenue and expenditure accounts, the balance sheet is based on the assets (fixed and current) and liabilities (current and long term) accounts of the nominal ledger.

The balance sheet, therefore, is an indication of a company's long-term financial standing and structure at a particular point in time. Figure 9.6 shows a balance sheet print out from the GBS package, which would again, form a very good basis for a company's accountant to produce a final amended balance sheet.

List VAT (option 8)

This option extracts five quarterly summaries of the company's VAT position as recorded through the VAT rated expenditure and revenue accounts. These will originally have been classified as VAT rated by the selection of the nominal ledger account codes (that is, codes ending 000–899). Figure 9.7 shows the VAT report produced by the GBS package. It could be used as the basis of a company's official VAT return.

Print nominal statements (option 10)

This option allows the user to examine the condition of any of the nominal ledger accounts at any time. The statement simply lists for each account:

   the balance brought forward;

   the current month's postings to the account;

   the current balance resulting from these two.

```
================================================================
                    BYTESOFT NOMINAL LEDGER
                    BALANCE  SHEET

                    Bykeshop Commuterland
                    2b Railway Arches
18/10/81            Birmingham B5 4TD                Page   1
================================================================
Fixed Assets
    LEASE                                    6500.00
    FIXTURES & FITTINGS                      2775.00
                                             --------
                                             9275.00
Current Assets
    STOCK OF WIDGETS                         1733.80
    STOCK OF BOOKS                           7269.96
    STOCK OF PAPER                           4510.29
    DEBTORS                                 29644.63
    CASH AT BANK                           (20833.19)
    VAT ON PURCHASES                         2323.50
    RENT PAID IN ADVANCE                      500.00
    RATES, IN ADVANCE                         220.00
    PETTY CASH FLOAT                           78.42
                                             --------
                                            25447.41
Total Assets                                34722.41  ***
Current Liabilities
    CREDITORS                                5231.77
    DEPOSITS TAKEN                           (200.00)
    VAT ON SALES                             2207.61
    PROVISION, TELEPHONE                       25.00
    PROVISION, PROFESS.                         5.00
    PROVISION, ELECTRIC.                       15.00
    PROVISION INCOME TAX                      129.60
    WORK IN PROGRESS                         (580.00)
                                             --------
                                             6833.98
Longterm Liabilities
    CAPITAL                       100.00
    P&L, BROUGHT FORWARD        17391.91
    MTD profit                    496.52
                                ---------
                                            17988.43
    LOANS                                    9900.00
                                             --------
                                            27888.43
Total Liabilities                           34722.41  ***
================================================================
```

Figure 9.6 *Balance sheet taken from assets, liabilities and trading accounts in the nominal ledger.*

End-of-month processing (option 11)

For the nominal ledger, the end-of-month processing simply updates the balance brought forward in line with the current month's postings, and then clears the latter. This processing also

```
===============================================================
                    BYTESOFT NOMINAL LEDGER
                       VAT REPORT

                    Bykeshop Commuterland
                    2b Railway Arches
18/10/81            Birmingham B5 4TD
===============================================================

Period ending              06/81      09/81      12/81     03/82     06/82

VAT-rated goods bought       .00   4,173.37     301.90       .00       .00

VAT paid out                 .00      35.70      22.80       .00       .00


VAT-rated goods sold         .00  16,297.20   4,164.00       .00       .00

VAT collected                .00        .00     573.60       .00       .00

===============================================================
```

Figure 9.7 VAT report extracted from VAT rated revenue and expenditure accounts in the nominal ledger.

ages the balance-brought-forward date by one month (or period). Any reports required from the nominal ledger should obviously be produced before end-of-month processing.

Sales ledger (main menu, option 2)

The sales ledger option offers a menu with eleven further options which are:

1 enter sales invoice transactions, print and post;
2 enter cash received, print and post;
3 enter credit notes sent, print and post;
4 list customers' names and addresses;
5 maintain customer file;
6 list aged debtor report;
7 list customer statements;
8 end-of-month processing;
9 sort customer file;
10 sales analysis;
11 customer invoice listing.

Sales, purchase and nominal ledger   181

  print = print audit trail;

  post = post to customer account and nominal accounts.

The various facilities offered by the sales ledger are dealt with in the sequence in which they would normally be used.

Maintain customer file (option 5)

This option allows the user to:

  create a new customer record;

  update existing records with changes (of address, telephone, etc.);

  delete existing customer records (only if the account balance is zero).

As with nominal accounts, each customer record is identified with a six digit code and, whilst it is not necessary to allocate codes to customers in a logical fashion, since the customer records can be sorted in ascending order of the record code using option 9, it is sensible to allocate codes on the basis of some categorization. It is also possible to create up to ten separate categories of customers by allocating codes in the range 000000–099999 to the first category, 100000–199999 to the second category and so on. Sensible allocation of codes to customer records at the initial stage results in a much more meaningful sales analysis report (option 10) because category subtotals can be produced.

It should be noted that this option only allows 'static' information such as address, telephone number, contact, etc. to be entered into the customer record. Financial ('live') information can only be entered into the account section of the record via the appropriate invoice transaction or the cash received or credit notes received options – all of which will ensure the printing of an audit trail and also postings of balanced credits and debits to the nominal ledger.

An existing customer record may only be deleted if the account stands at zero. In practice a deleted record will be removed from the sales ledger (and further space made available) when the file is next sorted.

Having created and sorted customer records, option 4 allows the user to print a list of all customers (see figure 9.8). Such a list is used to identify customers for processing invoices, etc.

182 Most popular business packages

```
===============================================================
                      BYTESOFT SALES LEDGER
                    CUSTOMER  LISTING

                      Bykeshop Commuterland
                       2b Railway Arches
  18/10/81            Birmingham B5 4TD                  Page 1
===============================================================

   1  100010  HIT & RUN (1980) LTD    2  200010  JONES THE WIDGET LTD
           5 GAS STREET                       5 GREEN VALLEY
           CHELTENHAM                         CARDIFF
           GLOUCS. CE3 4TT                    CA4 2SD
           0433-23232                         054-332-3456

   3  200030  SLOWPAY BROS LTD.       4  100020  QUALITY CARPETS LTD
           GOVERNMENT HOUSE                   119 MAYORS WALK
           PLUSH STREET                       ALLINGTON, NORHTANTS
           WIPLEY, CAMBS.
           056-789-1111                       0332-77668

   5  100052  J.T.ASPIN & SON         6  100060  BAXTON FUELS LTD.
           JUBILEE HOUSE                      SHERWOOD LODGE
           ST IVES, CAMBS                     BENNINGTON, CAMBS

           0774-99775                         0442-77889

   7  100070  LINCS COLD STORES       8  200030  PETER JONES NURSERIES LTD
           TEMPLE MEAD                        ABBEY ROAD
           FARLEY, NOTTS                      KESTEVEN, LINCS

           98-66442                           0442-54432

   9  200050  WHITMORE BUILDERS LTD. 10  200090  MORGAN BROS
           22 WESTBOURNE ROAD                 UNIT 7a
           STAUGHTON, LEICS                   LITTLE END, MORETON

           0311-4279                          3342221

  11  300020  BYTESHOP (GRIMSBY) LTD 12  300060  B. HENRY & SON LTD.
           MOUNTAIN WALK                      14 FOSTER AVENUE,
           GRIMSBY                            GRANTHAM. LINCS.



  13  400010  TAYLOR BROS (BUILDERS) 14  600030  APRIL COLD STORES LTD
           THE BUTTERLEYS                     15 MERVIEW ESTATE
           KIRTON, LINCS                      DODDINGTON, LINCS

           0332-12111                         0665-21334

  15  700030  DAMPROOF LTD           16  700040  JONES & SON
           CHAPEL STREET                      PLAGUE HOUSE
           BUCKDEN, HUNTS                     MORBID ROW

           0885-25252                         999
===============================================================
===============================================================
```

Figure 9.8 Customer listing.

Sales, purchase and nominal ledger   183

Some packages identify customers/suppliers by *alpha-matching* rather than, as here, by unique number codes. Alpha-matching usually uses the first three characters of a name to identify the required customer/supplier. Although this may make a package appear slightly easier to operate initially, this non-unique coding system does introduce a certain inefficiency into the functioning of the package.

Enter sales invoice transactions (option 1)

This option is routinely used to record all manually raised sales invoices sent to customers or, where an automatic facility for raising invoices on the customer is available, retaining details of those invoices.

Before using this option the operator needs:

a listing of customers' addresses created by option 4 (see figure 9.8);

a listing of all nominal accounts created by main menu, option 3 (see figure 9.3).

As each item of information from a sales invoice is entered it will be necessary to identify which nominal revenue account is to be credited such as:

sales;

hires;

repairs;

delivery;

VAT on sales etc.

To balance the nominal ledger, the total value of each sales invoice will be debited to the debtor's account.

Having identified the customer, the system informs the user of the number of the last sales invoice processed, which should tally with that produced by the last sales invoice audit trail. This check should ensure that sales invoices are never processed twice.

Identification of the customer to whom an invoice is to be sent via his listed identification number produces the following information on the screen:

184 Most popular business packages

customer's name and address (for final identification);

date and amount of last payment received;

sales turnover, year-to-date.

While sales invoices need not be entered in numbered sequence, in practice it is sensible to adopt such a discipline as an additional safeguard against duplicate entries and omissions. As the amount of each item on the sales invoice is entered, together with its associated nominal revenue account code, the current invoice total will be shown. Should this check total not eventually match that on the manually raised sales invoice, the user can make the requisite alterations or, if the original invoice was incorrect, a corrected invoice can be sent to the customer.

When a batch of sales invoices has been entered, a printed Audit Trail is produced, the customers' accounts debited and appropriate balanced postings made to the nominal ledger (see table 9.1).

Enter cash received (option 2)

This option allocates cash received from customers against previously posted sales invoices. Once a customer is identified, through his or her number, all the outstanding sales invoices posted to that customer are shown. The computer's cursor can be moved freely over the amounts displayed and with this facility the user can decide which previously invoiced amounts are to be covered by the cash payment received by hitting the 'P' (*post complete*) key when the cursor is opposite an amount to be cleared, or by keying in a specific amount in the case of part-payments.

Table 9.1 *Account transactions for sales and nominal ledgers*

		Sales invoice	Payment received	Credit note sent
Sales ledger	Customer accounts	debit	credit	credit
Nominal ledger Accounts	Sales (revenue)	credit		
	Bank (current assets)		debit	
	Returns inwards (revenue)			debit
	Debtors (current assets)	debit	credit	credit

Sales, purchase and nominal ledger 185

After this, yet another audit trail will be printed, customers' accounts credited and postings made to the nominal ledger.

Enter credit notes sent (option 3)

This option allows the user to issue credit notes to customers against items identified on previously raised invoices in much the same way as for cash received (option 2).

Table 9.1 summarizes how the various accounts in the sales and nominal ledgers should be credited and debited, as a result of the transactions made using options 1, 2 and 3, in what is – in effect – a triple entry accounting system.

List aged debtor report (option 6)

This option produces an extremely useful report which breaks down debtors by age of debt over the last four months. Within the

```
==================================================================================
                              BYTESOFT SALES LEDGER
                       AGED    DEBTOR    REPORT

                          Bykeshop Computerland
                          2b Railway Arches
                          Birmingham B5 4TD
18/10/81   File generation  7                                         PAGE   1
==================================================================================
Name                      October September    August     July+    Total due
==================================================================================
  1
HIT & RUN (1980) LTD      3017.60       .00       .00     572.15     3589.75
(  5000.00 paid on 15/10/81)
  2
JONES THE WIDGET LTD      1720.00       .00   2457.00    2006.83     6183.83
(   126.78 paid on 14/05/81)
  3
SLOWPAY BROS LTD.              .00      .00   1288.20    4509.85     5798.05

  6
BAXTON FUELS LTD.              .00  12552.00      .00        .00    12552.00

 16
JONES & SON                    .00      .00       .00    1521.00     1521.00
==================================================================================
Totals:                   4,737.60 12,552.00 3,745.20   8,609.83    29,644.63
Percentage breakdown         15.98     42.34    12.63      29.04      100.00
==================================================================================
==================================================================================
```

Figure 9.9 Aged debtor report from the sales ledger.

186 *Most popular business packages*

GBS package one can either opt for a complete list of all debtors or a selective list of debtors of more than a certain age (for example, owing over 90 days) or owing more than a certain amount (for example, owing more than £1,000). The report also identifies when each debtor's last payment was made. The full aged debtor report, an example of which is shown in figure 9.9, also gives the percentage breakdown of the debt over the last four months (the fourth month including debts of four months or older).

List customer statements (option 7)

This option allows the user to produce a statement of the current standing of any customer's account. This can be displayed on the computer screen (in response to a customer's telephoned query, for example) or can be printed and sent to the customer (at the end of a month). Statements can be produced either for individually identified customers or for all customers and indicate amounts owed for more than 90 days, 60–90 days and currently.

When customer statements are printed, the printing can be tailored to fit either pre-printed continuous stationery or to produce

```
                      Bykeshop Commuterland
                        2b Railway Arches
                        Birmingham B5 4TD

                             STATEMENT

SLOWPAY BROS LTD.
GOVERNMENT HOUSE
PLUSH STREET
WIPLEY, CAMBS.                                           18/10/81
==================================================================
90 Days +    :    4,509.85
60-90 Days   :    1,288.20
Current      :      564.80                 Total due :   6,362.85

Date       Invoice      Amount      Paid      Credited    Balance

06/03/81       3       1,421.40      .00        .00      1,421.40
14/05/81       8       1,843.45      .00        .00      1,843.45
23/03/81     128       1,245.00      .00        .00      1,245.00
31/08/81    2215       1,288.20      .00        .00      1,288.20
18/10/81  734345         564.80      .00        .00        564.80

                     Please pay this amount........:      6,362.85
```

Figure 9.10 Customer statement with printed letterhead.

its own letterhead on blank continuous stationery as in the example shown in figure 9.10.

From discussions with those who have successfully implemented a sales ledger system on a microcomputer, it appears that the greatest boon is the ability to produce all customers' statements in a matter of minutes rather than over several days.

End-of-month processing (option 8)

This option removes all fully cleared sales invoices, payments received and credit notes from the customer accounts in the sales ledger and also ages all debts with respect to the system date. Like most good ledger packages, the GBS system operates around an *open-order* discipline which only allows invoices that have been completely covered by a payment, and which from the system's point of view are therefore now only of 'historic' interest, to be cleared from the account. Readers should be wary of ledger packages which *claim* to be open-order or open-item but are essentially based on a brought forward balance.

Any reports required from the sales ledger should be produced before this option is invoked, as should the monthly backup disk. The GBS end-of-month processing does not produce any printout, but takes several minutes to run as clearances are made and files reorganized.

Sales analysis (option 10)

If a sensible allocation of customer code numbers has been made when establishing customer records (see p. 181) the sales contribution of different categories of customers can be readily identified from the customer analysis report produced by this option, an example of which is shown in figure 9.11. In this particular example, only four of the possible ten customer categories that can be identified through the code numbering system of the GBS package have been utilized.

Customer invoice listing (option 11)

This option prints a summary listing of all outstanding sales invoices (see figure 9.12). This would generally be produced only for internal use.

```
=====================================================================
                       BYTESOFT SALES LEDGER
             CUSTOMER   INVOICE   LISTING

                       Bykeshop Commuterland
                       2b Railway Arches
18/10/81               Birmingham B5 4TD              Page 1
=====================================================================
                     No.    Date     Invoice        Amount

HIT & RUN (1980) LTD  1   14/05/81     144          572.15
                          15/10/81    1213        3,017.60
                                                  3,589.75 **

JONES THE WIDGET LTD  2   06/03/81       2           17.43
                          10/03/81       5          691.27
                          22/03/81       7          611.80
                          14/05/81       9          418.03
                          14/05/81     127          268.30
                          24/08/81    1255        2,457.00
                          15/10/81    1212        1,720.00
                                                  6,183.83 **

SLOWPAY BROS LTD.     3   06/03/81       3        1,421.40
                          14/05/81       8        1,843.45
                          23/03/81     128        1,245.00
                          31/08/81    2215        1,288.20
                                                  5,798.05 **

BAXTON FUELS LTD.     6   23/09/81    1211       12,552.00
                                                 12,552.00 **

JONES & SON          16   23/03/81     129        1,521.00
                                                  1,521.00 **
=====================================================================
                                                 29,644.63 ***
=====================================================================
=====================================================================
```

Figure 9.11 Summary of sales made to categories of customer.

Purchase ledger (main menu, option 3)

The operation of the purchase ledger is similar to the sales ledger (already described) except that it deals with 'purchases' not 'sales', 'suppliers' not 'customers' and 'creditors' rather than 'debtors'. Because the operation of the two ledgers is so similar, I shall merely list the menu of the purchase ledger.

The purchase ledger option offers a menu with eleven further options which are:

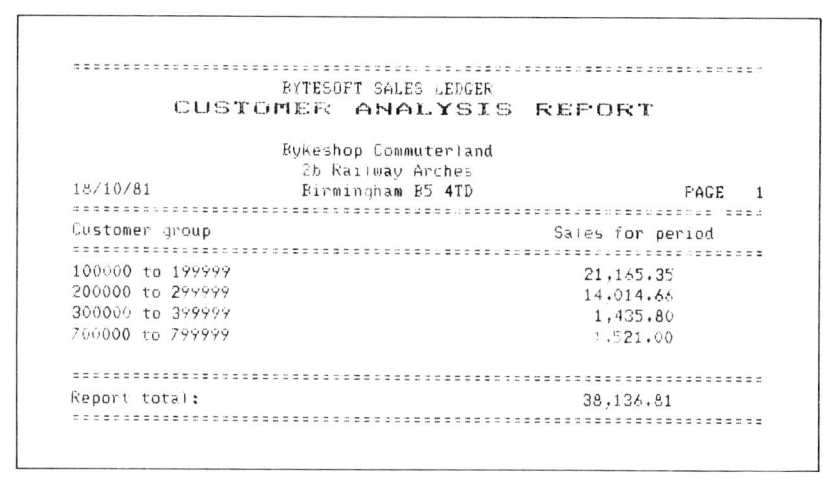

```
================================================================
                    BYTESOFT SALES LEDGER
               CUSTOMER  ANALYSIS  REPORT

                    Bykeshop Commuterland
                    2b Railway Arches
   18/10/81          Birmingham B5 4TD              PAGE   1
================================================================
   Customer group                         Sales for period
================================================================
   100000 to 199999                            21,165.35
   200000 to 299999                            14,014.66
   300000 to 399999                             1,435.80
   700000 to 799999                             1,521.00


================================================================
   Report total:                               38,136.81
================================================================
```

Figure 9.12 Listing of outstanding sales invoices.

1 enter purchase invoice transactions, print and post
2 enter cash paid, print and post
3 enter credit notes received, print and post
4 list suppliers' names and addresses
5 maintain supplier file
6 list aged creditor report
7 list supplier statements
8 end-of-month processing
9 sort supplier file
10 purchase analysis
11 supplier invoice listing

print = print audit trail

post = post to suplier and nominal accounts

The setting up, and weekly and monthly operations follow the same lines as those of the sales ledger.

Conclusion

This chapter has dealt with the accounting and other facilities offered by a fully integrated ledger package with sales, purchase

Most popular business packages

and nominal ledgers. Where a stand-alone sales or purchase ledger is used, the facilities provided are obviously much the same as the sales and purchase elements of an integrated system. But, as stand-alone ledger packages are not required to send postings to a nominal ledger, they are somewhat easier to operate. Invoices are treated as single transactions and do not usually have to be broken down into individual elements.

However, the additional effort required to incorporate a ledger of nominal accounts together with either or both a sales and purchase ledger in a well designed integrated microcomputer package, is well rewarded by the wealth of information as to the operating company's financial structure and standing that it provides.

The practical operation of an integrated ledger system tends to revolve around daily, weekly and monthly transactions which are typically as follows.

Daily

maintain sales and purchase ledger, if necessary by adding any new accounts or changes of address (it is not necessary to re-sort accounts and, in practice, since the operator(s) of the system generally become accustomed to associating customers and purchasers with particular identifying account numbers it is not sensible to be continually re-sorting and, hence, destroy this relationship);
enter sales invoices;
enter credit notes sent;
record cash payments received;
take backup record if frequency of transaction warrants.

Weekly

enter suppliers' (purchase) invoices;
enter credit notes received;
record cash payments made;
enter outstanding journal transactions for petty cash, etc.;
print aged debtor report.

Monthly

print and send all customer statements;
print aged debtor report;

Sales, purchase and nominal ledger

print sales invoice listing;
print sales analysis;
print aged creditor report;
print profit and loss and balance sheet to check for adjustments;
enter journal entries to nominal accounts to adjust;
print final profit and loss report and final balance sheet;
perform end-of-month procedures on all three ledgers (the end-of-month procedure appears as an option on each GBS ledger menu only because the sales and purchase ledgers can be used as stand-alone packages).

10

Stock control

Stock-control packages

Stock control versus stock recording

As can be seen from the survey of microcomputer applications packages (figure 1.16), stock control, at 12 per cent, appears to be the most popular single area of application of microcomputers. While most packages currently on offer are referred to as stock control, a very large majority are strictly speaking *stock recording* packages. My interpretation of the difference between the two is that, in the former, parameters which control the level of stocks, such as re-order levels, replenishment quantities, etc., are automatically updated in line with changes in demand, that is, an element of *forecasting* is a prerequisite. In stock recording, such parameters have to be set manually by the user and would, therefore, fail to control stocks effectively if demand were to change dramatically.

If forecasting is incorporated in a package, allowing true stock control, more information needs to be stored per stock record, which reduces the number of individual stock items that can be accommodated.

Having made my point about the distinction between stock control and stock recording, I shall, nevertheless, bow to market pressures and conventional usage and throughout this chapter call both 'stock control'!

Stand-alone versus integrated packages

Stock control packages for microcomputers can be either stand-alone or, to varying degrees, integrated. A stand-alone package simply controls the movements of stock and has no means of

Stock control   193

communicating with sales or purchase ledgers or aiding other management functions. An integrated package is designed to communicate with either one or several of these functions and, where integration is partial, the most common link is to a purchase or sales ledger package. A link with the purchase ledger could provide for the automatic raising of replenishment purchase orders (if, say, an allocation of stock causes a re-order level to be broken) and with a link to a sales ledger, an allocation of stock could automatically trigger a sales invoice.

Most of the stock control packages on the market can be obtained in a stand-alone form or integrated. As I warned in an earlier chapter, any later integration of a stand-alone system with other packages is a major undertaking and it is, therefore, sensible to think well ahead in making the initial choice (see chapter 2). Any degree of integration increases the number of disks required, which is an operating disadvantage. However, because all stock control packages require a file of supplier records which is also required for a purchase ledger, the integration of these two functions causes only a marginal reduction in the number of stock items that can be covered. This accounts for the relative popularity of this form of integration.

Stock control packages on the market which can stand alone (most of which can alternatively be integrated to varying degrees) have been written by TABS, CPS, ANAGRAM, OMICRON, Beam, MICROBITS, Bristol Software Factory, Triumph-Adler, Compact, Mediatech, Bytesoft Systems, Tridata Micros and many others. The examples shown in this chapter are produced by the stock control package written by Anagram Systems of Horsham.

Initial suitability of stock control packages

All stock control packages operate around a fixed record design format. It is, therefore, essential to ensure that the information for each stock item to be stored can be accommodated within that format. While software houses may be prepared, for instance, to increase the stock code from ten characters to twelve, such a change might well require further changes in the design of the package, all of which will have to be paid for.

As well as accommodating the information required for a single stock item it is obviously also essential that a stock control package must be able to accommodate the likely maximum number of stock items to be controlled by the system, together with their associated stock movements. In practice, the number of items to be held will control the number of floppy disks needed. A rough estimate can be made by assuming that 350–500 individual items can be accommodated per 100 kbytes of disk storage, table 10.1 gives a rough idea of that relationship in terms of operational disks.

If more than two 5¼ inch disks are to be used, additional hardware (disk drives) will be necessary if direct access to all items is required. With daily backup disks (see p. 14 for details of backup security), the actual number of disks to operate the system could be five times the number selected from table 10.1, and on top of that there would have to be twelve monthly backup disks. Thus, to control 6,000 stocked items with four disks operating simultaneously, some 30 floppy disks could be required, which shows why, at this level, it is sometimes preferable to opt for an admittedly much more expensive hard disk system.

Setting up a stock control system

Figure 10.1 shows diagrammatically the file structure of a typical microcomputer stock control package. Before it can be put to use, all the information for the records within these files will have to be transferred from the existing manual system – and for 3,000 items, the entry of this information could well occupy someone full-time for a week to a fortnight.

Having decided how many disks are needed, and having prepared or formatted the requisite number of new disks (see p. 13

Table 10.1 *Disk requirements as a function of items to be stocked (assuming an average of one purchase order and two allocations, or issues, per item per month)*

Disk configuration	Number of items	Number of suppliers
1 x 5¼" disk	1,500	200
2 x 5¼" disks	2,700	250
3 x 5¼" disks	4,400	300
4 x 5¼" disks	6,000	400
2 x 8" disks	8,000–10,000	500
1 x Winchester hard disk	30,000	1,000

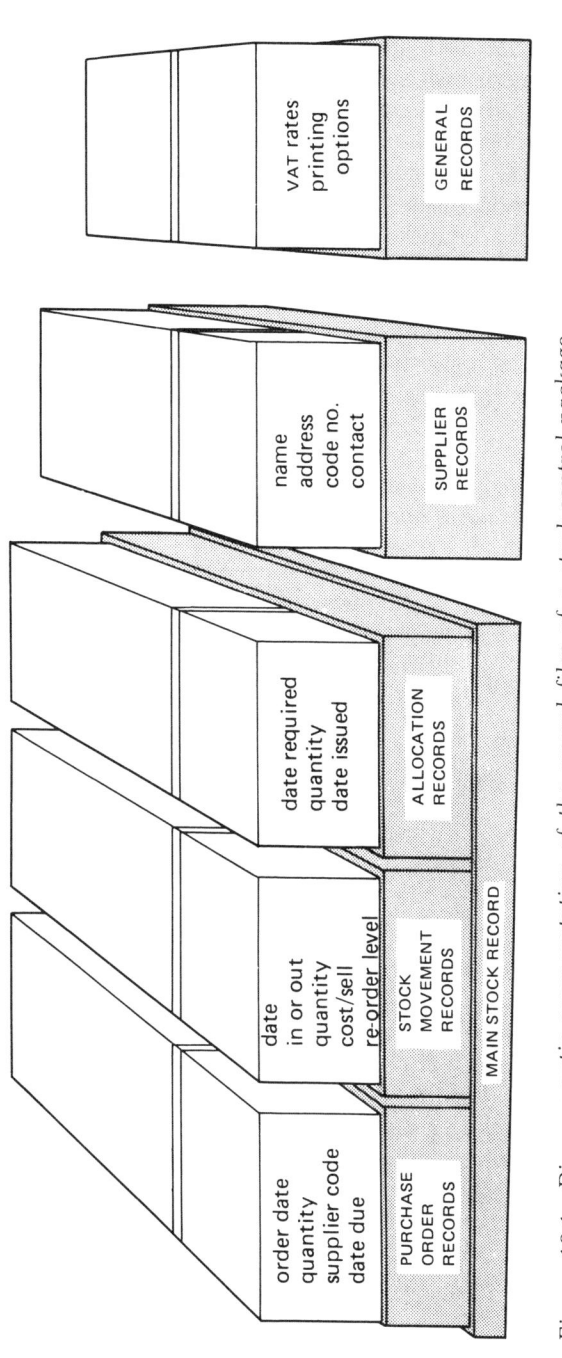

Figure 10.1 Diagrammatic representation of the record files of a stock control package.

for formatting procedures), the sequence of entering information would usually be as follows:

General

Enter company information, that is, the name, address, etc. of the company operating the stock control system.

Enter print facilities. Because a variety of printers might be used, the package must be told what type of printer is connected and in particular if a line-feed is required from the package. Details of how many lines can be printed per page will also have to be specified. At a normal printing of 6 lines to the inch, for 11 inch paper this cannot be greater than 66 and the norm is 60.

Supplier records

Each supplier will have his own individual record including information such as address, telephone number and possibly person to contact. To cut down on storage and to improve the package's efficiency, each supplier record is allocated a supplier code (either a number of alphanumeric abbreviation of the supplier's name) and references to suppliers from the stock records will be via this code.

Figure 10.2 shows a list of suppliers together with their allocated supplier codes, which in this case are numbers.

Stock records

The bulk of the information required by a stock control package will be for the individual stock records. While most of this information will be available from the existing manual system, it is sensible to perform a stocktake at the time of changing over from the manual to microcomputer-based system to ensure, in particular, that the figures entered for the quantities in stock, etc. are an accurate representation of the real life situation.

Figure 10.3 shows a typical record where

> *free stock* – represents the stock free to be issued and is equal to *in stock* plus *on order* minus *allocated* (i.e. 27+4−30=1);
>
> *in stock* – represents the actual physical stock held in stores and which, because it has been paid for by the stockist, represents capital tied up in stock;

```
Printed: 16 May 1981        SUPPLIER NAMES AND ADDRESSES            Page 1
--------------------------------------------------------------------------------

Supplier: 001         Name    : Commodore Business Machines
                      Address : 818 Leigh Road
                              : Slough
                              : Berks
                      Post code: BG2 3TR
                      Telephone: 0765-98321
                      Contact  : Julie North

Supplier: 002         Name    : Anadex Printer Co Ltd
                      Address : Exhall Trading Estate
                              : Slough
                              : Bucks
                      Post code: BU3 1CF
                      Telephone: 0981-4567
                      Contact  : Raymond Higgins

Supplier: 003         Name    : Software Services Limited
                      Address : 12 The Green
                              : Ballsover
                              : Kent
                      Post code: KE3 1SD
                      Telephone: 0987-7654
                      Contact  : Jane Frisbey

Supplier: 004         Name    : XYZ Electronics Ltd
                      Address : 45 North End Road
                              : Newbury
                              : Hants
                      Post code: HF2 1CF
                      Telephone: 0995-54545
                      Contact  : Penelope Arbuthnot

Supplier: 005         Name    : Brown's Multi-cables Ltd
                      Address : Unit 4
                              : Marley Trading Estate
                              : Telford
                      Post code: TF2 1CF
                      Telephone: 032-96868
                      Contact  : John Brown


+++ END OF PRINT +++
```

Figure 10.2 List of suppliers with allocated supplier codes.

```
Printed: 16 May 1981          STOCK CARD PRINT                      Page 1
--------------------------------------------------------------------------

Stock item: cbm8032    32K 12 in. computer
Free stock:  1     In stock: 27    On order: 4     Allocated: 30

Last activity : 10 May 1981  Minimum level : 10   Lead time days:
Bin / Location:              Maximum level : 30   Cost price    : 700.00
Supercedes   :               Re-order level: 15   Selling price : 895.00
Superceded by :              Re-order qty  : 15   V.A.T. rate   : 15
                             Quantity desc :

-------- SUPPLIER(s) --------

Main Supplier : 001     Name    : Commodore Business Machines
                        Address : 818 Leigh Road
                                : Slough
                                : Berks
                        Post code: BG2 3TR      Lead time days:
                        Telephone: 0765-98321   Cost price    : 700.00
                        Contact  : Julie North

-------- ORDER HISTORY --------

Order date   Reference  Ordered  Sup.  Date due   Received  Total value  Qty.O/S
-----------  ---------  -------  ----  ---------  --------  -----------  -------
10 May 1981  abc123        10    001                  6       7000.00       4

-------- MOVEMENT SUMMARY --------

   Date      Reference       Type         Cost/Sell    In     Out   Balance
-----------  ---------  ---------------   ---------  -----  -----  --------
 1 May 1981  BALANCE    Balance C/F         700.00    27                27
10 May 1981  abc123     Order received      700.00     6                33
10 May 1981  123456789  Allocation sent     895.00            6         27
10 May 1981  out1       Stock out           895.00            2         25
10 May 1981  STOCK-TAKE Stocktake (in)      700.00     2                27

-------- ALLOCATION SUMMARY --------

Required     Reference  Quantity  Centre  Issued  Total value   Qty.o/s
-----------  ---------  --------  ------  ------  -----------   -------
             123456789      5               6        4475.00
20 May 1981  asd           30               0       26850.00      30

+++ END OF PRINT +++
```

Figure 10.3   Typical stock record.

Stock control

on order – the amount of stock already ordered from suppliers which has yet to be delivered;

allocated – allocations which have been made against enquiries, etc. and for which confirmatory orders are awaited;

minimum and maximum stock levels – these are used to specify the acceptable levels of *in stock*. Stock items with *in stock* levels above the maximum or below the minimum will be highlighted in a stock level *highlights report* and, for this package, within the stock record itself;

re-order level – used to trigger the placing of purchase orders with suppliers when the *free stock* falls to, or below, this level. In a stand-alone stock control package, purchase orders are not raised automatically but the indication that a purchase order should be raised is signalled through a stock level highlights report and, for this package, within the stock record itself;

re-order quantity – the quantity normally purchased to replenish stocks;

cost price – the price at which stock is purchased. Many stock control packages allow for several cost prices and evaluate stock capital at an average price;

selling price – the price at which goods are valued when issued from stock.

In the example stock record shown, the *free stock* figure of 1 would be highlighted on the VDU screen since this is lower than the re-order level of 15. However, the *in stock* figure of 27 would not be highlighted since it is neither higher than the maximum level of 30 nor below the minimum level of 10.

Day-to-day transactions

The day-to-day transactions of a microcomputer-based stock control system are essentially concerned with stock movements, on very much the same basis as in a manual system. The big advantage of the microcomputer-based system – apart from its overall speed and its ability to store the data compactly on disks – is that, if any potentially *illegal* transactions are entered, the system immediately reacts and indicates why that proposed transaction just is not possible. Where *correct* information is entered into the stock control system which subsequently requires cancelling (for example, an allocation made to a customer who subsequently cancels) or where *incorrect* – but not illegal – information is entered (for example, an allocation is made against the wrong stock item), the design of the system must allow corrections to be made easily. Indeed, if the operator does not know, for example, to which stock item a piece of information relates, the system should be able to allocate this to a 'floating' location simply to allow the as yet unidentified information to be made available to the system. At a later stage, hopefully, the correct location will be identified and the information transferred to that location from the 'float'.

As figure 10.3 shows, day-to-day transactions may be concerned with:

> *purchase orders* – essentially recording that they have been placed and later that the goods are received. These records, therefore, represent the *input* to the stock control system;

> *allocations* – essentially recording the allocation of stock to potential customers and the subsequent despatch of those orders. These records, therefore, represent the *output* of the stock control system;

> *movement* – essentially recording the results of the stock balances replenished by purchase orders and depleted by customer allocations. To these must be added miscellaneous movements, such as corrections due to stocktaking. These records, therefore, represent the current state of the stock control system.

End-of-month processing (alternatively referred to as start-of-month processing)

Because of the relatively limited amount of disk storage space available on microcomputer systems, it is essential for such systems to remove non-essential information on a regular basis. This *purging* of the system usually takes place at the end of a month (or planning or accounting period) and essentially involves running an end-of-month program which removes any information which is now *historic* rather than *current* and which is, therefore, not essential for further day-to-day transactions.

Thus, an allocation made to a particular customer which was then followed by a withdrawal of stock against that customer's subsequent purchase order is (provided the quantities match exactly), as far as the system is concerned, of no further interest; both the original allocation and the subsequent withdrawal can be erased from the allocation record to make space for future allocation transactions. If the allocation and withdrawal figures do not match (as would occur with a partial fulfilment of a customer's order), the information obviously remains current and would not be removed by an end-of-month processing.

Similarly, information on purchase orders for which goods are subsequently received can be removed from the system if the quantities involved match exactly. If the quantities do not match (as in the case of a partial delivery against a purchase order) the information continues to be current and must, therefore, be retained on the relevant purchase order record.

Information deleted from both the purchase order and allocation record can also be removed from the stock movement record.

Before performing an end-of-month processing, it is absolutely essential to produce a backup copy of the stock control system on the last day of the month. In practice, this can best be achieved by withdrawing the relevant *daily* backup disks from the system and replacing those disks with new backup disks. Thus, if the end-of-month occured on a Friday, the Friday backup would become the end-of-month backup disks and the following Friday a set of new disks would become the Friday backup set. Such a procedure ensures that all daily backup disks are eventually withdrawn to become monthly backup disks, and thereby limits the number of times an individual disk will be used (which in practice should not exceed 50 or 60).

The end-of-month backup disk represents the state of the stock control system at that point in time. If the stock control system subsequently crashes (due to a disk failure, etc.), the latest end-of-month disk will be the backstop from which the current state of the stock control system can be re-restablished. If any reports are required from the stock control system, these must be produced either before end-of-month processing is undertaken, or later from the end-of-month backup disk.

Reports available

With a microcomputer-based stock control system containing information on up to 6,000 items, one of management's main concerns is to be able to take rapid and effective decisions for those stock items requiring action. The microcomputer-based stock control system's ability to produce *exception reports* of various kinds can, therefore, become a very powerful tool in effecting such 'management by exception'. Some of the reports produced by the ANAGRAM stock control package are described here.

Stock level highlights report

This report lists all the stock items held on file for which:

the *free stock* figure is less than the re-order level and, hence, a purchase order to replenish stocks should be raised;

the *in stock* figure is either greater than the maximum or less than the minimum figures previously set.

In the stock level highlights report shown in figure 10.4, item ad1981 has been included because the *in stock* figure of 15 is above the maximum of 10. Since no items appear on this report indicating a *free stock* figure below that of the re-order level, one can assume that no items are in need of replenishment and, hence, that no purchase order need to be raised.

```
Printed: 16 May 1981         STOCK LEVEL HIGHLIGHTS                    Page 1
-----------------------------------------------------------------------------

Stock item  Bin no  Qty desc  Re-order  Minimum  Maximum  In stock  Free stock
----------  ------  --------  --------  -------  -------  --------  ----------

ad1981              each         15        7       27        4          18
cbm76767            each          5        2       10       15          15

+++ END OF PRINT +++
```

Figure 10.4 Stock level highlights report.

```
Printed: 21 May 1981         STOCKTAKING LIST                      Page 1
-------------------------------------------------------------------------
                                                      Recorded   Actual
Stock item  Description                Qty desc Bin/Loc In stock  In stock
----------  -----------------------    -------- ------- --------  --------

A123456789  Clever Word Package        each              4
ad1981      IEEE Cable                 each             18
bcf100009   Payroll Package            each              1
bgh23343    Network cable system       each              0
bvf544444   IEEE/Centronics Interface  unit              2

C10         Cassette in Packs of 10    packs            18
C2N         Cassette Unit              unit              6
C30         Cassettes in Packs of 10   packs            19
cbm4016     40 col PET, 4 K in ROM     unit              4
cbm76767    8032 Brochure              each             10

cbm8032     32K 12 in. computer                         16
cbm8050     dual floppy disk unit      unit             12
M42         Midelectron Paper Tape St  unit              0
swq65446    40 column printer          unit              1
WX4671      X-Y Plotter                unit              0

yte76767    22 inch monitor unit       unit              1

+++ END OF PRINT +++
```

Figure 10.5   Stocktaking list.

Stocktaking report

This report, shown in figure 10.5, indicates the amount of stock for each item which the stock control system has recorded as being *in stock*. It includes a blank column for actual *in stock* values to be recorded manually, a task made easier if bin location information is available. Once any discrepancies between the recorded and actual figures are established, the recorded figures must be brought into line with the actual by effecting a miscellaneous stock movement which would not appear either as a purchase or an allocation.

Outstanding orders report

This report lists all the stock items for which purchase orders have been placed with a specified supplier and from whom goods have yet to be received in full. The outstanding orders report, therefore, can be used by a purchasing department as an action list for chasing suppliers. In the report shown in figure 10.6, because the value of outstanding orders is also given, this indicates the company's future financial commitment to stock.

Outstanding allocations report

This report lists all the stock items for which customer allocations have been made but for which a confirmatory customer order has yet to be received, or the quantity issued is less than the quantity required. As such this report can represent an action list for the sales department. As shown in figure 10.7, the value of the outstanding customer allocations is an indication to the accounting department, in particular, of the prospective sales that have yet to be converted into firm orders and, hence, cash payments to the company.

```
Printed: 16 May 1981          OUTSTANDING ORDERS                   Page 1
-------------------------------------------------------------------------

Supplier: 001 Commodore Business Machines

                      Date of   Date    Qty.   Order   Qty.   Outstanding
Stock item  Order ref. Order    due     desc.  qty.    o/s    order value
----------  ---------- -------  ------- -----  ------  ------ -----------

cbm8032     abc123     10May81                  10      4       2800.00
cbm8032     ucs6566    16May81  01Jun81         15     15      10500.00
                                                               -----------
Total outstanding order value                                  13300.00
                                                               -----------

+++ END OF PRINT +++
```

Figure 10.6 Outstanding orders report.

```
Printed: 21 May 1981          OUTSTANDING ALLOCATIONS                  Page 1
------------------------------------------------------------------------------

            Allocation  Date     Cost    Qty.  Quantity  Quantity Outstanding
Stock item  reference   required centre  desc. required  issued   alloc value
----------  ----------  -------- ------  ----- --------  -------- -----------

A123456789  Saif Tech   4Jun81           each     5                  2000.00
ad1981      Gas Bd      3Jun81           each    15                   315.00
bcf100009   Brit Gas    7Jun81           each     1                   345.00
bvf544444   BLMG        7Jun81           unit     1                    76.00
cbm76767    Brit Ley    7Jun81           each     6                    36.00
                                                                  -----------
Total outstanding allocation value                                   2772.00
                                                                  -----------

+++ END OF PRINT +++
```

Figure 10.7 *Outstanding allocations report.*

Stock valuation analysis report

This report, shown in figure 10.8, lists each stock item, together with in stock figures, the item's cost value (in stock × cost price) and the item's selling value (in stock × selling price). The total cost value and total selling value represent, respectively, money tied up in stock and potential sales (or issues).

Stock movement valuation analysis report

This report, shown in figure 10.9, gives the value of stock items moved in and out of stock since the start of the month (period). Issued at the end of a month (period), it shows the difference between the selling value of stock issued and cost value of stock acquired, that is, the operating profit of the stock system.

Inactive stock report

Sometimes referred to as a slow movers report, this lists items for which there has been no stock movements – in or out – since a date

```
Printed: 21 May 1981          STOCK VALUATION ANALYSIS
-----------------------------------------------------------------
                  Qty.                        Selling
  Stock item      desc.   In stock  Cost value  value
  ----------     -----   --------  ---------- -------

  A123456789     each        4      1380.00    1600.00
  ad1981         each       18       270.00     378.00
  bcf100009      each        1       300.00     345.00
  bgh23343       each        0         0.00       0.00
  bvf544444      unit        2       100.00     152.00

  C10            packs      18        90.00      99.00
  C2N            unit        6       270.00     330.00
  C30            packs      19       104.50     118.75
  cbm4016        unit        4      2000.00    2200.00
  cbm76767       each       10        50.00      60.00

  cbm8032                   16     11200.00   14320.00
  cbm8050        unit       12      8400.00   10740.00
  M42            unit        0         0.00       0.00
  swq65446       unit        1       400.00     460.00
  WX4671         unit        0         0.00       0.00

  yte76767       unit        1       200.00     273.00

                                   ----------  ----------
  Total stock value                  24764.50   31075.75
                                   ----------  ----------

  +++ END OF PRINT +++
```

Figure 10.8 *Stock valuation analysis report.*

specified by the user. Such a report identifies those stock items that have either become or are rapidly becoming obsolete and thus provides valuable information to prevent the retention of redundant stock. If it is decided to delete these items from the stock control system, a fictitious withdrawal of stock will have to be made before the system will allow the item to be actually deleted.

```
Printed: 21 May 1981     STOCK MOVEMENT VALUATION ANALYSIS          Page 1
------------------------------------------------------------------------

              Qty.   'IN'                    'OUT'     Selling
Stock item    desc.  movements  Cost value   movements  value    Difference
----------    -----  ---------  ----------   ---------  -------  ----------

A123456789    each      3        1062.00        0         0.00    1062.00-
ad1981        each     20         300.00        7       147.00     153.00-
cbm76767      each      0           0.00        5        30.00      30.00
cbm8032                27       18900.00       38     34010.00   15110.00
                                ---------              --------   --------
Totals                          20262.00              34187.00   13925.00
                                ---------              --------   --------

+++ END OF PRINT +++
```

Figure 10.9 Stock movement valuation analysis report.

Cost centre reports

Where a system of cost centres is in existence, many of the reports already described can be restricted to the stock items associated with a particular cost centre. A similar facility is provided in some packages for stock items associated with product groups.

Future trends and developments

Pareto analysis

One of the advantages of a computerized stock control system compared with a manually operated one is the ability of the computer to sort stock items into ascending or descending order on the basis of, say, cost value. Such a facility could be used to perform a Pareto analysis for all stock items to establish which are:

A type items – few in number but often representing up to 80 per cent of the capital invested in stock;

B type items – more in number than A items but representing less in investment terms;

C type items – the majority of items, often 70–80 per cent but representing sometimes as little as 5 per cent of capital invested.

Such a Pareto (or ABC) analysis is widely used in stock control to identify which stock items are more important than others. Few of the microcomputer stock control packages on the market offer this facility as yet, but since it is such a useful tool in stock management and is relatively simple to incorporate in a package, it will assuredly become more common in the next generation of microcomputer stock control packages currently under development.

Figure 10.10a shows a printout of just 20 stock items ordered by cost value, and figure 10.10b the resulting Pareto (or ABC) analysis which is derived from this. Even on this limited sample of twenty

Listing of all stocked items ordered by cost value.

CODE	DESCRIPTION	COST VALUE	CUMULATIVE VALUE
f45454	Manual	16.00	16.00
h64646	Nut	125.00	141.00
g97979	Bolt	168.00	309.00
h78787	Nut	210.00	519.00
g45454	Flange	340.00	859.00
h45454	Nut	350.00	1209.00
a45454	Casting	404.00	1613.00
g454541	Bracket	408.00	2021.00
g43435	Flange	585.00	2606.00
f34343	Flange	585.00	3191.00
b56565	Bracket	672.00	3863.00
h67676	Bracket	702.00	4565.00
g65657	Bracket	360.00	4925.00
f46464	Flange	1008.00	5933.00
a2003	Casting	1088.00	7021.00
g73535	Casting	1242.00	8263.00
f676760	Casting	1530.00	9793.00
a1000	Casting	1360.00	11153.00
g76767	Bracket	1870.00	13023.00
g20021	Bolt	3000.00	16023.00

Figure 10.10a   Printout of stock items listed in order of cost value to produce a Pareto analysis.

items it can be seen that 20 per cent of the items (that is, four: namely, g20021, g76767, a1000, and f676760) represent 50 per cent of the cost value and that 40 per cent of the items (eight: namely, f45454, h64646, g97979, h78787, g45454, h45454 and g454541) represent only 10 per cent of the cost value.

Forecasting

As I stressed at the beginning of the chapter, because most microcomputer based stock control packages do not incorporate an element of demand forecasting, they are strictly speaking stock recording rather than true stock control packages. A few packages on the market do incorporate a forecasting function, based on exponential smoothing techniques (see figure 5.8), and these forecasts are then used to establish the stock control parameters such as re-order levels, replenishment quantities, etc. As storage facilities on microcomputers becomes both larger and cheaper, I would expect to see an increasing move in the direction of true stock control for microcomputer-based packages.

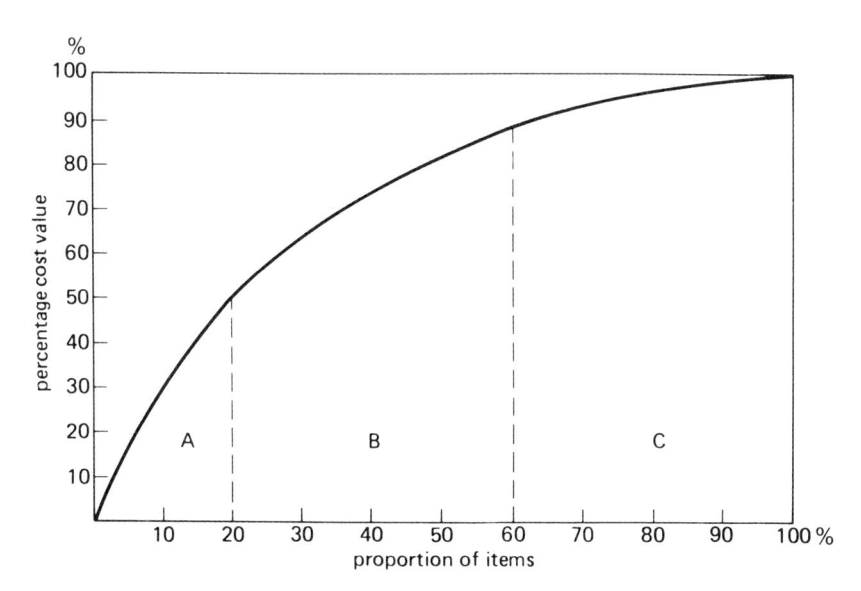

Figure 10.10b Pareto analysis of stock items as derived from figure 10.10a.

Decentralized stock control via microcomputer networks

Many large organizations hold stock on several sites and in the past have exercised control over those dispersed stocks using regional inter-active terminals accessing a central mini- or mainframe computer. The main disadvantages of such a system are the running expenses of connecting terminals to the central computer for up to eight hours every day via dedicated lines and the total dependence of all regional sites on the central computer.

In such decentralized stock control situations, independent microcomputers are increasingly being used to control regional stocks, with only occasional reporting to a central minicomputer to update the overall situation. Such a system considerably reduces running expenses and also allows regional control to continue if the central computer crashes.

Material requirements planning

In many manufacturing situations, where several components or subassemblies are used in the production of a main assembly, it is apparent that the demand for these components does not operate independently, as is assumed in conventional stock control. In such situations it is more efficient to control stocks of components and subassemblies using a procedure called material requirements planning (MRP). While MRP is more efficient at controlling stocks in such dependent demand situations, to achieve that improved control the system requires far more information about what components and subassemblies are needed to produce final assemblies and at what level in the manufacturing process. This has so far meant that microcomputers, with their limited storage facilities, have not proved suitable for this type of application. However, I can visualize the inclusion of MRP packages in the next generation of microcomputers. Already the latest versions of the ANAGRAM package discussed earlier in this chapter incorporates a single-level *parts explosion* which allows the user to identify shortages of components one level down from the main assembly when a proposal to build a certain quantity of that main assembly is investigated. It can only be a matter of time before, with increased storage facilities, microcomputer-based MRP packages are available with multiple-level parts explosions, such as are currently available on mini-and mainframe machines.

Conclusion

Stock control is currently the largest area of application of microcomputer packages. Some sixty packages are available on the market in the UK which means that, for the more popular types of microcomputer, potential users have a choice of four or five packages.

While no microcomputer package will exactly mimic an existing manual stock control system, because the costs of having a bespoke package written can prove prohibitive, many existing users have found that the relatively small restrictions placed on them by a particular stock control package are more than offset by the advantages offered by such a microcomputer-based system.

Glossary of Terms

Access time	Time taken to transfer data from disk to computer memory.
Address	Identifier of internal storage location
Alphanumeric	A character set which includes only alphabetic and numeric characters and in some interpretations can also include punctuation marks and other symbols.
Applications package	A proprietary program or suite of programs, usually developed by a software house, for a specific application (canned software – American)
Assembler	Systems software which translates an assembly language into a machine-readable code.
Assembly language	A programming language which is 'lower' than a high level language such as BASIC (which uses understandable English words) but which is 'higher' than a machine-readable code. Assembly languages are usually the province of professional programmers, are more difficult to use than higher level languages but are more efficient in terms of processing and size.
Backup	Data retained, usually on disk, separate from the operational systems. Used to reinstate the system if a failure should occur.
BASIC	The most used high level language for programming microcomputers. Stands for Beginners All-purpose Symbolic Instruction Code.
Baud	Measurement of the speed of transmitting data in bits per second.
'Boot up'	A euphemism for reading in systems software (operating system) from disk.

Glossary of terms 213

Bit	Abbreviation for binary digit – a character or byte being usually made up of 8 bits.
Bug	A euphemism for a fault, usually in a program. Hence to debug is to correct a fault.
Bus	Etched circuits (wires) providing electrical connections between chips.
Byte	Equivalent to a character and composed generally of 8 or 16 bits on current microcomputers.
Cassette	Physically exactly the same as a music cassette and used as a storage medium (instead of disks) on smaller microcomputers.
Central processing unit (CPU)	The main control unit of a computer incorporating processor, main memory and input/output controller.
Character	Equivalent to a byte. Can be alphanumeric or numeric.
Chip	A small piece of etched silicon which contains circuits which perform processor and memory functions. Usually mounted in plastic with metal legs which can be plugged into sockets within the computer.
Compiler	Systems software which translates an entire program in a high level language into a machine readable code program.
Correspondence quality typefont	Acceptable typefont as produced by a dot-matrix printer.
CP/M (Control Program for Microprocessors)	An operating system, originally developed by Digital Research Inc., which is used in numerous microcomputers.
Cursor	Position on computer screen where character currently being entered will appear. Often represented by an underline character and in some configurations, flashes on and off.
Daisy-wheel printer	A fairly slow but high quality printer.
Data	Information
Database	A file of data structured to allow a number of applications to access the data and update it without dictating or constraining the overall design of the content.
Digital	Representation of data in form of digits taking discrete forms, i.e. binary form of 0 or 1.
Disk (or disc)	A disk(ette) with a magnetic surface used for

214 Glossary of terms

	storing data which can be accessed directly (rather than serially as with tapes). For microcomputers floppy disks are cheap, removable and can store up to 500 kbytes on a single side, whereas Winchester hard disks are expensive and non-removable but can store up to 30 Megabytes.
Disk operating system (DOS)	Programs in the systems software which control the operation of the disk storage system and other internal operations.
Dot-matrix printer	A relatively fast printer.
EDI	Electronic data interchange.
EPROM	Erasable programmable read only memory – a ROM chip that can be erased and programmed.
Field	A group of alphanumeric or numeric characters.
File	A collection of many records.
Floppy disk	See disk.
Formatting	The process by which a new disk is prepared to accept programs and or data.
Hard copy	Printed computer output.
Hard disk	See disk.
Hardware	The physical components making up a computer.
Hexadecimal	A number system to base 16 as opposed to digital to base 2.
Host Organisation	Computer offering database facilities.
High level language	A computer language that uses English and mathematical notation and which is translated into a machine code by a compiler or interpreter.
Hobbyist	A home-based computer user.
Ink-jet printer	A relatively expensive and fast printer using ink jets to produce the printed image. Very quiet operation.
Input	Data entered into the computer.
Interface	A device and the appropriate programs that allow different electronic devices (such as printers) to communicate with a computer's CPU.
Interpreter	Program which translates a high level language line by line to a machine readable code.
I/O	An abbreviation used to cover input and output processes.

Glossary of terms

k	A measure of memory capacity; $1 \text{ k} = 2^{10} = 1024$ (approximated to 1000).
LAN	Local Area Network.
Letter quality	High quality typefont as produced by a daisy-wheel printer.
Machine code	The numeric codes in 0s and 1s which are the only code which the CPU can understand.
Macro programming	Very high level programming.
Mainframe computer	A large computer usually marketed by companie which have traditionally supplied comprehensive applications and systems software together with appropriate support.
Mega	A measure of memory capacity: 1 Mega $= 2^{20} = 1{,}048{,}576$ (approximated to 1,000,000 or 1,000k)
Memory	Elements of the computer system that store data and program instructions. Internal memory is directly accessible by the CPU.
Menu	A form of design used in an applications program indicating what alternative sub-program options are on offer.
Microcomputer	A computer based on a single microprocessor unit (MPU) or chip.
Microprocessor	An integrated circuit which contains several computational elements on a single chip.
Microprocessor unit (MPU)	A microprocessor designed specifically to control the components of a microcomputer.
Mini-computer	A computer between a microcomputer and a mainframe computer in both price and performance.
Modem	MOdulator/DEModulator – a device which translates digital signals into an analogue form for transmission down an analogue telecommunications line.
Nano second	One-billionth of a second (i.e. 10^{-9} seconds).
Near letter quality	A typefont better than correspondence but not as good as letter quality.
Operating system	A suite of programs that controls the overall operation of the computer.
Output	Data produced by the computer.
Package	A set of programs offering computing facilities for a particular application.

216 *Glossary of terms*

Parallel	A method of signal transmission in which all bits are transferred simultaneously.
Password	A personal codeword used for security purposes and known only to a restricted set of users.
Period	American word for a fullstop (.) – hence 'type of period' in VISICALC etc.
Peripheral	Hardware devices other than the CPU.
Printer	An output device which prints results on paper.
Printout	Output from a printer (hard copy).
Program	A collection of computer instructions – usually spelt as here, not as programme.
Programmer	A person who writes a program.
PROM	Programmable read only memory – a memory chip permanently programmed by the user which cannot subsequently be altered.
RAM	Random access memory – a memory chip which can be written to and read from. Loses contents when computer is switched off.
Random access	The retrieving of information from memory or storage via an index – direct access as opposed to serial access.
Read to or into	Enter information into memory or storage.
Record	Part of a file with a predetermined format and containing several fields.
Register	A high speed storage device in the MPU for the temporary storage of small amounts of data.
Resident monitor	Small resident program which will load the systems software from disk.
ROM	Read only memory – a memory chip programmed by the manufacturer which can only be read from, not written to.
S100 bus	The most popular bus used to interconnect sections of a microcomputer.
Serial	A method of signal transmission in which bits are transferred one at a time.
Software	A generic term for programs.
Software house	A computer services company exclusively developing and marketing software.
Stand-alone	A computer system or package which operates independently.

Glossary of terms

Store	See memory.
Systems software	Programs which provide the computer's operating system.
Systems house	A computer services company which buys in hardware and produces a total computing system for sale under its own marketing label using its own software.
True descenders	The tails of characters such as p, q, z etc. which occur below the print line.
'Turn-key' system	A computer system delivered complete and ready for the user to 'turn the key'. Likely to be supplied by a systems house.
Upward compatible	A program or suite of programs that will operate on larger machines in the same range of microcomputers.
User	General term for a computer user.
User-friendly	Designed to appeal to the user, particularly used of programs.
VDU	Visual display unit – a television-like screen for the temporary display of data.
Volatile memory	Memory which loses its contents when the power is turned off.
Winchester disk	A hard disk system in which the disk cannot be removed (see disk).
Word	A group of bits treated as a single unit, can be the same as a byte.
Word processor	A computer system for manipulating text.
Zeroize	An (unsuccessful) attempt to abbreviate 'to set to zero' – American.

Index

acoustic coupler 63
address points 78
after sale support 49
aged debtor report 185
AJ ink-jet printer 33
alphanumeric field 105
Apple II 17
Apple Macintosh 25
applications software 37
Apricot 20
audit trail 171

balance sheet 178
bar-chart 99
buffered keys 75
build up to gross 149
buses 10
byte 105

centring text 73
character 105
choice of microcomputer
    system 52
classification of database
    packages 105
clock 9
COMPAC Plus 24
corrections 73
correspondence quality print 82
cost centre reports 207
CPU (central processing unit) 4
customer invoice listing 187
customer statements 186

daisy-wheel printer 27
database provision 64

database terminology 104
deletion 73
dial-up systems 64
disk based packages 132
disk storage 12
dongle protection 41
DOS (disk operating system) 37
draft quality 82

Easylink 66
editing facilities 73
8-bit 6
electronic mail 64
Epson printers 29

fields 105
fill points 78
flexible database packages 103
floppy disk 13
forecasting 209
forward referencing 101

global record transactions 121
graphics 98
greeting points 78
gross-to-net calculation 150
hardware 3
    choice 53
    reliability 51
    support 49
headers 75

IBM compatibles 22
IBM PC 21
impact dot-matrix printers 27
inactive stock report 205

indentation 75
indexing 111
ink-jet printers 28
input/output interface 9
insertion 73
integrated business packages 128
integrated ledger packages 167
integration, from user's point of
    view 131
internal memory 8
iteration control 101

justification 73

key field 105
keyboard 11

LAN (Local Area Networks) 59
laser printers 28
ledger packages 163
letter quality 82
letters 81
line graph 100
line spacing 73

macroprogramming, database 123
macroprogramming,
    spreadsheet 100
mailmerging 78
major dealers 47
Material requirements 210
merging files of text 77
micro to mainframe
    communications 62
Micro to micro
    communications 59
microcomputer
    communications 59
    dealers 47
    industry 45
    sizes 54
    systems 16
    users 50
minor dealers 48
modems 63
mouse 12
moving text 74
MPU (microprocessor unit) 4
MRP (material requirements
    planning) 210

near letter quality print 83
NEC spin writer printer 32
nominal ledger 164
North Star Advantage 18
numeric field 105

One-to-One 67
outstanding allocations report 204
outstanding orders report 204

page numbering 75
page offset 75
page width 74
paging 74
Pareto analysis 207
password access 111
payroll
    cycle 157
    operations 149
    packages 139
    setting up a system 142
peripheral hardware 10
pie-chart 99
presentation facilities 73
Prestel 65
print bank giros 156
print cheques list 153
print coin analysis 152
print payslips 151
print quality 81
printers
    classification of 34
    daisy-wheel 27
    dot-matrix 27
    general 28
    ink-jet 28
    laser 28
    thermal 28
printing files 77
printing labels 80
profit and loss account 177
programming language 38
programming languages 36
PSS (Packet Switch Stream) 63
purchase ledger 167
RAM (random access memory) 8
RAM based packages 132
record structure 107
records 105
registered user 41

report writing   115
retail outlets   48
ROM (read only memory)   8
ROM protection   39

sales analysis   187
sales ledger   166
searching for records   113
selective record transactions   121
service contractors   48
setting headers   75
setting trailers   75
simple database facilities   101
Sirius   19
16-bit   6
software   32
   choice   52
   houses   49
   protection   39
   support   51
sorting   111
spellchecking   82
spreadsheet
   built-in functions   90
   concept of   86
   examples   92
   formulae   88
   graphics   98

macroprogramming   100
   packages   86
stationery   77
stock control packages   192
stock level highlights report   202
stock valuation report   205
stocktaking reports   202
supplier records   196
system integrity   169
systems houses   45
systems software   35

tabbing   75
Tandy Daisy-wheel printer   31
Tandy TRS-80 printer   30
Telecom Gold   65
trailers   75
   trial balances   175

uncopiable disks   41
upward compatibility   58

VAT   178
VDU (visual display unit)   10

Wang PC   26
word processing packages   71
WORDCRAFT   77